# Multimodal Biometric and Machine Learning Technologies

**Scrivener Publishing**
100 Cummings Center, Suite 541J
Beverly, MA 01915-6106

*Publishers at Scrivener*
Martin Scrivener (martin@scrivenerpublishing.com)
Phillip Carmical (pcarmical@scrivenerpublishing.com)

# Multimodal Biometric and Machine Learning Technologies

## Applications for Computer Vision

Edited by
**Sandeep Kumar**
**Deepika Ghai**
**Arpit Jain**
**Suman Lata Tripathi**
and
**Shilpa Rani**

Scrivener
Publishing

# WILEY

This edition first published 2023 by John Wiley & Sons, Inc., 111 River Street, Hoboken, NJ 07030, USA
and Scrivener Publishing LLC, 100 Cummings Center, Suite 541J, Beverly, MA 01915, USA
© 2023 Scrivener Publishing LLC
For more information about Scrivener publications please visit www.scrivenerpublishing.com.

**Wiley Global Headquarters**
111 River Street, Hoboken, NJ 07030, USA

For details of our global editorial offices, customer services, and more information about Wiley products visit us at www.wiley.com.

**Limit of Liability/Disclaimer of Warranty**
While the publisher and authors have used their best efforts in preparing this work, they make no representations or warranties with respect to the accuracy or completeness of the contents of this work and specifically disclaim all warranties, including without limitation any implied warranties of merchantability or fitness for a particular purpose. No warranty may be created or extended by sales representatives, written sales materials, or promotional statements for this work. The fact that an organization, website, or product is referred to in this work as a citation and/or potential source of further information does not mean that the publisher and authors endorse the information or services the organization, website, or product may provide or recommendations it may make. This work is sold with the understanding that the publisher is not engaged in rendering professional services. The advice and strategies contained herein may not be suitable for your situation. You should consult with a specialist where appropriate. Neither the publisher nor authors shall be liable for any loss of profit or any other commercial damages, including but not limited to special, incidental, consequential, or other damages. Further, readers should be aware that websites listed in this work may have changed or disappeared between when this work was written and when it is read.

*Library of Congress Cataloging-in-Publication Data*

ISBN 978-1-119-78540-8

Cover image: Pixabay.Com
Cover design by Russell Richardson

Set in size of 11pt and Minion Pro by Manila Typesetting Company, Makati, Philippines

Printed in the USA

10 9 8 7 6 5 4 3 2 1

# Contents

Preface                                                                    xiii

1  **Multimodal Biometric in Computer Vision**                              1
   *Sunayana Kundan Shivthare, Yogesh Kumar Sharma*
   *and Ranjit D. Patil*
   1.1  Introduction                                                        2
   1.2  Importance of Artificial Intelligence, Machine Learning
        and Deep Learning in Biometric System                              2
   1.3  Machine Learning                                                    4
        1.3.1  Supervised vs Unsupervised Model                            5
        1.3.2  Classification and Regression Problem                       6
   1.4  Deep Learning                                                       6
        1.4.1  Steps to Create the Machine and Deep Learning Model         8
   1.5  Related Work                                                        8
        1.5.1  Discussions                                                  11
   1.6  Biometric System                                                    11
        1.6.1  Biometrics in Physical Form                                  11
        1.6.2  Biometrics with Behavior                                     13
        1.6.3  Evaluation Parameters (Metrics) Used by
               Biometric Systems                                           14
   1.7  Need for Multimodal Biometric                                       15
        1.7.1  Perks of Multimodal Biometric                                15
        1.7.2  The General Outline of a Multimodal
               Biometric System                                            17
   1.8  Databases Used by Biometric System                                  17
        1.8.1  Confusion Matrix                                            18
   1.9  Impact of DL in the Current Scenario                                19
        1.9.1  Computer Vision                                             20
        1.9.2  Natural Language Processing                                 21
        1.9.3  Recommendation System                                      23
        1.9.4  Cyber Security                                             23

                                                                            v

1.10 Conclusion                                                        24
     References                                                        24

2  **A Vaccine Slot Tracker Model Using Fuzzy Logic
   for Providing Quality of Service**                                  **31**
   *Mohammad Faiz, Nausheen Fatima and Ramandeep Sandhu*
   2.1  Introduction                                                   32
   2.2  Related Research                                               33
   2.3  Novelty of the Proposed Work                                   37
        2.3.1  Age                                                     38
        2.3.2  Availability of Vaccination Slots                       38
        2.3.3  Vaccination Status                                      38
   2.4  Proposed Model                                                 38
        2.4.1  Role of the CoWIN App                                   40
        2.4.2  Process for Signing Up for the CoWIN App                41
   2.5  Proposed Fuzzy-Based Vaccine Slot Tracker Model                42
        2.5.1  Fuzzy Rules                                             43
   2.6  Simulation                                                     44
   2.7  Conclusion                                                     47
   2.8  Future Work                                                    50
        References                                                     51

3  **Enhanced Text Mining Approach for Better Ranking
   System of Customer Reviews**                                       **53**
   *Ramandeep Sandhu, Amritpal Singh, Mohammad Faiz,
   Harpreet Kaur and Sunny Thukral*
   3.1  Introduction                                                   53
   3.2  Techniques of Text Mining                                      55
        3.2.1  Sentiment Analysis                                      55
        3.2.2  Natural Language Processing                             55
        3.2.3  Information Extraction                                  56
        3.2.4  Information Retrieval                                   56
        3.2.5  Clustering                                              57
        3.2.6  Categorization                                          57
        3.2.7  Visualization                                          58
        3.2.8  Text Summarization                                     58
   3.3  Related Research                                               58
   3.4  Research Methodology                                           63
   3.5  Conclusion                                                     67
        References                                                     67

4   Spatial Analysis of Carbon Sequestration Mapping Using
    Remote Sensing and Satellite Image Processing                71
    *Prashantkumar B. Sathvara, J. Anuradha, R. Sanjeevi,*
    *Sandeep Tripathi  and Ankitkumar B. Rathod*
    4.1   Introduction                                            72
    4.2   Materials and Methods                                  75
          4.2.1   Materials                                      75
          4.2.2   Methodology                                    75
                  4.2.2.1   Formula for the Mathematical Extraction
                            of the Vegetation Area               76
    4.3   Results                                                77
    4.4   Conclusion                                             79
          Acknowledgment                                         80
          References                                             81

5   Applications of Multimodal Biometric Technology              85
    *Shivalika Goyal and Amit Laddi*
    5.1   Introduction                                           85
          5.1.1   Benchmark for Effective Multimodal
                  Biometric System                               86
    5.2   Components of MBS                                      87
          5.2.1   Data Store(s)                                  88
          5.2.2   Input Interface                                88
          5.2.3   Processing Unit                                88
          5.2.4   Output Interface                               89
    5.3   Biometrics Modalities                                  89
    5.4   Applications of Multimodal Biometric Systems           89
          5.4.1   MBS in Forensic Science                        90
          5.4.2   MBS in Government Applications                 90
          5.4.3   MBS in Enterprise Solutions and Network
                  Infrastructure                                 92
          5.4.4   MBS in Commercial Applications                 93
    5.5   Conclusion                                             97
          References                                             97

6   A Study of Multimodal Colearning, Application in Biometrics
    and Authentication                                          103
    *Sandhya Avasthi, Tanushree Sanwal, Ayushi Prakash*
    *and Suman Lata Tripathi*
    6.1   Introduction                                          104
          6.1.1   Need for Multimodal Colearning                105

|  |  |  |  |
|---|---|---|---|
| | 6.1.2 | Why Multimodal Biometric Systems? | 106 |
| | 6.1.3 | Multimodal Deep Learning | 107 |
| | 6.1.4 | Motivation | 108 |
| 6.2 | | Multimodal Deep Learning Methods and Applications | 108 |
| | 6.2.1 | Multimodal Image Description (MMID) | 110 |
| | 6.2.2 | Multimodal Video Description (MMVD) | 110 |
| | 6.2.3 | Multimodal Visual Question Answering (MMVQA) | 111 |
| | 6.2.4 | Multimodal Speech Synthesis (MMSS) | 112 |
| | 6.2.5 | Multimodal Event Detection (MMED) | 112 |
| | 6.2.6 | Multimodal Emotion Recognition | 113 |
| 6.3 | | MMDL Application in Biometric Monitoring | 113 |
| | 6.3.1 | Biometric Authentication System and Issues | 113 |
| | 6.3.2 | Multimodal Biometric Authentication System and Benefits | 115 |
| 6.4 | | Fusion Levels in Multimodal Biometrics | 116 |
| | 6.4.1 | Fusion at Feature Level | 117 |
| | 6.4.2 | Fusion at Matching Score Level | 118 |
| | 6.4.3 | Decision-Level Fusion | 118 |
| 6.5 | | Authentication in Mobile Devices Using Multimodal Biometrics | 119 |
| | 6.5.1 | Categories of Multimodal Biometrics | 120 |
| | 6.5.2 | Benefits of Multimodal Biometrics in Mobile Devices | 121 |
| 6.6 | | Challenges and Open Research Problems | 122 |
| 6.7 | | Conclusion | 123 |
| | | References | 123 |

**7 A Structured Review on Virtual Reality Technology Application in the Field of Sports** 129
*Harmanpreet Kaur, Arpit Kulshreshtha and Deepika Ghai*

| 7.1 | Introduction | 130 |
|---|---|---|
| 7.2 | Related Work | 132 |
| 7.3 | Conclusion | 142 |
| | References | 142 |

**8 A Systematic and Structured Review of Fuzzy Logic-Based Evaluation in Sports** 145
*Harmanpreet Kaur, Sourabh Chhatiye and Jimmy Singla*

| 8.1 | Introduction | 146 |
|---|---|---|
| 8.2 | Related Works | 148 |
| 8.3 | Conclusion | 159 |
| | References | 159 |

**9 Machine Learning and Deep Learning for Multimodal Biometrics** — 163
*Danvir Mandal and Shyam Sundar Pattnaik*
9.1 Introduction — 163
9.2 Machine Learning Using Multimodal Biometrics — 165
    9.2.1 Main Machine Learning Algorithms — 165
    9.2.2 A Hybrid Model — 165
    9.2.3 Semisupervised Learning Method — 166
    9.2.4 EEG-Based Machine Learning — 166
9.3 Deep Learning Using Multimodal Biometrics — 167
    9.3.1 Based on Score Fusion — 167
    9.3.2 Deep Learning for Surveillance Videos — 167
    9.3.3 Finger Vein and Knuckle Print-Based Deep Learning Approach — 167
    9.3.4 Facial Video-Based Deep Learning Technique — 168
    9.3.5 Finger Vein and Electrocardiogram-Based Deep Learning Approach — 168
9.4 Conclusion — 169
    References — 170

**10 Machine Learning and Deep Learning: Classification and Regression Problems, Recurrent Neural Networks, Convolutional Neural Networks** — 173
*R. K. Jeyachitra and Manochandar, S.*
10.1 Introduction — 174
10.2 Classification of Machine Learning — 174
10.3 Supervised Learning — 175
    10.3.1 Regression — 175
    10.3.2 Fuzzy Classification — 190
    10.3.3 Bayesian Networks — 193
    10.3.4 Decision Trees — 195
    10.3.5 Artificial Neural Network — 195
    10.3.6 Classification — 197
10.4 Unsupervised Learning — 201
10.5 Reinforcement Learning — 203
10.6 Hybrid Approach — 204
    10.6.1 Semisupervised Learning — 204
    10.6.2 Self-Supervised Learning — 205
    10.6.3 Self-Taught Learning — 205
10.7 Other Common Approaches — 205
    10.7.1 Multitask Learning — 206

|  |  |  |  |
|---|---|---|---|
|  | 10.7.2 | Active Learning | 206 |
|  | 10.7.3 | Outline Learning | 206 |
|  | 10.7.4 | Transfer Learning | 207 |
|  | 10.7.5 | Federated Learning | 207 |
|  | 10.7.6 | Ensemble Learning | 207 |
|  | 10.7.7 | Adversarial Learning | 208 |
|  | 10.7.8 | Meta-Learning | 208 |
|  | 10.7.9 | Targeted Learning | 208 |
|  | 10.7.10 | Concept Learning | 209 |
|  | 10.7.11 | Bayesian Learning | 209 |
|  | 10.7.12 | Inductive Learning | 209 |
|  | 10.7.13 | Multimodal Learning | 210 |
|  | 10.7.14 | Curriculum Learning | 210 |
| 10.8 | DL Techniques | | 210 |
|  | 10.8.1 | Recurrent Neural Network (RNN) | 211 |
|  | 10.8.2 | Convolutional Neural Network | 214 |
|  | 10.8.3 | Real-Time Applications of DL | 218 |
| 10.9 | Conclusion | | 219 |
|  | Acknowledgment | | 219 |
|  | References | | 219 |

**11 Handwriting and Speech-Based Secured Multimodal Biometrics Identification Technique**     227
*Swathi Gowroju, V. Swathi and Ankita Tiwari*
| 11.1 | Introduction | | 228 |
| 11.2 | Literature Survey | | 230 |
| 11.3 | Proposed Method | | 231 |
|  | 11.3.1 | SVM-Based Implementation | 235 |
|  | 11.3.2 | DTW-Based Implementation | 235 |
|  | 11.3.3 | CNN-Based Method | 236 |
|  | 11.3.4 | Proposed Model Implementation | 236 |
| 11.4 | Results and Discussion | | 237 |
|  | 11.4.1 | Data Exploitation | 237 |
|  | 11.4.2 | Data Sets Used | 238 |
|  | 11.4.3 | Validation and Training | 239 |
|  | 11.4.4 | Results on CNN-Based Methods | 239 |
|  | 11.4.5 | Results of Deep Learning-Based Method | 241 |
|  | 11.4.6 | Results of the Proposed Method | 244 |
|  | 11.4.7 | Measure of Accuracy | 245 |
| 11.5 | Conclusion | | 248 |
|  | References | | 249 |

12  Convolutional Neural Network Approach for Multimodal
    Biometric Recognition System for Banking Sector on Fusion
    of Face and Finger                                          251
    *Sandeep Kumar, Shilpa Choudhary, Swathi Gowroju*
    *and Abhishek Bhola*
    12.1   Introduction                                         252
    12.2   Literature Work                                      253
    12.3   Proposed Work                                        256
           12.3.1   Pre-Processing                              257
           12.3.2   Feature Extraction                          257
           12.3.3   Classification                              258
           12.3.4   Ensemble                                    259
    12.4   Results and Discussion                               260
           12.4.1   Data Set Used                               260
           12.4.2   Evaluation Parameter Used                   261
           12.4.3   Comparison Result                           262
    12.5   Conclusion                                           265
           References                                           265

13  Secured Automated Certificate Creation Based
    on Multimodal Biometric Verification                        269
    *Shilpa Choudhary, Sandeep Kumar, Monali Gulhane*
    *and Munish Kumar*
    13.1   Introduction                                         270
           13.1.1   Background                                  271
    13.2   Literature Work                                      274
    13.3   Proposed Work                                        276
    13.4   Experiment Result                                    278
    13.5   Conclusion and Future Scope                          279
           References                                           280

14  Face and Iris-Based Secured Authorization Model Using CNN  283
    *Munish Kumar, Abhishek Bhola, Ankita Tiwari*
    *and Monali Gulhane*
    14.1   Introduction                                         284
    14.2   Related Work                                         285
    14.3   Proposed Methodology                                 287
           14.3.1   Pre-Processing                              288
           14.3.2   Convolutional Neural Network (CNN)          289
           14.3.3   Image Fusion                                290

| | | |
|---|---|---|
| 14.4 | Results and Discussion | 291 |
| 14.5 | Conclusion and Future Scope | 296 |
| | References | 297 |
| **Index** | | **301** |

# Preface

This book provides relevant information on multimodal biometric and machine learning technologies in order to help students, academics, and researchers from the industry who wish to know more about real-time applications. It focuses on how humans and computers interact to ever-increasing levels of complexity and simplicity. The book provides content on the theory of multimodal biometric design, evaluation, and user diversity, and aims to explain the underlying causes of the social and organizational problems that are typically devoted to descriptions of rehabilitation methods for specific processes. Furthermore, this book describes new algorithms for modeling accessible to scientists of all varieties.

Multimodal biometric and machine learning technologies have revolutionized the field of security and authentication. These technologies utilize multiple sources of information, such as facial recognition, voice recognition, and fingerprint scanning, to verify an individual's identity. The need for enhanced security and authentication has become increasingly important, and with the rise of digital technologies, cyber-attacks and identity theft have increased exponentially. Traditional authentication methods, such as passwords and PINs, have become less secure as hackers devise new ways to bypass them. In this context, multimodal biometric and machine learning technologies offer a more secure and reliable approach to authentication.

Multimodal biometric technology utilizes multiple sources of information to verify an individual's identity. For example, facial recognition technology uses unique facial features to identify an individual, while voice recognition technology uses unique voice patterns. By combining these different sources of information, multimodal biometric technology can provide a more robust and accurate identification process.

Machine learning technology is another powerful tool used in authentication systems. Machine learning algorithms are designed to learn from data and improve over time. In authentication systems, machine learning algorithms can learn to identify patterns and anomalies in user behavior, which can help to detect and prevent fraud. The combination of multi-modal biometric and machine learning technologies has enabled the development of highly secure and reliable authentication systems. These systems can provide a seamless user experience while maintaining high security. For example, a user can look at their phone to unlock it without the need to enter a password or PIN. The system uses facial recognition technology to verify the user's identity and machine learning algorithms to detect and prevent fraud.

A primary advantage of multimodal biometric and machine learning technologies is their ability to adapt to changing circumstances. For example, if a user's face is injured or their voice varies due to illness, the system can still verify their identity using other sources of information. Machine learning algorithms can also adapt to new types of fraud and cyber-attacks, making it more difficult for hackers to bypass the system. However, there are also some challenges associated with the use of these technologies.

Privacy concerns are a significant issue, as the collection and use of biometric data can raise ethical questions. It is essential to ensure that user data is collected and stored securely and that users are fully informed about how their data is used. In addition, the accuracy of these technologies can vary depending on the quality of the data and the algorithms used. It is essential to continually improve and refine the algorithms to ensure high accuracy and reliability.

In conclusion, multimodal biometric and machine learning technologies have revolutionized the field of security and authentication. These technologies offer a more secure and reliable authentication approach while providing a seamless user experience. However, addressing privacy concerns and improving these technologies' accuracy and reliability is essential.

Some features of multimodal biometric-based machine learning technologies include:

- Improved accuracy and reliability: By combining multiple biometric modalities, multimodal biometric systems can provide higher accuracy and reliability than systems that rely on a single biometric modality. This is because the use of multiple modalities reduces the likelihood of a false match.
- Enhanced security: Multimodal biometric systems can provide improved security compared to traditional authentication systems (such as passwords or PINs), as biometric traits are unique to individuals and cannot be easily replicated or stolen.

- Adaptability: Multimodal biometric systems are highly adaptable and can be customized to meet the needs of various applications and user groups. For example, a system could be designed to recognize a user based on their face, voice, fingerprint, or any combination of biometric traits.
- Scalability: Multimodal biometric systems can be scaled up to handle large volumes of users without compromising on accuracy or speed.
- Machine learning-based: Multimodal biometric systems often use machine learning algorithms to analyze biometric data and improve the accuracy and reliability of the system over time.
- User-friendly: Multimodal biometric systems are often designed to be user-friendly, requiring minimal effort on the user's part. For example, a system could be designed to recognize a user's face, voice, and fingerprint simultaneously without requiring the user to perform any specific actions.

We thank all contributing authors who helped us tremendously with their contributions, time, critical thoughts, and suggestions to assemble this peer-reviewed edited volume. The editors are also thankful to Scrivener Publishing and their team for the opportunity to publish this volume. Lastly, we thank our family members for their love, support, encouragement, and patience during this work.

**Sandeep Kumar**
**Deepika Ghai**
**Arpit Jain**
**Suman Lata Tripathi**
**Shilpa Rani**
August 2023

# Multimodal Biometric in Computer Vision

**Sunayana Kundan Shivthare[1]\*, Yogesh Kumar Sharma[2] and Ranjit D. Patil[3]**

*[1]MAEER's MIT Arts, Commerce and Science College, Alandi, Pune,
Maharashtra, India
[2]Department of Computer Science and Engineering, Koneru Lakshmaiah
Education Foundation, Vaddeswaram, Guntur, AP, India
[3]Dr D.Y. Patil ACS College, Pimpri, Pune, Maharashtra, India*

## Abstract

In conjunction with the growing requirement for security regulations and information security worldwide, biometric technology is more prevalent daily than ever. Multimodal biometrics technology has gained popularity due to overcoming several significant drawbacks of unimodal biometric systems. Using numerous biometric markers by personal identification systems to identify individuals is multimodal biometrics. Unlike unimodal biometrics, which uses only one biometric feature, such as a fingerprint, face, palm print, or iris, multimodal authentication is more secure different biometrics systems aid in confirming that only authentic users are using the services. Using cutting-edge approaches like ML, computer vision, object detection and recognition, image analysis pattern recognition, and CNN is the general idea behind biometric identification methods. Machine learning and deep learning are widespread fields in today's digital era. While surfing the Internet, algorithms for machine learning and deep learning are used in every aspect of the online world. This shows that these fields have become an inseparable part of our lives. Abundance data produced through online mediums are classified through these techniques. In computer vision, these algorithms have prominently left their footprints. Deep learning is a subset of machine learning that studies and applies artificial neural networks (ANNs). Deep learning is at the heart of modern artificial intelligence, and its applications rapidly spread across industries and domains. In this chapter, the authors have tried to illuminate applications of

*\*Corresponding author*: sunayanashivthare@gmail.com

Sandeep Kumar, Deepika Ghai, Arpit Jain, Suman Lata Tripathi and Shilpa Rani (eds.)
*Multimodal Biometric and Machine Learning Technologies: Applications for Computer Vision,*
(1–30) © 2023 Scrivener Publishing LLC

machine learning and deep learning concepts and algorithms in connection with multimodal biometrics.

*Keywords*: Machine learning, deep learning, computer vision, biometric systems, multimodal biometrics, authentication

## 1.1   Introduction

Biometrics is the scientific method of identifying individuals based on their qualities or characteristics [1]. It is also used to locate people in groups that are being watched. Unique, quantifiable qualities called biometric identifiers identify and specifically define people. Biometric systems are crucial to finding a person and increasing worldwide security. Many biometrics, including height, DNA, handwriting, and others, could be used, but computer vision-based biometrics have become increasingly significant in human identification [2, 3]. The ability to identify a person's face, fingerprints, iris, and other biometrics using computer vision is used to build effective authentication systems.

## 1.2   Importance of Artificial Intelligence, Machine Learning and Deep Learning in Biometric System

Personal biometric authentication has developed into a necessary and in-demand technology with the development of intelligent artificial systems and e-technologies today. Artificial neural networks (ANN) with numerous hidden layers have been designed to extract low-level to abstract-level characteristics for deep learning (DL), a new subcategory of machine learning. DL approaches include distributed and parallel data processing, adaptive feature learning, dependable fault tolerance, and resilient resilience properties [4]. It is extensively employed in buildings, airports, mobile phones, identity cards, etc. Robust recognition systems must be learned using biometric data. A person can be recognized by various physical characteristics (hand geometry, fingerprint, face, palm print, iris, and ear) and behavioral factors (such as gait, signature, and voice). These qualities can be utilized to separate one person from another and will not be forgotten or lost with time [5]. Combining two or more of these traits helps to increase security, demonstrate excellent performance, and address the shortcomings and limitations of unimodal biometric systems.

Machine learning techniques have been used for recognition by several biometrics researchers. Before classifying the raw biometric data, machine learning algorithms must transform it into a suitable format and extract its characteristics. Before feature extraction, machine learning techniques call for some preprocessing operations [6].

Deep learning has recently had a significant impression and achieved outstanding achievements in biometrics systems. A lot of the drawbacks of traditional machine learning techniques, particularly those related to feature extraction methods, have been solved by deep learning algorithms. Deep learning techniques can handle biometric image changes, take raw data, and extract features [7–9].

Language is the primary means of inter-human communication. Humans are superior to all living things because they communicate using language. Humans can communicate via language because they have the senses of sight and sound. The idea for the intelligent thinking machine was closely related to the inspiration for the computer's invention. The five senses of sight, hearing, smell, taste, and touch enable us to observe, comprehend, appreciate, and engage with our environment [10, 11]. The two senses most contributing to a human's intelligence are sight and sound. The human brain receives information about the company and sound through the eyes and hearing, processes it, and then executes the required actions [12].

Artificial intelligence (AI) should be able to process human language and auditory and visual input. Artificial intelligence was also being developed concurrently with creating generic software consisting of wholly programmed instructions and logic. Making software that simulates the human brain was one of the goals of researchers and programmers in artificial intelligence. Artificial intelligence underwent a revolution with the creation of Deep Neural Networks and the necessary sophisticated technology to process enormous amounts of data. When computers first entered the world in the early 1900s, they were utilized to solve complicated equations [13, 14]. Later, when other technology emerged, people began to view computers as more than just calculators. One of the leading technologies that are replacing human labour is artificial intelligence. Deep learning is a subdomain of artificial intelligence subset of machine learning and was first introduced in 1943 [1, 15, 16].

These deep neural networks contributed to the ability of computers to process speech, images, videos, and other types of natural language. Deep learning is the name of the branch of computer science that deals with these deep neural networks. This chapter aims to explore many facets of machine and deep learning. Deep learning aims to use mathematical algorithms to learn how human brain networks work. Deep learning was created with the core goal of simulating the complicated cognitive process of the human brain to empower machines with independent thought and decision-making [3, 17, 18]. Deep learning is a method for using neural networks to handle massive amounts of data. Several issues in natural language processing, image recognition, and speech recognition can be solved best by this stage. One of the key benefits of adopting deep learning over different machine learning algorithms is that it can create new features from a small number of existing characteristics in the training data set. As a result, deep learning algorithms can solve current problems by creating new tasks [4, 19, 20].

Artificial neural networks, a type of algorithm used in deep learning, are inspired by the structure and operation of the brain. An input layer, a hidden layer, and an output layer make up artificial neural networks. Deep neural networks, which feature numerous hidden layers, are the more sophisticated iterations of artificial neural networks. Deep learning mimics how human brains work, in other words. The nervous system's structure, where every neuron is connected to the others and advances different input types, is precisely how the deep learning algorithm works [21]. The layer system in deep learning is its best asset. Between machine learning and deep learning, there are significant differences. While deep learning models tend to perform exceptionally well with massive data collections and continuously improve, machine learning models reach a saturation point where they cease improving [22]. The feature extraction zones are the other distinction in the future. Machine learning requires people to extract features every single time manually, but deep learning models can learn on their own without human intervention [7]. More significance is placed on computation power in the deep learning process [23, 24]. It depends on our layers; the necessary GPU and CPU quantity are required if the coating is practical. Otherwise, it may be challenging to obtain the outcome after a day, a month, or even a year [8, 9].

## 1.3    Machine Learning

The system is given input in traditional programming, producing output based on the logic. In machine learning, input and output are provided to the system, and models are built using machine learning algorithms. That model makes predictions and solves complex problems such as data analysis, business, and real-world problems [25]. Machine learning programs learn from experience and different examples and perform related

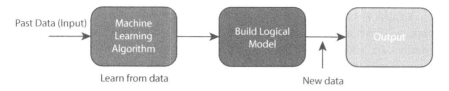

**Figure 1.1** Machine learning working strategy.

tasks accordingly. The machine learning algorithm is implemented using a training data set to create a model. When the machine learning algorithm is presented with new input (test data), it predicts results based on the model shown in Figure 1.1. The prediction is evaluated for accuracy, and the machine learning algorithm is used if it meets expectations. If the machine learning algorithm does not reveal the expected precision, it is trained again with a more extensive training data set [5–9]. Some examples of machine learning are Google or Amazon Recommendation System, Facebook auto-tagging, and email filtering.

Machine learning is effective in data science. Data mining and machine learning processes are similar. Data mining is identifying patterns (forms) in large data sets using methods from database systems, statistics, and machine learning. Data mining is one of the practices used to perform analysis steps for knowledge discovery in databases. Supervised, unsupervised, and reinforcement learning are the three primary forms of machine learning.

## 1.3.1 Supervised vs Unsupervised Model

The model is trained on a labeled data set in supervised learning. A labeled data set is a data set that includes both input and output. The data set's features are extracted, and various algorithms are used to create a model based on the requirements. After constructing a model, it is tested on a new data set. This data set can include times of day, weather conditions, etc., and supervised learning is faster and more accurate than unsupervised learning. The model learning process in supervised learning is done offline. It is applied to two types of problems. There is no need to supervise the model in unsupervised learning [26]. It works with unlabeled data. To obtain the information, the model will learn on its own. It prefers to know in real-time. Unsupervised learning is capable of handling more complex tasks than supervised learning. It provides less accuracy than supervised learning and detects all kinds of unknown patterns in data.

A supervised model receives input and output data from performing a task, whereas an unsupervised model only receives feedback. Supervised models are trained with labeled data, whereas unsupervised models are trained with unlabeled data. The primary goal of a supervised model is to train the model to predict outcomes when new input is introduced [27]. The purpose of an unsupervised model is to extract valuable insights and hidden nodes from unknown data sets. The supervised learning model includes classification and regression, whereas the unsupervised learning model includes clustering and association [10–14].

### 1.3.2   Classification and Regression Problem

In classification, predictions are made on categorical, class, or discrete values. The accuracy of predicting discrete values belonging to a specific category is calculated. Labels specify outputs in classification, such as categorizing images like cat or dog, emails like Spam or not Spam, Promotions, Social etc. To solve the classification problem following algorithms are used Support Vector Machine (SVM), Naive Bayes, Logistic Regression, Decision Tree Classification, K-Nearest Neighbor (KNN), and Random Forest. The prediction in regression is made on continuous values or in the form of numbers. The model predicts values closer to the output values, and errors are calculated. If the error is small, the model performs better. Regression examples include forecasting the weather and stock market [28].

## 1.4   Deep Learning

Deep learning's rise as a new research direction has sparked widespread concern in the AI community. Deep learning is a division of machine learning that mimics human brain functionality. Deep learning, also known as representation learning, automatically discovers good representations from data [29]. Deep learning models are capable of concentrating on the extraction of correct features with minimal human intervention. Image recognition is a computer vision problem in which millions of pixels are present, but most are irrelevant. As a result, deciding and extracting meaningful features becomes difficult in this case. The algorithm will succeed regardless of quality if the extracted features are correctly selected. Deep learning is used to solve such problems. Deep understanding involves training a neural network to recognize images, voice, and handwriting,

**Figure 1.2** Workflow of deep learning.

among other things, as shown in Figure 1.2. In contrast to ML, the data fed can be much larger, more complex, and unstructured [15–21].

The neural network idea is used in deep learning. They are also known as Deep Neural Networks for this reason [30, 31]. With the help of input nodes and hidden nodes that have been trained using more extensive data sets and driving the features from the data itself, deep learning uses AI to predict the output. The model is introduced, and the features are derived using supervised and unsupervised learning [17]. Each node in the above Figure 1.3 depicts a network of interconnected neurons. There are three different kinds of layers, including input, hidden, and output layers. The computation is done linearly. The input layer passes the raw data to the hidden layer(s) so that they may do the necessary calculations, recognize features, and so forth. They are then moved to the output layer so they can respond. The most effective deep learning technique is the conventional neural network of supervised learning, which uses a two-dimensional con-volutional layer to generate two-dimensional data such as photographs and convolves the features recovered from the input layer. Therefore, CNN only sometimes requires manual extraction. Images' attributes can be discov-ered by adding complexity and hidden layer(s) [32, 33].

The data from the input data set and the data from the output data set are compared to train the neural network or AI. The output might be incor-rect if the AI is a data set that has yet to be introduced. The cost function is used to determine an AI output's flaw. The output of an AI system and a

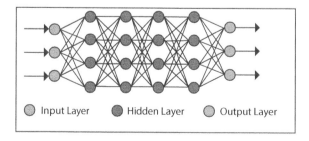

**Figure 1.3** Structure of deep learning model.

real data set will be identical if the cost function is zero. The cost function's value can be decreased by altering the weights between neurons. Gradient Descent methods, which keep the weight of neurons to a minimum after each iteration, are utilized when a practical approach is taken [34, 35].

### 1.4.1   Steps to Create the Machine and Deep Learning Model

The steps required to build ML and DL models are stated here.

**Step 1: Problem recognition**
Understanding the problem statement is the first step in identifying the problem's demands and requirements.
**Step 2: Data identification**
Regression or classification data from the provided data set may need to be recognized for selecting the best algorithm for model training. Various graphs are produced to learn the specific details about the attributes included in the data set.
**Step 3: Algorithm Selection**
Once the relevant data set has been understood, the best and most appropriate algorithm is selected based on regression or classification. Based on its accuracy, the best algorithm is selected.
**Step 4: Model Training**
The relevant factors are determined using the selected algorithm to train the model.
**Step 5: Model Testing**
After training the model, with the help of accuracy, the test data are tested to give the best model.

## 1.5   Related Work

Diverse research studies have suggested multimodal biometric systems that use several recognition methods. This section reviews recent studies using multimodal biometric systems, conventional machine learning, and deep learning techniques. This study by Vino *et al.* [32] seeks to thoroughly analyze the application of the convolutional neural network (CNN) algorithm in acknowledging a personality from three biometric qualities: the finger vein, iris, and face [36–38]. This is due to the excellent productivity of deep learning methods in many identification tasks. This study offers an effective multimodal biometric human reorganization system based on developing a deep learning model for photos of a person's finger vein, iris, and face. These characteristics were chosen because the face is arguably the most natural and visible person identification aspect and because the iris provides adequate recognition data that is both distinctive and very precise.

Chanukya *et al.* recently employed the neural network [39] to create a multimodal biometric verification system that could identify a person from their fingerprint and ear pictures. The design created a local Gabor Xor pattern to extract texture characteristics from the traits and a modified region growth technique to obtain form features from the aspects. The accuracy of the suggested system was 97.33%. However, several studies have concentrated on identifying users based on biometric behavioral factors. Due to the need for consistently repeatable patterns provided by behavioral features in these systems, feature detection and extraction are challenging. Panasiuk *et al.* [40] created a system that used a K-NN classifier to distinguish the user using mouse movement and keystroke dynamics to solve this issue. The proposed approach achieved a 68.8% accuracy rate.

IrisConvNet, a multimodal biometric system for person identification proposed by Al-Waisy *et al.* [41], integrated the left and right irises using ranking-level fusion. The system first identified the iris region in the eye picture, and this identified area was subsequently included in the CNN model. The recognition rate was 100% for the system. A novel feature extraction method for a multimodal biometric system based on iris and facial features was proposed by Ammour *et al.* [42]. With a multi-resolution 2D Log-Gabor filter, the iris feature extraction was completed. At the same time, normal inverse Gaussian and singular spectrum analyses were used to extract the facial features. Fuzzy k-nearest neighbour (K-NN) was utilized for classification, while score fusion with decision fusion was utilized for feature fusion.

A multimodal CNN that combined the features of the iris, face, and fingerprint at various CNN levels was proposed by Soleymani *et al.* [43]. The authors used weighted feature fusion algorithms and multi-abstract fusion as their two fusion techniques. According to the evaluation findings, using all three biometrics produced the most significant outcome. Ding *et al.* [44] conducted one of the experiments that employed deep learning algorithms to create a biometric system. A deep learning framework for face recognition is suggested in this study. The framework used numerous facial pictures and included a three-layer stacked auto-encoder (SAE) for feature-level fusion and eight CNNs for feature extraction. The CNNs were trained on two separate data sets, CASIA-Web face and LFW, and they were accurate to 99% and 76.53%, respectively.

A deep CNN mode for finger shape and finger vein was proposed by Kim *et al.* [45]. The finger photos were captured using the near-infrared camera sensor. The perceptron methods, weighted sum, and product combined the features' matching distance scores. In Gunasekaran *et al.* [46], deep learning template matching techniques were used to construct iris, fingerprint, and face biometrics identification systems. Contour let transform, and local derivative ternary approaches were used for feature extraction. The extracted features were combined using the weighted rank-level technique. Deep CNN models, however, performed poorly when there was a lack of training data. By transferring previously acquired insights from one origin to associated target domains, transfer learning (TL) is frequently employed to address problems with insufficient biometric data [25–28, 30].

Deep transfer learning algorithms were proposed for recognition based on coupled iris and periocular area modalities [47]. A VGG model was utilized for feature extraction, and the binary particle swarm approach was used for feature selection. Matching score-level and feature-level fusion techniques were employed for the fusion of the two modalities. In Daas *et al.* [48], finger vein and finger knuckle print characteristics were retrieved by combining transfer learning with three CNNs: Resnet50, VGG16, and Alexnet [29]. These features were integrated for categorization using the suggested fusion procedures. Zhu *et al.* [49] developed a CNN-based deep transfer learning method for the person identification framework. The framework picked up and communicated knowledge about the best dynamic representation of motion from the jobs in the origin domain.

Regarding [45–47], they created a system that combines voice, face, and iris recognition in this study, overcoming some of the inherent challenges of individual biometrics. Additionally, it is challenging for an outsider to take off several biometric features concurrently because of the integrated system. It reports a brand-new multimodal biometric system that combines many individual attributes for recognition and solves issues with unimodal systems while enhancing recognition performance. They created a multimodal biometric system that combined voice, face, and iris data at the match score level. Combining the information provided by various biometric features, they aim to address the pitfalls of unimodal biometric systems. In this study, scientists created a system that combines iris, face, and voice recognition to overcome some of the inherent challenges of individual biometrics. Additionally, it is challenging for an outsider to spoof several biometric features simultaneously because of the integrated system.

### 1.5.1    Discussions

This section is carried out for detailed discussion about biometric systems, evaluation parameters of biometric systems, need, and outline of multimodal biometric systems. Also, the authors explore the impact of machine learning and deep learning in multimodal biometrics [50].

## 1.6    Biometric System

One can frequently use passwords, PINs, smart cards, hard or soft credentials, etc., to confirm someone's identity. Another way to ensure a person's identification is biometric authentication. The focus of biometric systems is on identifying people, not only authenticating them to provide system access. Biometric techniques identify a person's identity by using physical or behavioral traits [51, 52]. These systems primarily function as identification, access control, and person recognition tools. Biometric systems use technologies that rely on distinctive identifiable characteristics to identify and authorize persons. DNA structure, face detection, iris pattern recognition, fingerprint recognition, hand geometry patterns, and speech recognition are some authentication techniques used to confirm a person's identification. The sensor, feature extraction, matching, and decision-making modules comprise most of the biometric recognition system's four components [32, 33]. Physical biometrics and behavioral biometrics make up the biometric system. Following are the data types used as a biometric system's authentication parameter.

### 1.6.1    Biometrics in Physical Form

The physical biometrics system allows for authentication and identification based on the physical traits of the person's physical components, which are enumerated as follows

a.    **Face Recognition**
A person can also be identified via face recognition. In this mode, a specific gadget collects information about a person's facial expressions and features, and the person is determined by comparing the information with previously saved data [53].

**b. Voice**

This analyzes a person's voice to validate their uniqueness. This procedure is rapid, and the user can be authenticated in seconds.

**c. Iris Recognition**

This biometric identification technique identifies a person by eye structure, ocular patterns, and interior features. The eyes' design does not match any other person's, just as each person's fingerprints may not fit another person's, which is why the iris recognition method is used to identify a person [54].

**d. Hand Vein**

This is a method for authenticating vascular patterns. Here, the vein of the hand (palm) vein pattern will be compared to a design that is stored in the database.

**e. Fingerprint**

This identification system records the fingerprint patterns used for verification and authentication on biometric devices, laptops, and smartphones.

**f. Gesture (Hand) Geometry**

It uses a biometric authentication method that scans the user's hand to determine their identity. In this technique, personal identification is carried out by comparing the information collected by scanning the palm with the information already stored [55].

**g. Authentication with Two Factors**

Two-step verification is the name of this two-factor authentication technique. Two components are employed in this authentication method to confirm the user's identity. The system user may determine which of the two components is used. The user might utilize a different element in the verification process besides the password in this verification and authentication method [56, 57]. A security token or a biometric component could comprise most of the second component. The user can employ hand or fingerprint scans, face scanning, and other biometric aspects as a second factor in addition to a password.

## 1.6.2    Biometrics with Behavior

The second type of biometrics is behavioral biometrics, which authenticates users based on patterns of behavior, such as voice, pulse, signature, keystroke, mouse activity, and touchscreen behavior patterns used to verify or identify an individual's authenticity [58, 59]. Behavioral biometrics addresses personal habits and unique movements.

a. **Pulse Reaction**

The pulse-reaction biometric works because each person's body reacts differently to a signal pulse applied to one hand's palm and measured on the opposite palm. Using a prototype setup, we demonstrate how users can be accurately identified quickly and with a high likelihood.

b. **Signing**

Another method for detecting an individual's behavior is based on the signature performed by the person. Every pattern or curve in a text evolved represents a person's behavior.

c. **Dynamics of Keystrokes**

This new, unique, and innovative biometric identification method identifies a person based on how they use the keyboard.

d. **Conversing (Voice Pattern)**

To confirm identification, the unique patterns in voice can be analyzed and compared.

Extrinsic biometric qualities, like the fingerprint and iris, and intrinsic biometric traits, like the finger and palm veins, can be divided into two categories. While external circumstances cannot influence inherent qualities, extrinsic attributes are noticeable and can be affected by them.

e. **Mouse Activity and Touchscreen Behavior**

An individual can be identified by their mouse activity and touchscreen behavior while operating a desktop, laptop, and other devices.

### 1.6.3    Evaluation Parameters (Metrics) Used by Biometric Systems

The biometric authentication system uses a variety of performance evaluation indicators to assess performance. The following list of frequently used performance evaluation metrics:

a. **Genuine Accept Rate (GAR)**
   It is the proportion of input samples correctly identified as authentic to all positive input samples. A superior GAR value suggests improved performance.

b. **Genuine Reject Rate (GRR)**
   It is the proportion of input samples successfully labeled as impostors to all input samples correctly labeled as impostors. A higher GRR value suggests improved performance.

c. **False Accept Rate (FAR)**
   It is the percentage of fake input samples incorrectly labeled as positive. You should be aware that FAR = 1- GRR. A lower FAR number indicates better system performance.

d. **False Reject Rate (FRR)**
   It is the percentage of numerous input samples that were wrongly labeled as forgeries. Note that FRR =1- GAR. A biometric authentication system performs better when its FRR value is lower.

e. **Equal Error Rate (ERR)**
   The ratio is the exact error rate when FRR and FAR become comparable. A lower ERR value indicates refined performance.

f. **Failure To Capture (FTC) or Failure To Acquire (FTA)**
   It measures how frequently a biometric system cannot recognize the biometric sample provided to it. A lower number suggests improved FTA acquisition efficiency.

g. **Failure To Enroll (FTE)**
   It is the proportion between the total number of users presented to a biometric system that cannot be successfully enrolled and the overall number of users. A lower FTE value indicates better population coverage.

## 1.7    Need for Multimodal Biometric

Unimodal authentication requires a single source of information. As the name implies, multimodal systems accept information from two or more biometric inputs. A multimodal biometric system broadens and diversifies the types of information collected from users for authentication [12]. Lack of confidentiality, non-universality of samples, user comfort and freedom in using the system, spoofing attacks on stored data etc., are challenged with unimodal systems. The multimodal method is more dependable when many qualities are available [31]. Data about users is more securely and secretively stored with a multimodal biometric system. Fusion techniques are used in the multimodal biometric system. Since a decade ago, deep learning research has been conducted internationally in various applications. The new learning method primarily uses cognitive applications that rely on machine learning. This will guide behavioral and physiological researchers and scientists for future work. Image processing and computer vision are frequently used in the field of biometrics [45–47]. Various categories for biometric techniques exist based on the modalities, fusion schemes, procedures, etc., employed. Face and fingerprint are the most often studied biometric characteristics in cognitive science applications. Biometrics is likewise categorized under A multimodal biometric is necessary for a better authentication system since it broadens the system's range and variety of input data. A multimodal biometric system can be used to tackle some of these issues.

### 1.7.1    Perks of Multimodal Biometric

In this section, the authors have sketched some of the perks of multimodal biometric

    a.  **Correctness**

        Compared to unimodal biometric systems, multimodal biometric systems nearly never experience false match rates (FMR) or acceptance rates (FAR). The performance indicators for biometric systems are false matches and false acceptance rates. It describes the instances in which the system either incorrectly matches it to a pattern found in the database or fails to match an existing design contained in the database. The level of accuracy is unquestionably high since multimodal biometric systems use more than one physiological feature, such as fingerprints, palm vein patterns, or iris patterns, to validate an individual [3].

b. **Noise-reduced data**

Occasionally, due to a finger being misplaced, which influences the matching process, the data obtained during authentication may differ from the input data during enrollment. Multimodal biometric systems can correct noisy data and intra-class variances using different biometric data for verification [44].

c. **Universality**

People with physical limitations cannot produce a solo biometric credential in some situations. However, a multimodal biometric system can accept any additional biometric authentication credential.

d. **Enhanced security and identification**

A secondary benefit of a multimodal biometric system is its ability to recognize individuals at more significant thresholds. Even if one of the system IDs cannot match a specific behavioral or physiological attribute, it can still identify the person using the remaining traits.

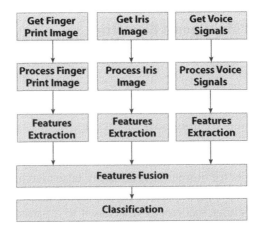

**Figure 1.4** Block diagram for multimodal biometric system using fingerprint, iris image, and voice [44].

### 1.7.2    The General Outline of a Multimodal Biometric System

Figure 1.4 depicts multiple biometrics traits, mainly a fingerprint, an iris image, and a voice, to design a multimodal biometric system for authenticating an individual. Each biometrics trait is recorded and processed in this system to extract features of different patterns. Ultimately, it is combined to get a more accurate authentication result.

Because of the automation of a person's identification and verification, biometrics is now used in many applications. Educational sectors, home security systems, legal applications, Banking systems, airport boarding, passes for personal identification, attendance and timing tracking, government applications, and commercial applications are just a few examples.

## 1.8    Databases Used by Biometric System

Personal identification is a vital human-computer interface activity in an increasingly digitalized world. Biometric methods, such as digital imprinting or face/voice probes, are rapidly gaining acceptance in the industry, administration, and personal life. Despite the rapid spread of databases, system development has previously focused on database precision rather than counting and speed issues for large database applications [51]. Apart from accuracy, these applications use increased response time, high-quality search, and recovery. Traditional databases classify records alphabetically or numerically to ensure efficient recovery. There is no natural order in biometric templates that could justify classification. We propose the group classification and restriction method, which uses general guidelines for designing templates before establishing exhaustive correspondences, to guide the search in a biometric database. Several biometrical characteristics can be used: for example, a single biometric characteristic, such as the face, can be used to identify preliminary virtual correspondences, followed by a more precise biometric characteristic, such as the digital imprint, for final identification. Active databases have demonstrated the potential of automatic reactions to specific occurrences. The dataset is distributed in three sections: Training, Validation, and Testing [52]. The learning model's parameters, features, and other choices are adjusted using the validation dataset. A testing data set is used to evaluate the performance of the model. Data distribution should be done wisely for authentic model learning and precise prediction. It can follow 80/20, 70/30, and 60/20/20 patterns as per the size of the dataset.

## 1.8.1  Confusion Matrix

The evaluation and testing of the model's efficacy come next after the model training phase. The model is anticipated to perform better along with the predicted outcome. A confusion matrix can be used to measure it. In it, the confusion matrix is essential. A confusion matrix is a handy tool for evaluating how well the classifier performs concerning the classification issue. Karl Pearson, a British statistician, created it in 1904. It is used to display the classes that the classifier recognizes.

It displays how effectively your classifier performs. It compares the actual values to those that the classifier predicted. More details are provided on the classifiers' mistakes and categories of errors. The X-axis in the confusion matrix represents expected values, whereas the Y-axis represents actual values. While non-diagonal numbers are wrong (mixed) forecasts, the diagonal values were accurately predicted. A more incredible performance of the model is shown if the numbers along the diagonal are higher. For N classes, the N X N confusion matrix can be assessed. Here, it is described as a binary classification problem using the example of two types.

Class A is Positive, and Class B is Negative. The terms TP (True Positive), FP (False Positive), FN (False Negative), and TN (True Negative) in the confusion matrix have a particular meaning. TP means the actual value is positive and is also predicted as positive shown in Figure 1.5. FN says that original values are positive, but it is given as unfavourable. FP intimates that the initial values are negative, which is also projected as positive. TN indicates that the actual value and resulted value both are negative. Accuracy, Precision, Recall, and F1-Score stemming from the confusion matrix are used to evaluate the classifier's performance. The following definitions are included:

| | | Predicted Values | |
|---|---|---|---|
| | | A (Positive) | B (Negative) |
| **Actual Values** | A(Positive) | TP (TP$_A$) | FN (E$_{BA}$) |
| | B(Negative) | FP (E$_{BA}$) | TN (TP$_B$) |

**Figure 1.5**  2X2 confusion matrix.

- **Accuracy**
  Accuracy tells how accurately the classifier performs well. It depicts the closeness or friendliness of the actual and predicted values. It is calculated as:

$$\text{Accuracy} = \frac{(TP + TN)}{(TP + TN + FP + FN)} \qquad (1.1)$$

- **Precision**
  The classifier model can recognize the relevant positive class. It depicts the proportion of the true positive values to the positive predictive values. It is given by:

$$\text{Precision} = \frac{TP}{(TP + FP)} \qquad (1.2)$$

- **Recall**
  It gives the ratio of the true positive values to the actual positive values. It is also called sensitivity or true positive rate. It is measured by:

$$\text{Recall} = \frac{TP}{(TP + FN)} \qquad (1.3)$$

- **F1-Score**
  It is a combination of precision and recall and tries to balance them. It is evaluated as follows:

$$\text{F1-Score} = 2 * \frac{(\text{Recall} * \text{Precision})}{(\text{Recall} + \text{Precision})} \qquad (1.4)$$

## 1.9 Impact of DL in the Current Scenario

Deep learning algorithms are associated with application development in various fields in the current era. Applications of DL are described shown in Figure 1.6.

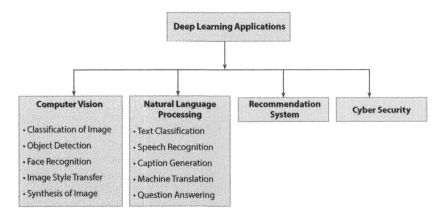

**Figure 1.6** Deep learning applications.

## 1.9.1   Computer Vision

The branch of AI and ML known as computer vision (CV) primarily gives computers the capability of seeing. Using computer vision, the contents of digital photographs are comprehended. DL addresses various computer vision issues, including picture categorization, object identification, image style transfer, and image synthesis [25–28, 30].

a.   **Classification of Image**
Giving a label to a set of pixels in an image is a supervised learning problem. The two image classification techniques frequently utilized in several applications are binary and multiclass classification. A classification method known as binary classification separates the provided collection of components into two classes following the principles of type. A famous example of binary classification is the issue of determining whether a given image is of a cat or a dog. The typical supervised machine learning task of multiclass classification involves categorizing the provided set of objects into more than two groups. Multiclass categorization is a difficulty that arises while naming a flower captured in photography. The CNN method is used to solve the image classification issue.

b.   **Object Detection**
This method primarily focuses on locating objects in still or motion pictures. This technique provides the location data

of a known set of items in an image. The object detection model is trained in a way that will enable it to recognize various object classes when given a particular input image. Each object in an image that is located and identified has a precision value assigned to it. The object identification methods include CNN, Fast RCNN, Faster RCNN, and Region-based CNN (RCNN).

c.  **Face recognition**
Face recognition is the process where, given a picture of one or more people, the system must either authenticate the person's identification in the image or identify the persons in the concept based on their faces.

d.  **Image Style Transfer**
The content and style reference images are the two types of photos combined to create a style image. Utilizing CNN, image style transfer is carried out.

e.  **Synthesis of Image**
Using a computer algorithm primarily refers to the process of creating realistic visuals. Image synthesis has several uses, including an image in the painting, texture synthesis, image super-resolution, and face image synthesis. A small digital image can create a vast digital image using texture synthesis. Converting a lower-resolution image into a higher-resolution image is known as image super-resolution. Reconstructing missing portions of an image is done via image in painting. Using this method, damaged sections of antique pictures are repaired. Face image synthesis is used to create images of faces that are photorealistic. Using this method, high-quality perceptual face images can be produced. Image synthesis is carried out by using Generative Adversarial Networks (GANs).

### 1.9.2   Natural Language Processing

Natural language processing (NLP) permits computers to manipulate, interpret, and comprehend human language. It serves as a link between spoken communication and computer comprehension. DL addresses NLP issues, including text classification, audio recognition, caption generation, machine translation, and question-answering.

a. **Text Classification**
Natural language documents are given tags with pertinent categories using them. Using text classifiers, the text is automatically analyzed. Sentiment analysis, subject identification, and language identification are the three most common applications for automatic text classification. Sentiment analysis examines the feelings (positive, negative, and neutral) underlying the chosen text. Topic detection technology is used to comprehend and organize extensive collections of text data. Language detection techniques are used to identify various languages and their variants.

b. **Speech Recognition**
It converts spoken language into written language and processes spoken language. Speech recognition software frequently uses NLP and DL to extract the constituent parts of speech. The collected speech-based elements are accurately translated into text. The speech recognition software is trained using a set of recognized spoken words. Measures of speech recognition performance include accuracy and speed.

c. **Caption Generation**
The method of caption generation is the automatic creation of natural language descriptions based on the image information. To address the issue of caption generation, NLP and CV are coupled.DL techniques like CNN and Long Short-Term Memory (LSTM) create an image captioning system. A unique type of artificial RNN, LSTM, is utilized to develop image captions from the CNN-obtained image attributes.

d. **Machine Translation**
Machine translation is translating stuff from its original language into one of the target languages. It is a fully automated piece of software that aids in the translation of speech and text into another language by people. Generic, configurable, and adaptive MT are the three types of machine translation systems. Generic MT systems are designed to be used by millions of individuals for various applications and are not constrained to a single domain. These systems have been trained using multiple types of data. The most well-known examples of generic MT systems are Microsoft

Translator and Google Translate. In the specified field, they offer translations of excellent quality. An example of an adaptable MT is WIPO Translate. Real-time in nature, adaptive MT systems pick up corrections as they are made. Machine translation is implemented using neural networks like RNN and recursive auto-encoders (RAE). When compared to other neural networks, these networks offer more significant results.

e.  **Question Answering**

It is a natural language processing and information retrieval system that automatically responds to queries given by people in that language. The close-domain and open-domain question-answering systems are the two different categories. While the open-domain question-answering system responds to inquiries from any field, the closed-domain question-answering system only addresses queries from a single domain. Cortana, Alexa, Siri, and Google Assistant are well-known examples of question-answering programs.

### 1.9.3  Recommendation System

The primary application of recommendation systems is to forecast customer preferences and make product recommendations based on data analysis. Examples of recommender systems that provide users with appropriate suggestions based on their past selections include Youtube, Netflix, Amazon, and Spotify. DL techniques such as the Deep Collaborative Filtering Model (DCFM), CNN, auto encoders (AE), and RNN can address issues with the recommendation system. These methods can be used to develop recommendation systems for social networks, educational resources, entertainment, and session-based suggestions.

### 1.9.4  Cyber Security

The core focus of cyber security is defending against and recovering from cyber attacks on systems, networks, and programs. Intelligent intrusion detection (ID) and intrusion prevention (IP) systems that can aid security teams in identifying malicious actions on the web can be made using CNN and RNN.DL algorithms can be effectively utilized to counteract more sophisticated network threats. DNN can be used to identify spam emails with greater accuracy.

## 1.10   Conclusion

A multimodal biometric system integrates more than one biometric data recognition results to improve the achievement of authentication systems, reducing the rate of false acceptance and preventing unauthorized users from authenticating. These systems use a variety of a person's physiological or behavioral traits for enrolment, verification, or identification. Applications for multimodal biometric systems, i.e., e-commerce, smart cards, passports, visas, etc. A person's fingerprint and iris are combined to identify a person automatically. For person authentication, multiple biometric traits of a personlike voice, fingerprint, and iris image are utilized to strengthen security. The central concept of biometric identification technologies uses cutting-edge techniques, including ML, computer vision, object detection and recognition, image analysis pattern recognition, and CNN. Machine learning and deep learning algorithms are used in every aspect of the online world. In this chapter, the authors have gone through aspects of machine learning and deep learning technologies, particularly the multimodal biometrics technique.

## References

1. Sharma, D.Y.K. and Pradeep, S., Deep learning based real-time object recognition for security in air defense. *Proceedings of the 13th INDIACom*, pp. 64–67, 2019.
2. Rokade, M.D. and Sharma, Y.K., MLIDS: A machine learning approach for intrusion detection for real-time network dataset, in: *2021 International Conference on Emerging Smart Computing and Informatics (ESCI)*, IEEE, pp. 533–536, 2021, March.
3. Uddin, A.H., Bapery, D., Arif, A.S.M., Depression analysis from social media data in bangla language using long short term memory (LSTM) recurrent neural network technique, in: *International Conference on Computer, Communication, Chemical, Materials and Electronic Engineering (IC4ME2)*, 2019.
4. Balakrishnan, S., Aravind, K., Ratnakumar, A.J., A novel approach for tumor image set classification based on multi-manifold deep metric learning. *Int. J. Pure Appl. Math.*, 119, 10c, 553–562, 2018.
5. Balaji, B.S., Balakrishnan, S., Venkatachalam, K. *et al.*, Automated query classification based web service similarity technique using machine learning. *J. Ambient Intell. Hum. Comput.*, 12, 6169–61.80, 2020. https://doi.org/10.1007/s12652-020-02186-6.

6. Balakrishnan, S. and Deva, D., *Machine intelligence challenges in military robotic control*, vol. 41, pp. 35–36, CSI Communications Magazine, CSI Publication, Chennai, India, January 2018.

7. JebarajRathnakumar, A. and Balakrishnan, S., Machine learning based grape leaf disease detection. *Journal of Advanced Research in Dynamical and Control Systems (JARDCS)*, 10, 08-Special issue, 775–780, 2018.

8. Prabha, D., Siva Subramanian, R., Balakrishnan, S., Karpagam, M., Performance evaluation of naive bayes classifier with and without filter based feature selection. *International Journal of Innovative Technology and Exploring Engineering (IJITEE)*, 8, 10, 2154–2158, August 2019.

9. Winston Paul, D., Balakrishnan, S., Velusamy, A., Rule based hybrid weighted fuzzy classifier for tumor data. *Int. J. Eng. Technol. (UAE)*, 7, 4.19, 104–108, 2018, https://doi. org/10.14419/ijet.v7i4.19.

10. Vasu, S., Puneeth Kumar, A.K., Sujeeth, T., Dr S. Balakrishnan, A., Machine learning based approach for computer security. *Journal of Advanced Research in Dynamical and Control Systems (JARDCS)*, 10, 11-Special issue, 915–919, 2018.

11. Rani, S., Lakhwani, K., Kumar, S., Construction and reconstruction of 3d facial and wireframe model using syntactic pattern recognition, in: *Cognitive Behavior & Human Computer Interaction*, pp. 137–156, Scrivener & Wiley Publishing House, Beverly, Mass. United States, 2021.

12. Rani, S., Ghai, D., Kumar, S., Kantipudi, M.V.V., Alharbi, A.H., Ullah, M.A., Efficient 3D AlexNet architecture for object recognition using syntactic patterns from medical images. *Comput. Intell. Neurosci.*, 2022, 1–19, 2022.

13. Rani, S., Ghai, D., Kumar, S., Reconstruction of simple and complex three dimensional images using pattern recognition algorithm. *Journal of Information Technology and Management (JITM)*, 14, 235–247, 2022.

14. Fogelman Soulie, F., Gallinari, P., Lecun, Y., Thiria, S., Generalization using back-propagation, in: *Proceedings of the First International Conference on Neural Networks*, IEEE, San Diego, California, 1987 June, 1987.

15. Gaetano, L., Are neural networks imitations of mind? *J. Comput. Sci. Syst. Biol.*, 8, pp. 124-126, 2015. 10.4172/jcsb.1000179.

16. Deng, J., Dong, W., Socher, R., Li, L.-J., Li, K., Fei-Fei, L., Imagenet: A large-scale hierarchical image database. *2009 IEEE Conference on Computer Vision and Pattern Recognition*, pp. 248–255, 2009.

17. Caruana, R., Silver, D.L., Baxter, J., Mitchell, T.M., Pratt, L.Y., Thrun, S., Knowledge consolidation and transfer in inductive systems, in: *Learning to Learn*, Springer New York, NY, 1995 December.

18. Sharma, Y.K., Yadav, R.N.B.V., Anjaiah, P., The comparative analysis of open stack with cloud stack for infrastructure as a service. *Int. J. Adv. Sci Technol.*, 28, 16, 164–174, 21 Nov. 2019.

19. Pan, S.J. and Yang, Q., A survey on transfer learning. *IEEE Trans. Knowl. Data Eng.*, 22, 10, 1345–1359, 2010.

20. Sarkar, D., Bali, R., Ghosh, T., *Hands-on transfer learning with python: Implement advanced deep learning and neural network models using TensorFlow and Keras*, Packt Publishing, Mumbai, Maharashtra, India, 2018.

21. Sharma, Y.K. and Khan, V., A research on automatic handwritten devnagari text generation in different styles using recurrent neural network (deep learning) especially for marathi script. *International Journal of Recent Technology and Engineering (IJRTE)*, 8, 2S11, 938–942, September 2019.

22. Jadhav, M., Sharma, Y., Bhandari, G., Forged multinational currency recognition system using convolutional neural network, in: *Proceedings of 6th International Conference on Recent Trends in Computing*, Springer, Singapore, pp. 471–479, 2021.

23. Sharma, Y. K. and Pradeeep, S., Performance escalation and optimization of overheads in the advanced underwater sensor networks with the internet of things. *International Journal of Innovative Technology and Exploring Engineering (IJITEE)*, 08, 11, 2299–2302, 2019. https://doi.org/10.35940/ijitee.k2073.0981119.

24. Pradeep, S., Sharma, Y.K., Verma, C., Dalal, S., Prasad, C., Energy efficient routing protocol in novel schemes for performance evaluation. *Appl. Syst. Innov.*, 5, 5, 101, 2022. (MDPI).

25. Patil, S., Sharma, Y.K., Patil, R., Implications of deep learning-based methods for face recognition in online examination system. *International Journal of Recent Technology and Engineering (IJRTE)*, 8, 3, 14–27, 2019.

26. Kumar, S., Jain, A., Agarwal, A.K., Rani, S., Ghimire, A., Object-based image retrieval using the u-net-based neural network. *Comput. Intell. Neurosci.*, 1–14, 2021. https://doi.org/10.1155/2021/4395646

27. Kumar, S., Haq, M.A., Jain, A., Jason, C.A., Moparthi, N.R., Mittal, N., Alzamil, Z.S., Multilayer Neural Network Based Speech Emotion Recognition for Smart Assistance. *CMC-Comput. Mater. Contin.*, 74, 1, 1–18, 2022. Tech Science Press.

28. Abhishek, and Singh, S., Visualization and modeling of high dimensional cancerous gene expression dataset. *J. Inf. Knowl. Manag.*, 18, 01, 1950001–22, 2019. World Scientific.

29. Shivthare, S., Sharma, Y.K., Patil, R.D., To enhance the impact of deep learning-based algorithms in determining the behavior of an individual based on communication on social media. *International Journal of Innovative Technology and Exploring Engineering (IJITEE)*, 8, 12, 4433–4435, October 2019.

30. Tidake, A.H., Sharma, Y., Deshpande, V.S., Design and implement forecast remedy techniques to maximize the yield of farming using deep learning, in: *2020 International Conference on Industry 4.0 Technology (I4Tech)*, IEEE, pp. 80–84, 2020, February.

31. Ren, C.-X., Dai, D.-Q., Huang, K.-K., Lai, Z.-R., Transfer learning of structured representation for face recognition. *IEEE Trans. Image Process.*, 23, 12, 5440–5454, December 2014.

32. Vino, T., Sivaraju, S.S., Krishna, R.V.V., Karthikeyan, T., Sharma, Y.K., Venkatesan, K.G.S., Manikandan, G., Selvameena, R., Markos, M., Multicluster analysis and design of hybrid wireless sensor networks using solar energy. *Int. J. Photoenergy*, 2022, 1–8, 2022. Hindawi.

33. Shao, L., Zhu, F., Li, X., Transfer learning for visual categorization: A survey. *IEEE Trans. Neural Networks Learn. Syst.*, 26, 1019–1034, 2015.

34. Sharma, Y.K., Web page classification on news feeds using hybrid technique for extraction, in: *Information& Communication Technology for Intelligent System*.

35. Rezende, E., Ruppert, G., Carvalho, T., Ramos, F., de Geus, P., Malicious software classification using transfer learning of resnet50 deep neural network. *16th IEEE International Conference on Machine Learning and Applications*, 2017.

36. Luttrell, J., Zhou, Z., Zhang, C., Gong, P., Zhang, Y., Facial recognition via transfer learning: Fine-tuning keras_vggface. *International Conference on Computational Science and Computational Intelligence*, pp. 576–579, 2017.

37. Sharma, Y.K. and Ranjeet, K., A review on different prediction techniques for stock market price. *Int. J. Control Autom.*, 13, 1, 353–364, 2020. Science and Engineering Research Support Society.

38. Alay, N. and Al-Baity, H.H., Deep learning approach for multimodal biometric recognition system based on fusion of iris, face, and finger vein traits. *Sensors*, 20, 19, 1–17, 5523, 2020. https://doi.org/10.3390/s20195523

39. Chanukya, P.S.V.V.N. and Thivakaran, T.K., Multimodal biometric cryptosystem for human authentication using fingerprint and ear. *Multimed. Tools Appl.*, 79, 659–673, 2020.

40. Panasiuk, P., Szymkowski, M., Marcin, D.A., Multimodal biometric user identification system based on keystroke dynamics and mouse movements, in: *Proceedings of the 15th IFIP TC 8 International Conference on Computer Information Systems and Industrial Management*, pp. 672–681, Vilnius, Lithuania, 14–16 September 2016

41. Al-Waisy, A.S., Qahwaji, R., Ipson, S., Al-Fahdawi, S., Nagem, T.A.M.A., multi-biometric iris recognition system based on a deep learning approach. *Pattern Anal. Appl.*, 21, 783–802, 2018.

42. Ammour, B., Boubchir, L., Bouden, T., Ramdani, M., Face–Iris multimodal biometric identification system. *Electronics*, 9, 85, 2020.

43. Soleymani, S., Dabouei, A., Kazemi, H., Dawson, J., Nasrabadi, N.M., Multilevel feature abstraction from convolutional neural networks for multimodal biometric identification, in: *Proceedings of the 2018 24th International Conference on Pattern Recognition*, pp. 3469–3476, 20–24 August 2018.

44. Ding, C., Member, S., Tao, D., Robust, face recognition via multimodal deep face representation. *IEEE Trans. Multimed.*, 17, 2049–2058, 2015.

45. Kim, W., Song, J.M., Park, K.R., Multimodal biometric recognition based on the convolutional neural network by fusing finger-vein and finger shape using a near-infrared (NIR) camera sensor. *Sensors*, 18, 2296, 2018.

46. Gunasekaran, K., Raja, J., Pitchai, R., Deep multimodal biometric recognition using contourlet derivative weighted rank fusion with a human face, finger-print, and iris images. *Autom. CasopisZaAutom. Mjer. Elektron. Računarstvo I Komuň.*, 60, 253–265, 2019.

47. Silva, P.H., Luz, E., Zanlorensi, L.A., Menotti, D., Moreira, G., Multimodal feature level fusion based on particle swarm optimization with deep transfer learning, in: *Proceedings of the 2018 IEEE Congress on Evolutionary Computation (CEC)*, Rio de Janeiro, Brazil, pp. 1–8, 8–13 July 2018.

48. Daas, S., Yahi, A., Bakir, T., Sedhane, M., Boughazi, M., Bourennane, E.-B., Multimodal biometric recognition systems using deep Learning based on the finger vein and finger knuckle print fusion. *IET Image Process*, 14, 3859–3868, 2020.

49. Zhu, H., Samtani, S., Chen, H., Nunamaker Jr, J.F., Human identification for activities of daily living: A deep transfer learning approach. *J. Manag. Inf. Syst.*, 37, 457–483, 2020.

50. El_Tokhy, M.S., Robust multimodal biometric authentication algorithms using the fusion of fingerprint, iris, and voice features. *J. Intell. Fuzzy Syst.*, 40, 1, 647–672, 2021.

51. Tolba, A.S. and Rezq, A.A., Combined classifier for invariant face recognition. *Pattern Anal. Appl.*, 3, 4, 289–302, 2000.

52. Prasanna, D.L. and Tripathi, S.L., Machine learning classifiers for speech detection, in: *2022 IEEE VLSI Device Circuit and System (VLSI DCS)*, pp. 143–147, Kolkata, India, 2022.

53. Thillaiarasu, N., LataTripathi, S., Dhinakaran, V. (Eds.), *Artificial Intelligence for Internet of Things: Design Principle, Modernization, and Techniques*, 1st ed, CRC Press, Boca Raton, Florida, United States, 2022, https://doi.org/10.1201/9781003335801.

54. Sandeep, K., Rani, S., Jain, A., Verma, C., Raboaca, M.S., Illés, Z., Neagu, B.C., Face spoofing, age, gender and facial expression recognition using advance neural network architecture-based biometric system. *Sen. J.*, 22, 14, 5160–5184, 2022.

55. Abhishek, and Singh, S., Gene selection using high dimensional gene expression data: An appraisal. *Curr. Bioinform.*, 13, 3, 225–233, 2018. Bentham Science.

56. Rani, S., Gowroju, Sandeep, K., IRIS based recognition and spoofing attacks: A review, in: *10th IEEE International Conference on System Modeling &Advancement in Research Trends (SMART)*, December 10-11, 2021.

57. Swathi, A., Sandeep, K., V. S., T., Rani, S., Jain, A., Ramakrishna, K. M.V.N.M, Emotion classification using feature extraction of facial expressiona, in: *The International Conference on Technological Advancements in Computational Sciences (ICTACS – 2022)*, Tashkent City Uzbekistan, pp. 1–6, 2022.

58. Bhaiyan, A.J.G., Shukla, R.K., Sengar, A.S., Gupta, A., Jain, A., Kumar, A., Vishnoi, N.K., Face recognition using convolutional neural network in machine learning, in: *2021 10th International Conference on System Modeling & Advancement in Research Trends (SMART)*, IEEE, pp. 456–461, 2021, December.

59. Bhaiyan, A.J.G., Jain, A., Gupta, A., Sengar, A.S., Shukla, R.K., Jain, A., Application of deep learning for image sequence classification, in: *2021 10th International Conference on System Modeling & Advancement in Research Trends (SMART)*, IEEE, pp. 280–284, 2021, December.

# 2

# A Vaccine Slot Tracker Model Using Fuzzy Logic for Providing Quality of Service

Mohammad Faiz, Nausheen Fatima and Ramandeep Sandhu*

*Department of Computer Science and Engineering, Lovely Professional University, Phagwara, Jalandhar, India*

## Abstract

In recent years, we have seen the outbreak of COVID, and vaccination has proved to be quite effective in this case. Vaccination of a large population in a country like India is a big hurdle. People wait for hours to get the slot for vaccination. However, most humans still need help getting the vaccination slot because the information about the place of vaccination and opening time is unavailable. We have proposed a vaccination tracker model for this problem, which provides instant communication to the users about the vaccination opening and location, which makes registering the vaccination very easy. The proposed model is based on object-oriented, database, and networking techniques that use fuzzy logic to get the availability of vaccination slots using three input parameters: age, availability of vaccine slot, and vaccination status. The proposed model is a web-based application that clients can access with a server. The registered users are given priority based on their possibilities, which are calculated using the fuzzy technique. According to the preference, which can be very low, low, medium, high, or very high, the user is informed how many slots are available and booked based on the information they gave when they signed up. After successfully vaccinating the first dose, the countdown is started for the following amount. The simulation results show the effectiveness of the proposed model.

*Keywords:* Vaccination, COVID-19, health care, fuzzy logic, economy, pandemic, quality of service

*Corresponding author*: ramandeep.28362@lpu.co.in

Sandeep Kumar, Deepika Ghai, Arpit Jain, Suman Lata Tripathi and Shilpa Rani (eds.)
Multimodal Biometric and Machine Learning Technologies: Applications for Computer Vision,
(31–52) © 2023 Scrivener Publishing LLC

## 2.1    Introduction

The SARS-CoV-2, is a type of  new coronavirus that causes coronavirus illness (COVID-19). It has caused an unparalleled healthcare catastrophe in recent times. It was declared a pandemic disease because of the significant spike in cases. Since the first case, 4 million infections and even above 300,000 death reports have been confirmed in various parts of the world, including the United States. COVID-19 has a high potential for progression. There needs to be more knowledge about its behavior patterns, pointing to the urgent need to solve this public health emergency. Corporations, Governments and private institutions worldwide are integrating their efforts to find a viable solution for preventing COVID-19 from spreading worldwide. It is critical to use digital technologies in this scenario because they are vital tools towards improvement regarding the health status of the population and the provision of essential services to them. The World Health Organization (WHO) released ten endorsements for improving healthcare quality and basic services through digital technologies. If we talk about technology and digitalization, mobile phones are currently estimated to be used by more than 5 billion people worldwide; additionally, as per the "State of Mobile in 2019" report issued in 2018, 194 trillion dollars in applications have been downloaded around the world in 2018 [1]. As a result, most of the world's population can easily access and use apps, making them extremely popular. The historical context must understand the breadth and depth of coronavirus disease (COVID-19)-related software. Furthermore, a comprehensive directory of all the apps developed to combat the COVID-19 pandemic has yet to be established.

For the vaccination drive, digitalization played a vital part in the scheduling and maintaining the necessary precautions to be taken possible. Now, a question arises: what does vaccination mean, why is it mandatory, or how do vaccines shield? The body's immunity is stimulated by vaccination, which protects people against later illnesses or diseases. Now, coming to digitalization and app development, The Govt. Agencies developed over half of the apps used during the pandemic. The use of the apps is to provide info on the number of infected, healthier, and dead patients, record signs, and trace patients' contacts, the public's ease of access, and the use of artificial intelligence stance apps as tools capable of identifying new COVID-19 transmission foci, analyzing the proportion of propagation, tracking possible symptoms, and roughly characterizing positive cases at a distance. Managing and monitoring vaccine stockpiles, logistics, and fair distribution are all essential aspects of vaccination. Immunization provides you with constant visibility and actionable data about vaccine distribution, observing it and ensuring that it is reasonable and equal. Immunization allows you to schedule vaccination appointments and track the vaccines being distributed [2]. Even during the current global epidemic, many governments have decided to implement apps to aid in slowing the rapid spread of the COVID-19 virus, which played a significant and appreciable role.

## 2.2    Related Research

In the study by Akshita *et al.* [3], the authors conducted a cross-sectional, descriptive observational study of all smartphone apps related to COVID-19. Between April 27 and May 2, 2020, and searched for COVID-19 apps in the App Store (for iOS) and the Google Play Store (for Android). As a result of the investigation, they discovered 114 applications on the explored platforms. There were 62 of 114 (54.4%) Android devices and 52 of 114 (45.6%) iOS devices. Three-quarters of the 114 apps were developed in Europe, 28% were designed in Asia, and 26% were produced in North America. Foreign language usage was most prevalent in English (65/114, or 57.0%), Spanish (34/114, or 29.8%), and Chinese (14/114, or 12.3%). The most popular categories were apps for health and well-being/fitness (41/114, 41.2%) and medicine (43/114, 37.7%). There were 113 (99.1%) free apps among the 114 total. The average time between the analysis date and the most recent update was 11.1 days (SD, 11.0 days). A total of 95 (83.3%), 99 (7.5%), and 3 (2.6%) of the 114 apps were designed for the general public, health professionals, or both. 64 of the 114 apps (56.1%) were created by governments, 42 by national governments (64.1 percentage), and 23 by regional governments (35.3 percentage). All but one app with more than 100,000 downloads (P=0.13) was developed by a government, except the World Health Organization app, which had more than 500,000 downloads (P=.13). The most common uses were to get general COVID-19 information COVID-19 news (53, 51.0%), record COVID-19 symptoms (53, 51.0%), and find people who have COVID-19 contacts (51, 47.7%). Their paper provides a comprehensive and one-of-a-kind review of all COVID-19 applications currently available.

In Arjun Kumar *et al.* [4], the author mentions invaluable insights shared by the Chief Executive Officer of the National Health Authority (NHA), Ministry of Health and Family Welfare of the Government of India, Dr R S Sharma, CEO of the National Health Authority (NHA), Ministry of Health and Family Welfare of the Government of India that the danger of such circumstances provides sufficient justification for the administration to depend on digital infrastructure despite the substantial concern about the digital divide that has been raised. Two main principles direct their work: the first is the goal of building the CoWIN platform—the tech backbone that ultimately operates underneath the entire policy regulations of the government; and the second is the goal of ensuring that the CoWIN framework—the technology backbone—is as secure as possible. Another is to focus on making the system more citizen-centric continuously. As a result, the framework has been working with third-party requirements and ensuring people can access improved user interfaces while providing a single point of contact. The third solution was promoting the idea of one-click vaccination through digital tools already in existence. The fourth solution proposes using CoWIN to allow corporations to organize health assessment and immunization campaigns, thereby incorporating the vaccination process into their corporate social responsibility efforts. The final recommendation made a case for the establishment of Vaccine Warriors through the use of financial incentives to encourage their participation.

In a study by Nath *et al.* [5], the author explains the working and functionality of the CoWIN App introduced by the Indian government. The COVID-19 virus was discovered in the marketplaces of Wuhan, China, and spread from there. Different countries have developed other vaccine strains distinct from one another. The Indian government has authorized two monoclonal antibodies. One is CoviShield, manufactured by Oxford University, and the additional is Covaxin, manufactured by the Indian pharmaceutical company named Bharat Biotech. To supervise and regulate the immunization prescribed, the Indian government has developed an application entitled CoWIN. The disadvantages and advantages of this application have yet to be determined. Their article can be concluded as an overview of the app's strengths and weaknesses and its opportunities and threats, which can be determined by a SWOT analysis (strengths, weaknesses, opportunities, threats).

In [6], the author analyzed the drive's initial phase to immunize the past three core healthcare workers. In March, the emphasis was on people older than 60 years and those with co-morbidities between 45 and 60. Self-registration was made possible through the AarogyaSetu mobile application or the CoWIN website. As a result, the vaccination drive in April was restricted to people over the age of 45 years. Vaccination for those over 18 is scheduled to begin in May 2019. However, as with technological advances, some glitches are still being worked on continuously. The portal can sometimes be unresponsive, resulting in a bottleneck that hinders the drive's progress. It is necessary to overcome the instability of web services and increase storage infrastructure for technological advancement to be efficiently streamlined. Additionally, at points in time, the official site has cross-platform navigational issues that make navigating challenging. As a result, using the software application on a smartphone is inefficient, which becomes even more difficult in vaccination sites due to the lack of access to desktop computers or laptops.

In a study by Chopra *et al.* [7], the authors explain their analysis as numerous reports have demonstrated how certain factors impact the economy and the reality that the economic system was significantly affected during the COVID-19 crisis when there were lockdown drills and all commercial activity were halted. The situation was highly critical, and everybody was in complete panic. However, smart devices such as smartphones and tablets were extremely useful in raising awareness during this crucial time when people required accurate information. Data science is used to analyze the situation and determine whether the spike in COVID-19 had either a positive or negative impact on the economy, with most of the results being negative. CoWIN and AarogyaSetu, two smartphone applications extremely useful in managing the data from millions of vaccination drives, were particularly beneficial. We used data science to analyze the economic impact of COVID-19, but the technology has a wide range of applications. To investigate the regional effects of COVID-19, big data can be used to determine which age category of the citizenry was the most adversely affected, allowing for the implementation of appropriate countermeasures to be implemented. The economic system will take time to regain momentum; however, on the positive side, India, as a developing economy, served as a torchbearer during this pandemic and assisted many other countries in doing so as well.

In Karopoulos *et al.* [8], as reputable evidence that an individual was vaccinated against COVID-19, tested negative for COVID-19, or healed from COVID-19, digital COVID-19 certificates aid in facilitating health care, occupational, educational, and travel-related activities during the pandemic. This paper contributes to our knowledge by providing the first state-of-the-art and thorough review of this ecological system. Ongoing global vaccination campaign; COVID-19 certificates are intended to relieve travellers of domestic and international travel restrictions, including entrance prohibitions, quarantine requirements, and testing. Similar proposals authored in the relevant papers are included in the survey. Because specific certification schemes are usually accompanied by mobile applications that make it easier for certificate holders to store, update, and verify their certificates, we also examine official Android apps for any element that risks user privacy. At least two different types of certificates are considered by approximately half of the existing schemes. The most widely accepted certificate is the immunity certificate, followed closely by the vaccination certificate. On the negative side, only a few plans consider scalability problems, critical considerations for real-world deployments. Fifty-four nations have already established their own national official COVID-19 quality assurance system (seven from America, 15 from Asia, three from Europe, and three from Africa/Oceania), with 36 of them being endorsed by smartphone apps; some of these schemes work in conjunction with more comprehensive measures (as in the case of EUDCC), while others are stand-alone initiatives. There is a large number of mobile app-based schemes that are aimed at both the Android and iOS platforms, and they endorse all three types of proof, which are immunization, diagnostic procedures, and immunity. Only four of them, however, are available as open-source.

In a study by Karandikar *et al.* [9], the author interprets the whole scenario as, so far, the COVID-19 global epidemic has been linked to 5.5 million reported deaths worldwide, with India accounting for 8.7% of all reported deaths. In the mentioned survey, the authors list and analyze the inequities during India's vaccination strategy drive and also computed the impact of new policies implemented due to these inequities. To better understand these potential inequities, use data made available through government portals to conduct qualitative and quantitative analyses.

To be more specific, (a) look for inequities that may exist inside the policies, (b) evaluate the influences of new policies that have been implemented to increase vaccine uptake, and (c) identify data discrepancies that may exist across various sources of information. The number of cases, vaccine availability, apps and automation tools being developed, vaccine distribution, and the strategy and implementation of guidelines at the health center scale were all discovered to be published in various sources, according to the research. Two significant policies were evaluated for their effectiveness and illustrations of how the distribution of vaccination policies failed to achieve equitable distribution in certain states. To ensure that policies and decisions are based on reliable information, it is also critical that the vaccination records that are made available to the public are consistent and accurate. Several inconsistencies in the vaccination records accessible on the CoWIN Dashboard have been brought to our attention [10]. With the help of quantitative analysis, identification of vital disparities in administering vaccinations and endorsement of future policies be developed with equity and transparency as primary considerations. More functional requirements need to be added, including those about kids and the assimilation of passports to make travel more convenient.

## 2.3    Novelty of the Proposed Work

Because India has the second largest population after China, keeping track of every citizen's vaccination is nearly impossible. While not a replacement for human oversight and management, the CoWIN App assists in gathering and storing all the required information for current and future use. With 12 languages supported by the app, the developers have created a user-friendly interface allowing people from all over the globe to interact with the application quickly and comfortably. This simplifies the process of working with the CoWIN application. Our greatest strength is our ability to experiment and develop an app in such a short period. The significant drawbacks are the failure to raise awareness among people, particularly those living in rural areas, and the inability to solve this problem. The proposed model provides various improvements to the existing system's slot booking process that might increase the system's effectiveness and user-friendliness. The steps are as follows: to register, the user must complete the fields on the homepage such as User Name, user_Contact Number, user_Aadhar Number (used for authentication purposes), user_ Email Address, and other user details like select state, select district, select the pin code, date range, user prefers for vaccination, select age, select paid or free, select availability, and select vaccine status. After verifying the information, the user can access the slot tracking tool. Based on the vaccination details provided by the user, i.e., if the user has not been vaccinated or it is the first dose, the user›s selected date determines the available slot at the PIN code. Depending on the user›s vaccination status, the second dose countdown begins 12 weeks after the first dose.

i.    If the user has not been vaccinated or it is the first dose, their selected date determines the available slot at the PIN code. Depending on the user's vaccination status, the second dose countdown begins 12 weeks after the first dose.

ii.    If the user has already taken the first vaccination dose, it displays a slot for the second vaccination dose.

iii.    If the user gets vaccinated for the first dose, a booster dose countdown automatically starts at six months.

Subsequently, every level, the user receives an email reminder for the next dose's time and place. The user's email is based on the details (PIN, email) in the database during registration.

### 2.3.1   Age

The government selected the following priority for the COVID 19 vaccination program: people older than 60 years, people older than 45 years, and people older than 18 years.

### 2.3.2   Availability of Vaccination Slots

A key consideration for determining an individual's priority based on these characteristics is the availability of vaccination slots.

### 2.3.3   Vaccination Status

During this stage, an individual's vaccination history is taken, including the first, second, and booster doses.

## 2.4   Proposed Model

The proposed model contains advanced features that can be included in the vaccination app to make it more user-friendly and straightforward. The model consists of a few steps to be followed by the user, such as after entering the homepage, the user must register by entering its essential details. The features include information on the availability of vaccine slots at various locations based on the selection of states, their districts, and their respective PIN codes. The portal also seeks the minimum age the user wants to access the information. There is the option of the vaccine you prefer, whether the user wants a free or a paid vaccination, and its availability. Once the user enters this information, the result is displayed on the screen in a tabular format. If in case the user has previously taken the first vaccine dose, then a reminder of the second dose is automatically set up at the break of 48 days from the date of the first vaccination. Once the interval is completed, the user is sent a mail on the registered email id for the availability of the slots based on its first dose vaccination details consisting of the date range, State, District, Pin code, Free/paid vaccination and preferred vaccine.

The mechanism of the proposed model is shown in the flowchart in Figure 2.1.

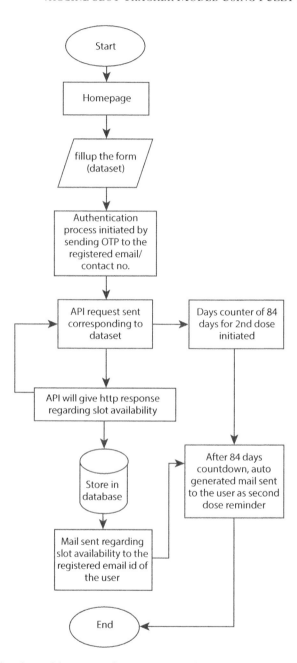

**Figure 2.1** Flowchart of the proposed vaccination tracker model.

An OTP will be sent to the user's mentioned contact number and email address for verification purposes; the authentication process is completed as soon as the user enters the OTP. And if not, the user is asked to restart from the beginning. Once the user details are verified, the user can access the slot tracker feature. If the user is partially vaccinated (has taken the first vaccination dose), the system automatically sets up a reminder on the backend, which is sent to the user once the duration of the second dose starts.

The algorithm of the proposed model is as follows:

---

**Algorithm: Designing a Model for Vaccine Slot Tracker**

---

H: homepage; R: Registration; R1, R2, R3…. Rn: Registration serial numbers; VS: Vaccination Slot; F1:First dose vaccinated; N1: Not vaccinated; r2: reminder for 2$^{nd}$ dose

1:   *Begin* by Homepage (H)
2:   Submit R
3:   *for* each  R(R1, R2, R3…. Rn):
4:    OTP sent to provided email & contact number;
5:   *If* (OTP==verified)
6:       *If* (user==N1):
7:       Display information regarding VS;
8:       Store the data of R
9:          else
10:          Redirect to H;
11:       *If* (user==F1):
12:    r2 starts for 48 days time interval from the date of F1
13:    Mail sent regarding slot availability to the registered email id of the user
14:    else
15:    Redirect to H;
16:   *end if*
17:   *end if*
18:   *end if*
19:   *End*

---

## 2.4.1   Role of the CoWIN App

According to our Honorable Prime Minister, the software will ensure that people receive the second dose of the vaccine on schedule. Certificates will be generated after administering the first and second vaccine doses.

According to the platform's description, it is a cloud-based information technology solution for organizing, executing, tracking, and assessing COVID-19 vaccines in India [13]. In addition to assisting with administrative management (through the Orchestration Module), the platform can also screen the vaccine amount supply chains (via the Vaccine Cold Chain Module), onboard citizens as vaccine recipients (via the Citizen Module), update their status vaccination (via the vaccinator module), and various issue certificates following vaccination (certificate, feedback, and AEFI module) [15, 16].

### 2.4.2   Process for Signing Up for the CoWIN App

Registration requires the presentation of a government-issued photo identification card of any type. Once candidates have registered, they will receive a schedule detailing when and where to receive their vaccine shots. The Vaccination Unit will verify the beneficiary's information and update the beneficiary's vaccination status [11].

The following are the steps in the overall process:

- Step 1: An SMS with the time and date is sent to the candidate registered on the CoWIN app.
- Step 2: The nominee must arrive at the vaccination venue and present the SMS to the officer.
- Step 3: The identification document is scanned by the vaccination officer.
- Step 4: The candidate's information on the CoWIN application is checked. The OTP (one-time password) received via SMS is used for verification.
- Step 5: The applicant is vaccinated, and the vaccination Officer reports the candidate's information in the CoWIN application.
- Step 6: The applicant receives another SMS with appointment information for the second dose and an OTP.
- Step 7: The recipient must wait approximately 30 minutes before being watched for any adverse reactions to the medication. If there are no allergic reactions, the candidate is free to leave.

Overall, India's peak is expected to result from the central government's strict implementation of mandatory face masks, social distancing, frequent handwashing, halting public transportation entirely during lockdown periods, and restricting internal and international movements only essential travel, and so on.

## 2.5   Proposed Fuzzy-Based Vaccine Slot Tracker Model

The proposed model uses fuzzy logic to allocate suitable vaccination slots to the people. The fuzzy approach is a method for processing variables that uses a single variable to process several possible truth values. It is multivalued logic is the subject of a mathematical discipline. It is a phenomenon that follows fuzzy rules and is powered by artificial intelligence, or AI. They are utilized in engineering and non-engineering applications, including stock trading and medical diagnostics, and are employed in any system, including input and output component systems [12].

The three essential factors: i) age, ii) availability, and accessibility of the slots for vaccine and iii) status or eminent personality of the person

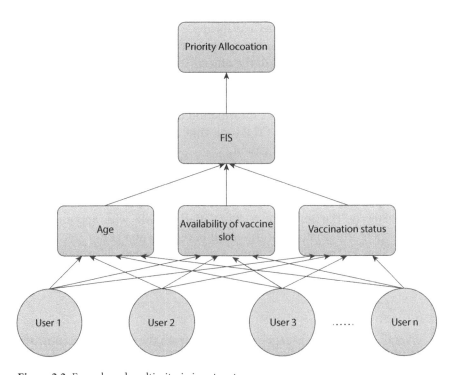

**Figure 2.2** Fuzzy based multicriteria input system.

**Table 2.1** Defined parameters used for simulation.

| Parameters | Low | Medium | High |
|---|---|---|---|
| Age | 0–35 | 30–55 | 50–100 |
| Vaccine slots status | 23–31 | 13–25 | 1–14 |
| Vaccination status | 15–28 | 12–18 | 0–14 |

for vaccination, are used as input parameters for vaccine slot tracking, as shown in Figure 2.2.

Using the parameters defined in Table 2.1, the model decides the output in likelihood.

If the likelihood is:

- High: In this situation, the user will be notified at the earliest stage.
- Medium: It is such a situation that the user will be notified after people have the priority high.
- Low: Here, the user will be informed if any slots remain available in the zone next to the Medium and high-priority booking.

In this study, the fuzzy value assignment to the first dose ranges from 0 to 14, and the second dose ranges from 12 to value 18. Apart from this, the booster dose ranges from 15 to 28.

## 2.5.1    Fuzzy Rules

Fuzzy rules are defined to determine the probability of availability of vaccine slots. The fuzzy rules are defined as follows [13]:

Rule 1: *If (Age is Medium) and (AVS is Medium) and also (VS is Medium), then (probability is Medium).*
Rule 2: *If (Age is Medium) and (AVS is Medium) and also Here, (VS is High), then (probability is High).*
Rule 3: *If (Age is High) and (AVS is High) and (VS is High) and also Here, (probability is exceptionally High).*

.
.
.

Rule 27: *If (Age is Low) and (AVS is Low) and (VS is Low) then (probability is extremely Low).*
where AVS, availability of vaccine; VS, vaccination status.

Here using fuzzy logic, three input variables(age, availability of vaccine, and vaccination status) are used, having three membership values each (low, medium, high); so, a total of 3 *3*3 = 27 fuzzy rules are generated.

## 2.6   Simulation

The database, object-oriented, and networking approaches are all used to develop the suggested model. Because we have many locations where we need to maintain entries in the database, we are utilizing SQLite software, among the best and most user-friendly programs available for storing information. As the front-end software, this project uses PHP, a real-world dealing with an object-based programming language, and it has a connection to the MySQL database. It is a web-based service that customers may access via a server [14] and a browser. The simulation of the proposed model is performed using Django as the basic backend, and the database is managed through SQLite [17]. The hardware and software configurations are represented using Table 2.2. At first, when the user visits the webpage, the user is asked to fill up the essential details such as name, email, pin code of the area, and the user's age. Before proceeding further, there is an authentication interface in which the authentication is done by sending an OTP to the registered mail id of the user. Once the user is authenticated, it is directed to another webpage, the service provider page, i.e., all the information and features can be accessed from this page. At first, the user is asked for the date range, i.e., how many days from the current date the user wants the information, as shown in Table 2.2. For example, if the date is January 3, 2022, and the user enters a range: of 3, then the slot availability will be displayed on the result from January 3, 2022, to January 5, 2022 [18].

Various input parameters are used to calculate the likelihood of getting a vaccination slot evaluation and allocation process. To virtually construct and distribute each crisp input to the proposed model, the fuzzy toolbox of MATLAB is used. The input variables utilized in the simulation are listed in Table 2.1. In the simulation process, the age of the registered user, vaccination slot availability, and the user's vaccination status are collected

Table 2.2 Hardware and Software configurations.

| Processor | Pentium 2.4 GHz or above |
|---|---|
| Memory | 256 MB RAM or above |
| Cache Memory | 128 KB or above |
| HardDisk | 3GB or above [at least 3MB free space required] |
| PenDrive | 5GB |
| Operating System | Windows 10 |
| Font-End Tool | JSP, Servlets, JavaScript, HtmlCss bootstraps |
| Backend | SQLite, Django, Python |

as inputs to the proposed model, where $U_1$ denotes the specific user. The occurrences of each of these factors are presented in Table 2.3.

In the computed results using the proposed model, the probability for the priority for $U_1$ is 0.5, for $U_2$ is 0.864, and for the $U_3$ 0.276, showing that user $U_2$ with the highest priority, whereas $U_1$ has a medium focus, and $U_3$ has the lowest priority.

The selected input parameters are shown in Figure 2.3, where "Mamdani-FIS" is used to create the fuzzy rule base.

Figure 2.4 shows the probability of allocating vaccine slots for the individual user using the selected parameters.

In Figure 2.5, the Priority of $U_1$ is 0.5, which shows that users' priority is Low. The inputs for different parameters used for $U_3$ are as follows: Age: 50, AVS: 14, and SV: 15.

In Figure 2.6, the priority of $U_3$ is 0.864, which shows that users' priority is exceptionally high. The inputs for the different parameters used for $U_3$ are age, 70 years; AVS, 8; and SV, 15.

Table 2.3 Input instances for vaccine slot tracking.

| Serial no. | User | Input values | Probability |
|---|---|---|---|
| 1. | $U_1$ | [50, 15,14 ] | 0.50 |
| 2. | $U_2$ | [70, 8,15 ] | 0.8640 |
| 3. | $U_3$ | [17, 5,15 ] | 0.2760 |

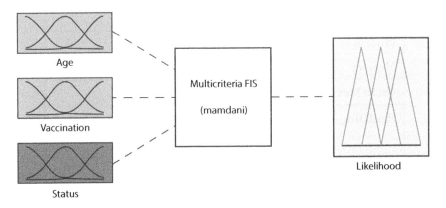

**Figure 2.3** Fuzzy-based vaccination slot tracker.

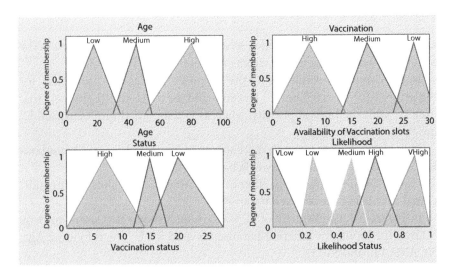

**Figure 2.4** Likelihood of vaccination slots with selected input parameters.

In Figure 2.7, the Priority of $U_3$ is 0.276, which shows that users' priority is Low. The inputs for different parameters used for $U_3$ are as follows: Age: 17, AVS: 5, and SV: 15.

Figure 2.8 shows the actual implementation of the vaccine slot tracker for the proposed model.

Even though wealthy countries are administering mass immunizations at record rates, developing countries continue to be affected by several complicating factors, including the spread of COVID-19, testing hurdles, mass vaccination challenges, and medical supply constraints [12].

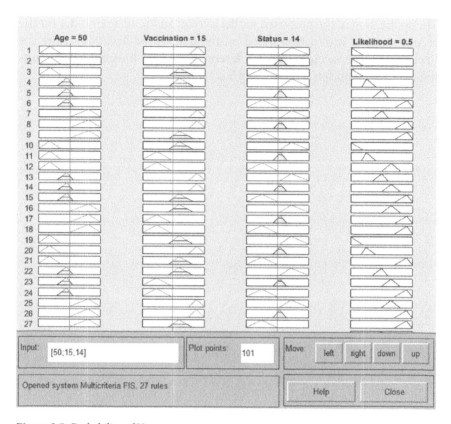

**Figure 2.5** Probability of $U_1$.

## 2.7 Conclusion

Due to the obstacles faced by vaccine delivery, tracking, and registration, the conventional COVID-19 vaccine strategy is deemed fragile. In the proposed model, the main emphasis is mainly on the features that still need to be introduced in the models of the existing vaccination drive platforms. We have discovered various sources of information being released on the number of cases, the availability of vaccines, the development of phone applications and bots, the dispensing of vaccines, and the planning process. The proposed model is tested using different random test cases with multiple users, and a small test case is demonstrated where for three other users. The model evaluated the likelihood of the vaccine slot allocation for users U1, U2, and U3 as 0.5, 0.864, and 0.276, respectively. Hence, the priority sequence for vaccination slot allocation is U2 > U1 >U3.

The application of the proposed model is to set and send a reminder for the second dose of vaccination based on the date of the first dose using the likelihood of the vaccine slot for different age groups. It would entail granting citizens reminders amidst their busy schedules.

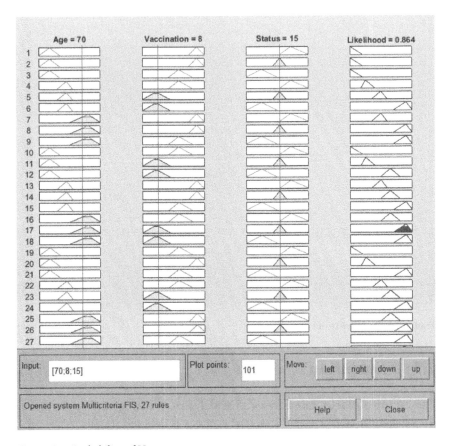

**Figure 2.6** Probability of $U_2$.

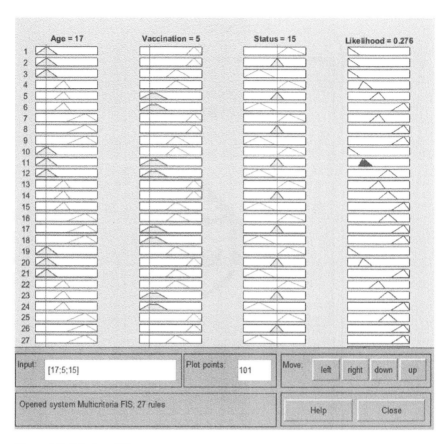

**Figure 2.7** Priority of $U_3$.

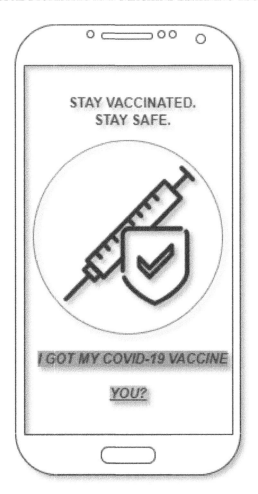

**Figure 2.8** Proposed vaccine slot tracker.

## 2.8   Future Work

In the future, our goal is to improve the model using machine learning that will be used for widespread awareness campaigns. We will make an effort to propose strategies to ensure that vaccinations are given fairly and evenly, that every country receives them, and that every nation can employ them to protect its citizens.

# References

1. WHO website 2019, *Coronavirus disease (COVID-19)*, https://www.who.int/emergencies/diseases/novel-coronavirus-2019/covid-19-vaccines.
2. Collado-Borrell, R., Escudero-Vilaplana, V., Villanueva-Bueno, C., Herranz-Alonso, A., Sanjurjo-Saez, M., Features and functionalities of smartphone apps related to COVID-19: Systematic search in app stores and content analysis. *J. Med. Internet Res.*, 22, 8, 2022.
3. Akshita, V., Dhanush J., S., Dikshitha Varman, A., Krishna Kumar, V., Blockchain-based covid vaccine booking and vaccine management system. *Proc. 2nd Int. Conf. Smart Electron. Commun. ICOSEC 2021*, 2021.
4. Mehta, R., Kumar, A., Gupta, R., Babbar, K., Kapoor, C., Center for ICT for Development (CICTD), IMPRI Impact and Policy Research Institute, New Delhi and The Dialogue organized a panel discussion on "Strengthening CoWIN Platform towards Universal Vaccination". *Strengthening CoWIN platform towards universal vaccination*, 2021.
5. Nath, S., Aravindkumar, K., Sahoo, J. P., Samal, K. C. and Chidambaranathan, A., Use of CoWIN app in vaccination program in India to fight COVID-19. *Vigyan Varta*, 2, 2, 10–13, 2021.
6. Gupta, M., Goel, A.D., Bhardwaj, P., The CoWIN portal–Current update, personal experience and future possibilities. *Indian J. Community Heal.*, 33, 2, 414, 2021.
7. Chopra, M., Singh, S.K., Mengi, G., Gupta, D., Assess and analysis Covid-19 immunization process: A data science approach to make india self-reliant and safe. *CEUR Work. Proc*, 9186, 0–2, 2021, http://ceur-ws.org/Vol-3080/10.pdf.
8. Karopoulos, G., Hernandez-Ramos, J.L., Kouliaridis, V., Kambourakis, G., A survey on digital certificates approaches for the COVID-19 pandemic. *IEEE Access*, 9, 138003–138025, 2021.
9. Karandikar, T., Prabhu, A., Mathur, M., Arora, M., Lamba, H., Kumaraguru, P., CoWIN: really winning? Analysing inequity in india's vaccination response. ArXiv, abs/2202.04433, 2022.
10. Hashmi, A.A. and Wahed, A., Analysis and prediction of Covid-19. *Commun. Comput. Inf. Sci.*, 1393, 381–393, 2021.
11. Grant, D., McLane, I., West, J., Rapid and scalable COVID-19 screening using speech, breath, and cough recordings. *BHI 2021 - 2021 IEEE EMBS Int. Conf. Biomed. Heal. Informatics, Proc*, 2021.
12. Faiz, M. and Daniel, A.K., A multi-criteria cloud selection model based on a fuzzy logic technique for QoS. *Int. J. Syst. Assur. Eng. Manag.*, 1–18, 2022. https://10.1007/s13198-022-01723-0.
13. Faiz, M. and Daniel, A.K., Multi-criteria based cloud service selection model using fuzzy logic for QoS. *International Conference on Advanced Network Technologies and Intelligent Computing*, Springer, Cham, 2021.

14. Faiz, M. and Daniel, A.K., Threats and challenges for security measures on the internet of things. *Law, State Telecommunications Review (LSTR)*, 14.1, 71–97, 2022.

15. Awasthi, S., Chauhan, R., Tripathi, S.L., Datta, T., COVID-19 research: Open data resources and challenges, in: *Biomedical Engineering Applications for People with Disabilities and Elderly in a New COVID-19 Pandemic and Beyond*, 93–104, Academic Press, 2022, https://10.1016/B978-0-323-85174-9.00008-X.

16. Singh, T. and Tripathi, S.L., Design of a 16-bit 500-MS/s SAR-ADC for low-power application, in: *Electronic Devices, Circuits, and Systems for Biomedical Applications*, pp. 257–273, Academic Press, 2021.

17. Dhinakaran, V., Varsha Shree, M., Tripathi, S.L., Bupathi Ram, P.M., An overview of evolution, transmission, detection and diagnosis for the way out of coronavirus, in: *Health Informatics and Technological Solutions for Coronavirus (COVID-19)*, CRC Taylor & Francis, 2021, https://10.1201/9781003161066.

18. Dhinakaran, V., Surendran, R., Shree, M. V., Tripathi, S. L., Role of modern technologies in treating of COVID-19, in: *Health Informatics and Technological Solutions for Coronavirus (COVID-19)*, pp. 145–157, CRC Press, 2021.

# 3

# Enhanced Text Mining Approach for Better Ranking System of Customer Reviews

Ramandeep Sandhu[1], Amritpal Singh[1], Mohammad Faiz[1]*, Harpreet Kaur[1] and Sunny Thukral[2]

*School of Computer Science & Engineering, Lovely Professional University, Punjab, India*
*PG Department of Computer Science and IT, DAV College, Amritsar, Punjab, India*

## Abstract

Most customers say that online reviews influence their decisions to purchase a new product. Therefore, it is no exaggeration to say that online reviews are critical to the success of a business. A star rating only cannot lead to decision making for a customer; text reviews play a vital role in product recommendations. Collecting online reviews and transforming them into valuable insights is highly beneficial for both the customer and the company. This chapter proposes an enhanced text-mining approach based on social media data. The proposed technique works on real-time customer reviews in the form of tweets, calculates the frequency-based ranking and has provided promising results.

*Keywords*: Online reviews, customer feedback, text analysis, data mining, text mining

## 3.1 Introduction

Text mining has become increasingly popular significantly over the past decade. Text mining primarily aims to derive relevant patterns and information from certain information. Text mining is continually changing when paired with big data analytics. Staying in touch with the needs of

---
*Corresponding author*: faiz.28700@lpu.co.in

Sandeep Kumar, Deepika Ghai, Arpit Jain, Suman Lata Tripathi and Shilpa Rani (eds.)
Multimodal Biometric and Machine Learning Technologies: Applications for Computer Vision,
(53–70) © 2023 Scrivener Publishing LLC

buyers and clients requires text-mining customer reviews to examine customer experience. Because of the widespread adoption of various forms of technology, vast quantities of unstructured text data are generated online. Consequently, a data professional will need to use mining techniques for textual data to extract such a massive amount of knowledge [1]. The text mining approach exploits a lexicon-based strategy, grammatical research, and sentence length to provide light on consumers' behavioral and emotional connections to brands [2].

There are various reasons related to customer evaluations that may be effective motivators for how you want to build your business. Text mining client reviews can give such rich insight into your organization's strengths and problems [3]. The final aim is long-term growth, greater customer loyalty, and clients choosing to do business with a particular company or association. These are benefits worth pursuing and maintaining a process made more accessible by text-mining customer evaluations for the rich depth of their dynamic content as more businesses see the benefits of text-mining consumer evaluations, which are turning to review platform titans for appropriate responses. Amazon review analysis provides fantastic insights into client purchasing behaviors and product goals.

Meanwhile, an excellent Google review analyzer is ideal for determining customers' thoughts on their brand experience. Customer reviews are for more than just customers to inform other prospective customers what they think about a product and brand experience. In the right hands, text-mining client evaluations mean crowdsourcing the future vision of your whole operation, informed by the individuals who matter the most to your organization. Text mining helps process massive amounts of unstructured data to extract actionable intelligence. Integrating it with machine learning can allow text analysis frameworks to classify data or extract key phrases from text based on previous training [4, 5].

Text mining refers to analyzing texts, such as emails, customer reviews, standard text, web ranking, indexing reports, and legal records to retrieve data, translate it into intelligence, and render it accessible for decision-making. Text mining allows for the rapid and easy analysis of vast and complicated data sets to extract meaningful information. Text mining will enable you to determine a product's overall approach in this scenario. A technique known as sentiment analysis is used to determine whether the reviews are positive, critical, or impartial. Ultimately, representation through images, infographics, incorporation with controlled information held in databases or warehouses, machine learning, etc., to its incorporation of linguistic, statistical, and machine learning methodologies. Although the study is based on unstructured material, one of the first goals is to arrange and organize it for subsequent qualitative and quantitative research. Text mining is a process for extracting useful information from large amounts of unstructured text. Information may be mined from unstructured text data by performing a series of steps that make up text mining. Text mining techniques are the procedures that conduct text mining and extract insights from data. Before implementing text mining algorithms, preprocessing the text is necessary. It is the procedure of inspecting and correcting information before its use. Many different methods, including language recognition, text categorization, and part-of-speech labeling, are used in text preprocessing, an essential aspect of natural language processing [6].

## 3.2    Techniques of Text Mining

High-quality information may be mined from any given text using "text mining." These methods will be instrumental in the financial sector, where analyzing large volumes of data is essential and advantageous for businesses, agencies, and the public. This section highlights several basic and extensively used strategies in textual data analysis [7–10].

### 3.2.1    Sentiment Analysis

Sentiment analysis (SA) is among the most well-known text mining methods. Opinion mining is another name for this kind of computing used to uncover hidden opinions in textual data. In addition to its obvious usage in e-commerce sites, posts, social networks, and content communities benefit from its popularity. Sentiment and valence identification are two of the main principles of sentiment analysis. Integrating deep learning methods with traditional machine learning strategies (such as sentiment lexicon development) has shown promising results for researchers.

### 3.2.2    Natural Language Processing

Natural language processing (NLP) focuses on the automated processing and interpretation of text documents input and allows computers to read by dissecting the syntax and semantics of phrases, as shown in Figure 3.1. Use internal and external data channels to gauge customer satisfaction and measure the impact of marketing campaigns. Businesses are motivated to interact with customers via sentiment analysis because it provides actionable insights into how those customers feel about a company's products and services [11–13].

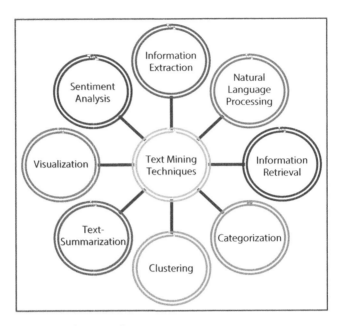

**Figure 3.1** Different techniques of text mining.

### 3.2.3   Information Extraction

In many other words, it is a method for gaining insight from massive data sets. Tokenization, named entity identification, sentence segmentation, and part-of-speech assignments are all a component of information extraction (IE), the initial step in a computer's ability to read unstructured text. Information extraction systems are used in this context to detect entities and their connections inside documents and extract specific information from them. The resulting corpora are then centralized into interconnected databases for analysis. The helpful information and consequences from the recovered data may be checked and evaluated with the help of precision and recall.

### 3.2.4   Information Retrieval

Information retrieval (IR) is the procedure of gleaning valid data and interconnected patterns from a collection of textual assets known as a corpus. Information retrieval uses various algorithms to track the user's actions and unearths the most relevant data and insights. Google's search engine, for instance, often employs information retrieval methods to locate appropriate content in response to user queries. Search engines use query-based algorithms that keep track of trends and provide more relevant results. Then, depending on the user's question, the search engine will provide a more relevant result to their needs.

### 3.2.5   Clustering

Clustering is an unsupervised method for organizing text into meaningful categories using clustering algorithms. Clustering may be performed top-down or bottom-up, including scheduling and retrieving similar words or patterns across several texts. Because of this, the documents are split into smaller groups called clusters. Each document's content inside the cluster is very similar, but the range of different clusters differs. Therefore, the efficacy of clustering can be more accurately measured. The process of text mining is shown in Figure 3.2.

### 3.2.6   Categorization

Documents written in an accessible format are categorized into one or more groups as part of the classification method. To learn how to classify new information, supervised learners employ feedback instances. The content of each text file is used to determine its classification. The purpose of text categorization is to automatically classify unidentified examples by training classifiers on recognizedinstances. This is accomplished by preprocessing, retrieval, function approximation, and classification [14–17]. In addition, the computational complexity of the feature space presents challenges for text categorization, as shown in Figure 3.3.

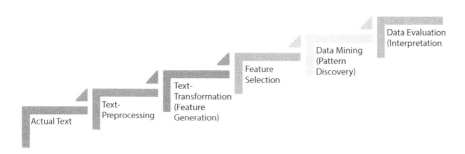

**Figure 3.2** Process of text mining.

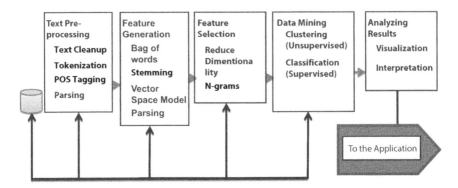

**Figure 3.3** Phases of text mining.

### 3.2.7  Visualization

Visualizing pertinent data may be facilitated and clarified using visualization approaches. When outlining single documents or groups of documents, text flags denote the document type, while colors depict the document density. A visual hierarchy organizes significant textual sources for easy user interaction. Information visualization has been used by the authorities, for instance, to map out terrorist networks and catalogue criminal activity.

### 3.2.8  Text Summarization

Text summarizing, which aims to reduce a document's length, features, and intricacy without losing its essential points and true meaning, helps assess if a long paper fulfils the user's needs and determines whether it is valuable reading for further information or not. However, groupings of documents may be able to replace text summaries [18].

## 3.3  Related Research

Capturing massive amounts of text data is within reach for most organizations today. Customers' opinions, ratings of products, and comments on social media postings are simply the edge of the iceberg regarding the massive amounts of data now available. This kind of text may provide valuable insights that can guide product development and provide a competitive advantage for businesses. Making use of the mentioned possibility without resorting to text mining is challenging. This is because the human brain cannot process such massive volumes of data. Companies may streamline their text classification processes with the use of text mining. Several factors, such as subject matter, purpose, emotional tone, and linguistic background, might be used to organize the data. Text mining is helpful because it may replace many time-consuming and laborious manual processes. The related research is as follows:

Sharma *et al.* [19] investigated the development of research leanings in information management by carefully examining articles using bibliometric analysis and STM. The data set contains bibliographic data from the Scopus database on 19,916 research articles, book chapters, and review papers relevant to information management from 1970 to 2019. Porturas *et al.* [20] identified theme subjects and research trends in emergency medicine using LDA, hierarchical clustering. The data set contains 20,528 abstracts of emergency medicine-related research publications from the OVID database published between 1980 and 2019. Karami *et al.* [21] used term frequency exploration and MALLET enactment to identify these issues and topic progression in Twitter research from 2006 to 2019. The data set contains abstracts from 18,000 research publications on Twitter from IEEE and Web of Science archives. Kim *et al.* [22] analyzed abstracts from 231 relevant research publications to identify these issues and trends in the blockchain technology sector using Word2vec and Spherical k-means clustering (W2V-LSA). The data set comprises abstracts of blockchain-related academic articles published between 2014 and 2018. The system extracted semantic analysis using the expert system with the latest tools in programming. Maeda *et al.* [23] utilized the AntConc software, TF-IDF, and keyword computation algorithms to inspect telemedicine exploration developments in South Africa. The data set comprises abstracts and labels from PubMed of 36 study publications on telemedicine published in 2019. Text mining techniques with different domains are shown in Table 3.1

Zuliani *et al.* [24] employed the XLSTAT tool to analyze mountain livestock agricultural research patterns using TF-IDF, LDA with Gibbs specimen, and hierarchical clustering. The data set contains abstracts from Scopus of 2,679 research publications on Mountain cattle production from 1980 to 2018. Ding *et al.* [25] investigated trending issues in the significant data sector using the MALLET version of LDA with 1800 Gibbs sampling rounds. The data set contains abstracts, titles, and keywords from 17,599 big data–related research papers printed between 2009 and 2018 in Elsevier's Scopus database. Ahmad *et al.* [26] took a somewhat different method, focusing on sentiment analysis of economic news streams in many dialects. Automatic sentiment analysis was replicated using three frequently spoken languages. The authors accessed a local archive of the

**Table 3.1** Text mining techniques with different domains.

| Author's | Techniques | Application domain | Results |
|---|---|---|---|
| Sharma et al. [19] | Information retrieval technique | Information management | Extract bibliometric database analysis |
| Porturas et al. [20] | Clustering, Linear discriminant analysis | Medical Domain | Identified themes in emergency medicine |
| Karami et al. [21] | Term Frequency Analysis and Linear discriminant analysis | Twitters Progression | Recognized theme issues based on 18000 abstracts |
| Kim et al. [22] | K-means Clustering | Blockchain technology | Extract semantic analysis using programming tools |
| Maede et al. [23] | Keyword computation algorithm | Telemedicine domain | Utilized the AntConc software to investigate telemedicine research trends in South Africa |
| Zuliani et al. [24] | Research patterns, clustering | Farming domain | Analyzed research patterns with hierarchical clustering based on cattle production data sets |
| Ding et al. [25] | Linear discriminant analysis approach | Big data | Observed trending issues in big data using the MALLET version |
| Ahmad et al. [26] | Text collection, Keyword detection | Languages extraction | Differentiated Arabic, Chinese, and English languages with an accuracy of around 75% |

*(Continued)*

**Table 3.1** Text mining techniques with different domains. (*Continued*)

| Author's | Techniques | Application domain | Results |
|---|---|---|---|
| Nazir [27] | Text-Summarization | Noun phrase mining | Investigated term frequency using existing data sets |
| Ding [28] | Linear discriminant analysis approach | Saving energy domain | Analyzed 1600 building energy-saving research |
| Youssef and Rich [29] | Sentiment Analysis | Bioinformatics domain | Discovered theme subjects using text mining |
| Dehghani [30] | Text mining and multilayer dimension reduction | Financial domain | J48 algorithm proved the best system accuracy for text mining |
| K. Patel *et al.* [31] | Sentiment Analysis, KNN, SVR algorithm | Social networking domain | 70–75% Accuracy was obtained with sentiment analysis |
| Nguyen *et al.* [32] | Natural language processing (NLP) | Stock prediction | 87% Specificity and 92% accuracy were achieved using NLP |

three languages to implement a regional grammar strategy. The discovery of keywords was helped by statistical criteria included in the training text sample. The English corpus was the most widely accessible, followed by the Chinese and Arabic ones. The most popular words were ranked and selected based on how often they were used. The extraction accuracy varied from 60% to 75% based on manual examination. For implementation in real-time markets, a more rigorous analysis of this model would be required, including adding more than one news source at a time. Nazir [27] investigated data mining research trends using noun phrase mining and term frequency. The data set contains abstracts and information from 5,843 science direct data mining publications published between 2014 and 2018. Ding [28] investigated building-saving energy exploration tendencies using TF-IDF, n-grams, and LDA. Between 1973 and 2016, 1,600 building energy-saving investigations were collected from three databases: Web of Science, Science Direct, and JSTOR.

Youssef and Rich [29] to discover theme subjects in bioinformatics research on 143,000 bioinformatics studies published between 1987 and 2018 is included in the data set's titles from the PubMed database. Stock prices are affected by the behavior of investors after reading about a firm in the news. Thus Wu *et al.* developed a model that combines technical stock analysis with sentiment research. They put their efforts into identifying the dominant mood associated with each news item and giving it the right emotions according to its significance. The model was applied to the forecasting of the Taiwanese stock market, and it outperformed models that relied only on either factor. This suggests an effective system that has room to grow and add features.

The model proposed by Dehghani [30] may predict foreign exchange (FX) trends based on the headline news. News articles that appeared around the same time as significant movements in forex currency pairs in the past were also evaluated in the hopes of predicting future market behavior. The targeted prediction algorithm was employed for optimal feature reduction, while the J48 algorithm was used in the decision tree construction phase of text mining. Aside from using historical data to make predictions, fundamental analysis (which primarily dealt with unstructured textual data) was also heavily relied upon. The J48 algorithm enhanced the system's precision, performance, efficiency, and throughput.

The primary model acquired the data set for prediction, preprocessed it using logistic regression to eliminate redundancies, and utilized a genetic algorithm, KNN, and support vector regression, while Patel *et al.* [31] created a hybrid and integrated two models. Their predictions were based on KNN, and when the three methods were compared, it was found that KNN was the most accurate. Later, the optimizer was used to enhance precision further. To aid the genetic algorithm even further, SVR was enlisted to provide the genetic algorithm with the future opening price. Since Twitter was rated the most prominent source of linked news, it was used for sentiment analysis. Using a vast set of terms, the algorithm divided tweets in half and predicted whether the market would increase or decrease. Ultimately, the model's precision was around 70% to 75%, which we expect in a dynamic environment.

Nguyen *et al.* [32] focused on analyzing online commenters' moods. They learned the sentiments underlying trending topics at established companies and generated encouraging results compared to the previous year's stock accuracy. The percentage of positive emotions was calculated for each class after analyzing human-annotated social media posts concerning stock prediction. Based on natural language processing [33], the system is 87% precise and 92% accurate. A classification model was created for texts without exact sentiments that use the annotated emotions from the data set.

## 3.4    Research Methodology

The steps in the proposed method "Enhanced Text Mining Approach for Better Ranking System of Customer Reviews" are shown in Figure 3.4. RStudio has been used to perform the various operations.

Various steps of the proposed system, as shown in Figure 3.4, are explained below.

(a) The first stage reads the real-time data from a Twitter website. The data has been collected using Twitter APIs. Figure 3.5 represents the configuration file used to manage the data. The underlying tool used for collecting data is Apache Flume. Apache Flume is a data ingestion tool in the Apache Hadoop ecosystem. It is used to manage unstructured data from various sources.

(b) The second stage of the proposed work starts with extracting data and corpus creation. Statement (i) is used for this process for various reviews.

review1=Corpus(VectorSource(myreview$Review.Text))
........................(i)

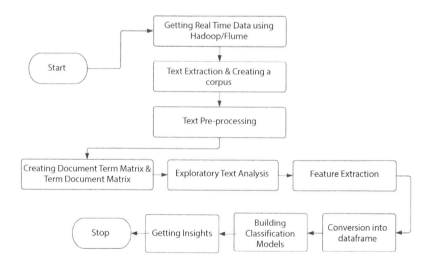

**Figure 3.4** Proposed methodology.

(c) The next step is to preprocess the text. Here are a few typical preprocessing steps: conversion into lowercase, removal of punctuation, removal of stop words and stemming document.

(d) The further step of the approach transforms text into a data frame which consists of words and their frequencies. Document term matrix (DTM) and text document matrix (TDM) have been generated here. Figure 3.6 represents the frequency rate of the ten most common words. The ratio of terms is selected from 1:10. It provides the frequency rate of the most popular text mining-based word arrangement in its descending order.

(e) Further, exploratory text analysis (ETA) has been applied.

    a. Here are a few typical preprocessing steps: conversion into lowercase, removal of punctuation, removal of stop words and stemming document.

(f) Based on various text data features, data has been converted into a data frame for applying classification models, as shown in Figure 3.7.

```
Open      ▼   ⊡                                          *twitter.conf
tw.sources = e1
tw.channels = c1
tw.sinks = s1

tw.sources.e1.type = com.cloudera.flume.source.TwitterSource
tw.sources.e1.consumerKey = G9TxQLWHLoH2rWxxxxxxxxxxxxx
tw.sources.e1.consumerSecret = c4DgPknw4PUaSV6bAxxxxxxxxxxxxxxxxxxxx
tw.sources.e1.accessToken = 1274610960641097728-zt0kDUWQ7tH2nxxxxxxxxxxxxxxx
tw.sources.e1.accessTokenSecret = WVRjqFTvoCmEynp17FYPgZxxxxxxxxxxxxxxxxxxxxxxxxxx

tw.sources.e1.keywords = productreviews,clothingreviews,onlineshoppingreviews

tw.sinks.s1.type = hdfs
tw.sinks.s1.channel = c1
tw.sources.e1.channels = c1
tw.sinks.s1.hdfs.path = /user/amrit/my_tweets1
tw.sinks.s1.hdfs.fileType=DataStream
tw.sinks.s1.hdfs.writeFormat=Text

tw.sinks.s1.hdfs.batchSize = 1000
tw.sinks.s1.hdfs.rollCount = 10000

tw.channels.c1.type = memory
tw.channels.c1.capacity = 10000
tw.channels.c1.transactionCapacity = 10000
```

**Figure 3.5** Apache flume configuration file screenshot.

> review_term_freq[1:10]
 love     fit    size    look     top    wear   color   great perfect   order
11351   11310   10597    9276    8261    8047    7191    6084    5224    4983

**Figure 3.6** Ten most common words.

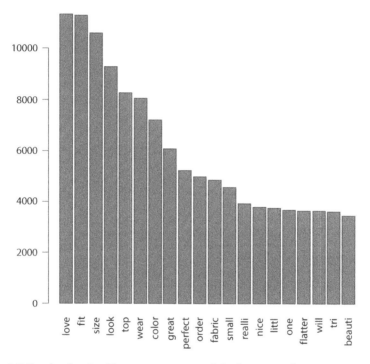

**Figure 3.7** Barplot showing 20 most common words in the extracted text.

One of its main goals is to analyze the differences in keyword usage between individuals who suggest the product and those who do not, as shown in Figure 3.8.

Based on the distance in frequency, word clustering helps find word groups that are frequently used together. Dendrograms are used to depict word clusters, as shown in Figure 3.9.

The next step in the proposed methodology is feature extraction. It is to be done by removing sparsity. One frequently encounters huge matrices in text mining, many of which include zeros. Keep only a few non-zero entries and their positions rather than the entire set of cells one at a time to save memory. The construction of a data frame follows feature extraction.

The final step is to build the classification model. We will apply regularization with a lasso and logistic regression for model development

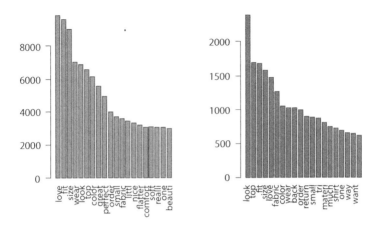

**Figure 3.8** Separate bar plots (one for recommend-yes [green] and another for recommend-no [red]).

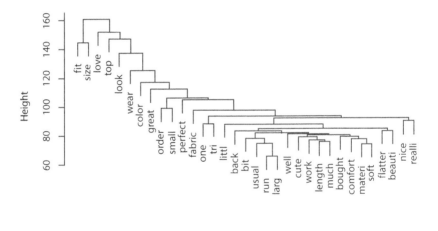

dist(review_tdm2, method = "euclidean")
hclust (*, "complete")

**Figure 3.9** Dimension reduction technique (word clustering).

and classification to reduce the number of features. The logistic regression model's odds ratio will provide numerous insightful classification insights, as shown in Table 3.2.

Here is the interpretation: a product review that uses the phrase "compliment" has a 4.9 times higher probability of being recommended than one that does not. The word "disappoint" has a negative coefficient, meaning it is doubtful that the product will be advised if it appears in the review.

Table 3.2 Ratio of various product reviews.

| Variable | Odds ratio |
|----------|------------|
| Compliment | 4.9 |
| Perfect | 2.36 |
| Return | −1.18 |

## 3.5   Conclusion

In this work, a classification model for real-time text mining is proposed. While posting the reviews using Twitter API, the most common and frequent words used by customers are captured. The research spotlights selecting two studies' insights, one recommended and another not recommended by customers submitting reviews online. Feature-based and opinion-based word clustering has been implemented to make the research more effective. Using the lasso logistic regression model, better results have been provided as it successfully reduced the dimensions of text reviews.

## References

1. Buenano-Fernandez, D., Gonzalez, M., Gil, D., Lujan-Mora, S., Text mining of open-ended questions in self-assessment of university teachers: An LDA topic modeling approach. *IEEE Access*, 8, 35318–35330, Feb. 2020. Sandhu, R., A novel method to find score value for online opinions. *International Journal of Compuugggtational Science and Information Technology* (*IJCSITY*), 1, 1, 2320–8457, February 2013.
2. Campbell, J.C., Hindle, A., Stroulia, E., Latent dirichlet allocation: Extracting topics from software engineering data, in: *The Art and Science of Analyzing Software Data*, vol. 3, no. 4–5, pp. 139–159, 2015.
3. Al Moubayed, N., Breckon, T., Matthews, P., McGough, A.S., Sms spam filtering using probabilistic topic modeling and stacked denoising autoencoder, in: *Lecture Notes in Computer Science (including subseries Lecture Notes in Artificial Intelligence and Lecture Notes in Bioinformatics)*, vol. 9887 LNCS, pp. 423–430, 2016.
4. Bastani, K., Namavari, H., Shaffer, J., Latent dirichlet allocation (LDA) for topic modeling of the CFPB consumer complaints. *Expert Syst. Appl.*, 127, 256–271, Jul. 2019.
5. Bennett, R., Vijaygopal, R., Kottasz, R., Attitudes towards autonomous vehicles among people with physical disabilities. *Transp. Res. Part A Policy Pract.*, 127, 1–17, Sep. 2019.

6. Sandhu, R., A novel method of opinion extraction for product opinions. *International Journal of Foundation in Computer Science and Tenchnology (IJFCST)*, 2, 5, 17–24, September 2012.

7. Eler, D.M., Grosa, D., Pola, I., Garcia, R., Correia, R., Teixeira, J., Analysis of document pre-processing effects in text and opinion mining. *Information*, 9, 100, 2018.

8. Elshendy, M. and FronzettiColladon, A., Big data analysis of economic news: Hints to forecast macroeconomic indicators. *Int. J. Eng. Bus. Manag.*, 9, 1847979017720040, 2017.

9. Jin, M., Wang, Y., Zeng, Y., Application of data mining technology in financial risk analysis. *Wirel. Pers. Commun.*, 102, 3699–3713, 2018.

10. Klopotan, I., Zoroja, J., Meško, M., Early warning system in business, finance, and economics: Bibliometric and topic analysis. *Int. J. Eng. Bus. Manag.*, 10, 1847979018797013, 2018.

11. Liu, D. and Lei, L., The appeal to political sentiment: An analysis of Donald Trump's and Hillary Clinton's speech themes and discourse strategies in the 2016 US presidential election. *Discourse, Context Media*, 25, 143–152, Oct. 2018.

12. Lotto, J., Examination of the status of financial inclusion and its determinants in Tanzania. *Sustainability*, 10, 2873, 2018.

13. Thukral, S. and Rana, V., Versatility of fuzzy logic in chronic diseases: A review. *Med. Hypotheses*, Elsevier, 122, 150–156, 2019.

14. Sandhu, R., Applying opinion mining to organize web opinions. *International Journal Computer Science, Engineering and Applications* (*IJCSEA*), 1, 82–89, 2011, https://doi.org/10.5121/ijcsea.2011.1408, https://www.scilit.net/article/8738c7c4b56ac78cc270d8500ffc8166.

15. Roh, T., Jeong, Y., Yoon, B., Developing a methodology of structuring and layering technological information in patent documents through natural language processing. *Sustainability*, 9, 2117, 2017.

16. Arner, D.W., Barberis, J., Buckley, R.P., The evolution of Fintech: A new post-crisis paradigm. *George. J. Int. Law.*, 47, 1271, 2015.

17. Karami, A., Ghasemi, M., Sen, S., Moraes, M.F., Shah, V., Exploring diseases and syndromes in neurology case reports from 1955 to 2017 with text mining. *Comput. Biol. Med.*, 109, 322–332, Jun. 2019.

18. Dehghani, M., Johnson, K.M., Garten, J. *et al.*, TACIT: An open-source text analysis, crawling, and interpretation tool. *Behav. Res.*, 49, 538–547, 2017, https://doi.org/10.3758/s13428-016-0722-4.

19. Sharma, A., Rana, N.P., Nunkoo, R., Fifty years of information management research: A conceptual structure analysis using structural topic modelling. *International Journal Information Management* (*IJIM*), 58, 2021.

20. Porturas, T. and Taylor, R.A., Forty years of emergency medicine research: Uncovering research themes and trends through topic modelling. *Am. J. Emergency Med.*, 45, 213–220, Aug. 2020.

21. Karami, A., Lundy, M., Webb, F., Dwivedi, Y.K., Twitter and research: A systematic literature review through text mining. *IEEE Access*, 8, 2020.

22. Kim, S., Park, H., Lee, J., Word2vec-based latent semantic analysis (W2V-LSA) for topic modelling: A study on blockchain technology trend analysis. *Expert Syst. Appl.*, 152, 2020.

23. Maeder, A., George, M., Naveda, B., Identifying recent telemedicine research trends using a natural language processing approach, in: *2020 International Conference on Artificial Intelligence, Big Data, Computing and Data Communication Systems (icABCD)*, Durban, South Africa, pp. 1–6, 2020.

24. Zuliani, A. *et al.*, Topics and trends in mountain livestock farming research: A text mining approach. *Animal*, 15, 1, 2021.

25. Gurcan, F. and Sevik, S., Big data research landscape: A meta-analysis and literature review from 2009 to 2018, in: *2019 1st International Informatics and Software Engineering Conference (UBMYK)*, Ankara, Turkey, pp. 1–5, 2019.

26. Ibrahim, M. and Ahmad, R., Class diagram extraction from textual requirements using natural language processing (NLP) techniques. *2010 Second International Conference on Computer Research and Development*, Kuala Lumpur, Malaysia, pp. 200–204, 2010.

27. Nazir, S., Asif, M., Ahmad, S., The evolution of trends and techniques for data mining, in: *2019 2nd International Conference on Advancements in Computational Sciences (ICACS)*, Lahore, Pakistan, pp. 1–6, 2019.

28. Ding, Z., Li, Z., Fan, C., Building energy savings: Analysis of research trends based on text mining. *Autom. Constr.*, 96, 398–410, Oct. 2018.

29. Youssef, A. and Rich, A., Exploring trends and themes in bioinformatics literature using topic modelling and temporal analysis, in: *2018 IEEE Long Island Systems, Applications and Technology Conference (LISAT)*, Farmingdale, NY, U. S. A., pp. 1–6, 2018.

30. Sandhu, R. and Khanna, K., Satisfaction: A scale to fulfil consumer's expectations on cloud computing. *International Journal of Research in Electronics and Computer Engineering (IJRECE)*, 5, 3, 362–365, 2017.

31. Patel, K. *et al.*, Facial sentiment analysis using AI Techniques: State-of-the-art, taxonomies, and challenges. *IEEE Access*, 8, 90495–90519, 2020.

32. Nguyen, E.T., Xie, F., Chen, Q., Zhou, Y., Chen, W., Bautista, J. *et al.*, Characterization of patients with advanced chronic pancreatitis using natural language processing of radiology reports. *PLoS One*, 15, 8, e0236817, 2020, https://doi.org/10.1371/journal.pone.0236817.

33. Prasanna, D.L. and Tripathi, S.L., Machine learning classifiers for speech detection. *2022 IEEE VLSI Device Circuit and System (VLSI DCS)*, Kolkata, India, pp. 143–147, 2022.

# 4

# Spatial Analysis of Carbon Sequestration Mapping Using Remote Sensing and Satellite Image Processing

**Prashantkumar B. Sathvara, J. Anuradha, R. Sanjeevi\*,
Sandeep Tripathi and Ankitkumar B. Rathod**

*Nims Institute of Allied Medical Science and Technology
(Nims University Rajasthan), Jaipur, India*

## Abstract

As a result of modernization and urbanization, carbon emissions are becoming a significant issue for society. Agents for storing carbon include soils, oceans, forests, and the atmosphere. They act as sinks or sources at various periods and emit more carbon than they absorb. Carbon sinks eliminate carbon dioxide ($CO_2$) from the surroundings through a process known as carbon sequestration. On a global scale, trees are better at storing carbon than crops, but on a smaller scale, crops have a purpose. Green plants use photosynthesis' atmospheric carbon dioxide ($CO_2$) to store carbon in their tissues. Satellite data can calculate ground vegetation, seasonal production, and carbon sequestration. The carbon cycle and vegetation can both be monitored using global remote sensing technologies. This study includes open and closed shrubs, agricultural land, healthy vegetation patterns, and biomass. This study provides a quick way to access the value of biomass and carbon sequestration. Given the importance of carbon sequestration, it is essential to consider crops when modelling a region's carbon balance because they can act as small-scale carbon sinks.

*Keywords*: Carbon sequestration, geospatial imaging, remote sensing, net primary productivity, LANDSAT, MODIS terra

---

\**Corresponding author*: r.sanjeevi@nimsuniversity.org

Sandeep Kumar, Deepika Ghai, Arpit Jain, Suman Lata Tripathi and Shilpa Rani (eds.)
*Multimodal Biometric and Machine Learning Technologies: Applications for Computer Vision,*
(71–84) © 2023 Scrivener Publishing LLC

## 4.1   Introduction

The most significant feared issue in the world, global warming, is partly caused by carbon emissions from various sources. Due to human actions like burning fossil fuels, deforestation, and urbanization during the past century, the atmosphere now contains a lot of $CO_2$ and other greenhouse gases [1]. Global warming is brought on by one of the most common greenhouse gases, $CO_2$, which also causes draughts, deforestation, and rising sea levels [2]. Agents for storing carbon include soils, oceans, forests, and the atmosphere. Global warming is brought on by one of the most common greenhouse gases, $CO_2$, which also causes draughts, deforestation, and rising sea levels [3]. This is measured *in situ* following the estimation of plant species' biomass. Remotely sensed satellite data is a technology that can quickly and efficiently assess the value of plants for carbon sequestration over a broader region in terms of biomass [4].

Carbon sequestration involves storing carbon dioxide or other types of carbon to slow down global warming. $CO_2$ is removed from the atmosphere through biological, chemical, or physical processes [5]. One kind of greenhouse gas is $CO_2$. The atmospheric build-up of greenhouse gases brought on by Carbon sequestration can reduce the burning of fossil fuels and other anthropogenic factors. A reservoir that gathers and stores chemical compounds containing carbon may be called a carbon sink. Carbon sinks absorb $CO_2$ to remove it from the atmosphere. Natural sinks include forests, soil, oceans, plants, and algae [6]. The amount of carbon sequestration should be measured using an exact, accurate, and economical method. As a result, we can use traditional techniques like GIS, and remote sensing could offer a better solution in this situation [7]. Remote sensing has been used to develop methods for assessing plant biomass and carbon content, although evaluation of land surface predictive or diagnostic factors has generally received relatively little attention [8].

Around the world, many cubic tons of carbon dioxide is trapped in organic matter. Natural processes transform this organic material into fuels like gasoline, diesel, coal, wood, and peat. When the energy is burned, the carbon dioxide that has been stored is released into the environment [9]. Naturally, carbon dioxide is stored away once more, though more quickly than now. Sinks absorb the released gas and keep it there for a longer duration. Carbon is stored in the lithosphere, ocean, soil, atmosphere, biosphere, and biomass [8].

There are numerous traditional techniques for measuring stored carbon. Many of these techniques have constrained coverage, are costly and are complex. Such restrictions make it difficult to quantify and monitor carbon accurately. Remote sensing can overcome such measurement and monitoring constraints [10]. The use of remote sensing can help meet carbon sequestration requirements, like having permanent sample plots. Green, Red, and near-infrared (NIR) wavelength reflection contains essential data on plant biomass [11, 26, 27].

This study's primary goal is to calculate carbon sequestration using satellite data. The entirety of Ahmedabad's districts makes up the research area (Figures 4.1 and 4.2). Latitude 23.033863 N and longitude 72.585022 E are its coordinates. It has 8,086 square kilometres in India's north-central state of Gujarat. The site is selected near the Sabarmati River's banks. Census data indicates that Ahmadabad's metro area will have 8,450,000 residents in 2022, an increase of 2.39% from 2021. 8,253,000 people called Ahmadabad's metro region home in 2021, a 2.41% rise from 2020. Winter, monsoon season and summer are the three main seasons. Except for the

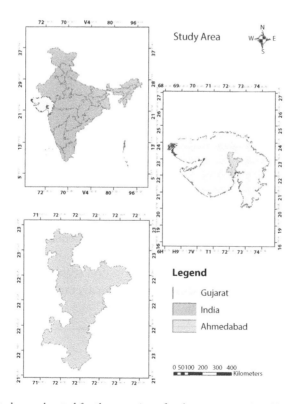

**Figure 4.1** Study area located for the mapping of carbon sequestration (*Source:* Figure generated by the researcher).

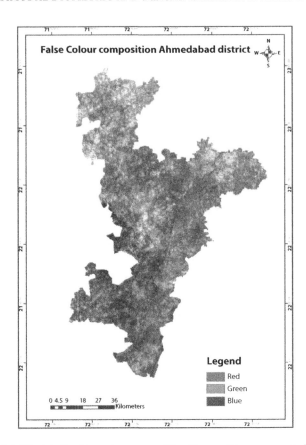

**Figure 4.2** Satellite date for false color composition (*Source:* Figure generated by the researcher).

monsoon season, the climate is arid. Summertime maximum temperatures often range from 43 °C (109 °F) to 24 °C (75 °F). March through June is hot months. From November to February, the median high temperature is 30 °C, and the average low is 13 °C (55 °F). Brisk winds from the north bring on a minor chill in January. The monsoon season produces a humid climate from mid-June to mid-September. On average, there is 800 mm of rain every year [12, 13, 28, 29].

## 4.2    Materials and Methods

### 4.2.1    Materials

Moderate Resolution Imaging Spectroradiometers (MDOIS) remotely sensed is used for the inquiry due to its 500-m resolution. NASA's Terra satellite, possessing the MODIS sensor, is a scan measurement system with 36 wavelength channels covering the visible to thermal IR spectra [14–16]. Band 1 (red, 620-670 nm), band 2 (near infrared, 841-876 nm), band 3 (near infrared, 841-876 nm), band 7, and band 8 (near infrared, 841-876 nm) are the first seven bands that are mainly meant for distant sensing of terrestrial surfaces. Maps of the areas of study were created using MODIS bands 1, 2, and 7 [17–19]. NASA provided the study region with MODIS data for the entire Ahmedabad region for January, June, and October during the consecutive year 2021 and 2022. QGIS 3 was the programme used to analyze images and geoinformation. In this investigation, 16 topographic maps at a scale of 1:250,000 were employed [20–22].

### 4.2.2    Methodology

The following methodology studies revealed that the equation could accurately capture the rise in plant biomass total primary output (NPP) [23–25]:

$$NPP = APAR.LUE$$

where NPP, net primary production; APAR, absorbed photo-synthetically active radiation; LUE, light use efficiency factor; PAR, photo-synthetically active radiation.

The normalized difference vegetation index (NDVI), which utilizes the frequency in the red (RED) and infrared (NIR), can be used to extract PAR and APAR from remote sensing data [19, 20].

Normalized Difference Vegetation Index = near infrared – Red/ near-infrared + Red (NDVI = NIR – RED / NIR + RED)

Absorbed Photosynthetically Active Radiation/Photosynthetically Active Radiation ~ Normalized Difference Vegetation Index

$$(APAR/PAR \sim NDVI)$$

Productivity is the measure of the production of biomass rate per time step expressed as in the equation.

Net primary productivity = Normalized Difference Vegetation Index × photosynthetically active radiation × light use efficiency

$$(NPP = NDVI \times PAR \times LUE)$$

The vegetation acreage extraction procedure uses 250-m resolution MODIS Terra satellite pictures. The technique makes use of six photos. On satellite data, digital image processing techniques are applied. Satellite data are enhanced and processed using image processing tools [21].

The image of January reveals the winter season, June is represented the summer season, and October shows the monsoon season.

### 4.2.2.1   *Formula for the Mathematical Extraction of the Vegetation Area*

Area (m²) = Number of clusters' pixels * the image's resolution Square

$$\text{Area (ha)} = \text{area (m}^2) / 10,000$$

The MODIS Terra 250 m sensor took this picture, so Area (m²) = Value of cluster pixels multiplied by 250 by 250.

The algorithms utilized are represented mathematically. The following are the theoretical, computational procedures involved in calculating biomass using remote sensing data:

**NDVI = NIR-RED/NIR+RED**

**Biomass = *NDVI\*PAR\*LUE***

The FPAR Estimation technique is employed for integrating straight-forward leaf-level models of photosynthesis, light absorption, light scattering, and stomata conductance. The FPAR-Simple Ratio (SR) Vegetation Index correlation analysis offered a solid mechanical underpinning, and the correlations between FPAR and SR were deduced by land cover class as follows [18]:

$$FPAR_{SR} = \frac{(SR - SRmin)(FPARmax - FPARmin)}{SRmax - SRmin} + FPARmin$$

where FPAR*max* = 0.95, FPAR*min* = 0.001, SR*max* and SR*min* are the SR values related to 98% and 2% of the Vegetation indices frequency analysis, respectively, and SR = (1 + NDVI)/ (1 − NDVI). This equation is known as the SR-FPAR model.

The following formula provides the NDVI-FPAR model, an alternative model.

$$FPAR_{NDVI} = \frac{(NDVI - NDVImin)(FPARmax - FPARmin)}{NDVImax - NDVImin} + FPARmin$$

$$FPAR = \frac{(FPAR(SR) - FPAR(NDVI)}{2}$$

Comparing the ground-measured FPAR with the estimated FPAR produced by the above models. This work evaluated the FPAR from 2021 and 2022 using this intermediate model. Several vegetation types' 98% and 2% NDVI and accompanying SR values were estimated from MODIS Vegetation indices from 2021 to 2022.

$$\varepsilon = \varepsilon^{\circ}*T1*T2*W \ (g/MJ)$$

Where $\varepsilon^{\circ}$ = 2.5g/MJ and
*T1* and *T2* relate temperature adaptation to plant development [21].

## 4.3   Results

The research area of the present study is the Ahmedabad district. The recorded results are shown in Figures 4.3 and 4.4 and in Table 4.1. In the current work, we used remote sensing and GIS to compute the carbon sequestration and compare it to 2021 and 2022. The estimated biomass of vegetation is 163,442 kg/ha during the 2021 winter season, 169,559 kg/ha during the summer season, and 242,100 kg/ha during the monsoon season.

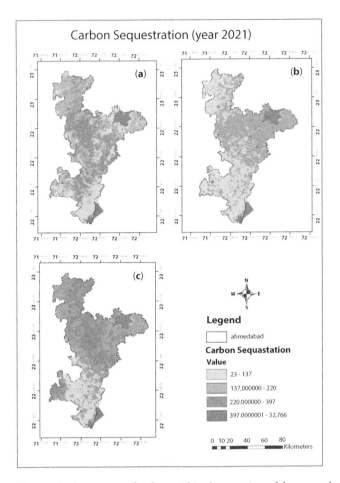

**Figure 4.3** Changes in the amount of carbon within the premises of the research area for the time (a) January 2021 (b) June 2021 (c) October 2021.

During the 2022 estimation, the district recorded vegetation biomass as 190,177 kg/ha in winter, 111,743 kg/ha in summer and 199,139 kg/ha in monsoon season. The result estimated value of carbon sequestration is higher during the monsoon season. Whole scene pixel values are added together to calculate the carbon for the entire study site.

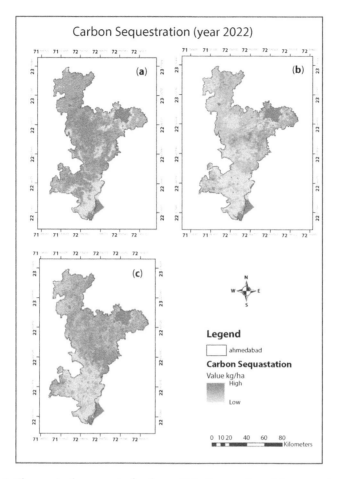

**Figure 4.4** Changes in the amount of carbon within the premises of the research area for the time (a) January 2022, (b) June 2022, (c) October 2022. (*Source:* Figure generated by the researcher).

## 4.4   Conclusion

The current study offers a workable result for carbon quantification using remotely sensed data. We can analyze findings over a large study area with a one-time investment with built-in map-producing qualities. The overall quantity of carbon sequestered in the study region is 67,260,000,000 kg/ha,

**Table 4.1** Carbon sequestration data concerning time and study area*.

| Month | kg/ha | tonne/ha |
|---|---|---|
| January 2021 | 163,442 | 163.442 |
| June 2021 | 169,559 | 169.559 |
| October 2021 | 242,100 | 242.1 |
| January 2022 | 190,177 | 190.177 |
| June 2022 | 111,743 | 111.743 |
| October 2022 | 199,139 | 199.139 |

* (*Source:* Tabulation above details generated by the researcher).

although it is evident that the research areas sequester a lot of carbon. This study leaves a lot of potential for further investigation. Agricultural carbon sequestration reduces greenhouse gas emissions and improves environmental quality. Therefore, the idea of carbon trading also has substantial financial potential.

The foundation of the agricultural sector builds up the Indian economy [24, 25]. Although agricultural land is available, little is known about its capacity to operate as a carbon sink during the growing season. After all the factors and qualities have been considered, it is clear that the present investigation on carbon sequestration has major scientific significance.

Globally, India, in particular, needs to wake up to the fact that there are alternative carbon sinks outside the traditional ideas of forests/oceans as a sink [18]. To lessen the impacts of global warming, we desperately need to increase the modes of carbon sinks as alternatives to forests, as the forest cover area is quickly vanishing.

## Acknowledgment

The remote sensing and GIS lab of Nims University Rajasthan, Jaipur, provided the lab space and motivation for the current investigation, for which the authors are grateful. The authors are pleased to use the USGS Earth Explorer Online Platform for the MODIS data sets utilized in this investigation.

# References

1. Houghton, R.A., Converting terrestrial ecosystems from sources to sinks of carbon. *Ambio*, 25, 4, 267–272, 1996.
2. Arias, D., Calvo-Alvarado, J., Richter, D. de B, Dohrenbusch, A., Productivity, aboveground biomass, nutrient uptake and carbon content in fast-growing tree plantations of native and introduced species in the Southern Region of Costa Rica. *Biomass Bioenergy*, 35, 5, 1779–1788, May 2011.
3. MacDicken, K.G., A guide to monitoring carbon storage in forestry and agroforestry projects, Winrock International Institute for Agricultural Development, Forest Carbon Monitoring Program, 1997. [Online] Available: https://www.osti.gov/biblio/362203
4. Arya, A., Shalini Negi, S., Kathota, J.C., Patel, A.N., Kalubarme, M.H., Garg, J.K., Carbon sequestration analysis of dominant tree species using geo-informatics technology in Gujarat State (INDIA). *International Journal of Environment Geo-informatics (IJEGEO)*, 4, 2, 79–93, May 2017.
5. Anaya, J.A., Chuvieco, E., Palacios-Orueta, A., Aboveground biomass assessment in Colombia: A remote sensing approach. *For. Ecol. Manag.*, 257, 4, 1237–1246, 2009.
6. Sellers, P.J. *et al.*, Remote sensing of the land surface for studies of global change: Models — Algorithms — Experiments. *Remote Sens. Environ.*, 51, 1, 3–26, Jan. 1995.
7. Deng, S., Shi, Y., Jin, Y., Wang, L., A GIS-based approach for quantifying and mapping carbon sink and stock values of a forest ecosystem: A case study. *Energy Procedia*, 5, 1535–1545, 2011.
8. Bindu, G., Rajan, P., Jishnu, E.S., Ajith Joseph, K., Carbon stock assessment of mangroves using remote sensing and geographic information system. *The Egyptian Journal of Remote Sensing and Space Science (EJRS)*, 23, 1, 1–9, Apr. 2020.
9. Goward, S.N. and Huemmrich, K.E., Vegetation canopy PAR absorptance and the normalized dit erence vegetation index: An assessment using the SAIL model. *Remote Sens. Environ.*, 39, 2, 119–140, 1992, https://10.1016/0034-4257(92)90131-3.
10. Pareta, D.K. and Pareta, U., Forest carbon management using satellite remote sensing techniques a case study of sagar district (M. P.). *Int. Sci. Res. J.*, 4, 14, 2011.
11. Frazao, L.A., Silva, J.C., Silva-Olaya, A.M., $CO_2$ Sequestration, IntechOpen, 2020 [cited 2022 Sep 25]. Available from: https://www.intechopen.com/books/co2-sequestration/introductory-chapter-co-sub-2-sub-sequestration
12. Wikipedia contributors. (2023, June 16). Ahmedabad. In Wikipedia, The Free Encyclopedia. Retrieved 19:07, June 17, 2023, from https://en.wikipedia.org/w/index.php?title=Ahmedabad&oldid=1160451925

13. Wikipedia contributors. (2023, June 16). Ahmedabad. In Wikipedia, The Free Encyclopedia. Retrieved 19:07, June 17, 2023, from https://en.wikipedia.org/w/index.php?title=Ahmedabad&oldid=1160451925

14. Olofsson, P., Eklundh, L., Lagergren, F., Jönsson, P., Lindroth, A., Estimating net primary production for Scandinavian forests using data from Terra/MODIS. *Advances in Space Research (ASR)*, 39, 1, 125–130, Jan. 2007.

15. Zhao, M., Running, S., Heinsch, F.A., Nemani, R., MODIS-derived terrestrial primary production, in: *Land Remote Sensing and Global Environmental Change*, vol. 11, B. Ramachandran, C.O. Justice, M.J. Abrams (Eds.), pp. 635–660, Springer New York, NY, 2010.

16. Hassan, Q.K., Spatial mapping of growing degree days: An application of MODIS-based surface temperatures and enhanced vegetation index. *J. Appl. Remote Sens.*, 1, 1, 013511, Apr. 2007.

17. Liu, J. *et al.*, Crop yield estimation in the canadian prairies using Terra/MODIS-derived crop metrics. *IEEE J. Sel. Top. Appl. Earth Obs. Remote Sens.*, 13, 2685–2697, 2020.

18. Zhu, Q. *et al.*, Remotely sensed estimation of net primary productivity (NPP) and its spatial and temporal variations in the greater Khingan Mountain Region, China. *Sustainability*, 9, 7, 1213, Jul. 2017.

19. Asrar, G., Fuchs, M., Kanemasu, E.T., Hatfield, J.L., Estimating absorbed photosynthetic radiation and leaf area index from spectral reflectance in wheat [1]. *Agron. J.*, 76, 2, 300–306, Mar. 1984.

20. Sanjeevi, R., Rathod, A.B., Sathvara, P.B., Tripathi, A., Anuradha, J., Tripathi, S., Vegetational cartography analysis utilizing multi-temporal ndvi data series: A case study from rajkot district (GUJARAT), India. *Tianjin Daxue Xuebao (Ziran Kexue yu Gongcheng Jishu Ban)/ J. Tianjin Univ. Sci. Technol.*, 55, 04, 490–497, 2022.

21. Field, C.B., Randerson, J.T., Malmström, C.M., Global net primary production: Combining ecology and remote sensing. *Remote Sensing of Environment (RSE)*, 51, 1, 74–88, Jan. 1995.

22. Supriya Devi, L. and Yadava, P.S., Aboveground biomass and net primary production of the semi-evergreen tropical forest of Manipur, north-eastern India. *J. For. Res.*, 20, 2, 151–155, Jun. 2009.

23. Kumar, S., Rani, S., Jain, A., Verma, C., Raboaca, M.S., Illés, Z., Neagu, B.C., Face spoofing, age, gender and facial expression recognition using advance neural network architecture-based biometric system. *Sens. J.*, 22, 14, 5160–5184, 2022.

24. Kumar, S., Jain, A., Agarwal, A.K., Rani, S., Ghimire, A., Object-based image retrieval using the U-net-based neural network. *Comput. Intell. Neurosci.*, 2021, 1–14, 2021 Nov 10.

25. Kumar, S., Haq, M., Jain, A., Andy Jason, C., Moparthi, N.R., Mittal, N., Alzamil, Z.S., Multilayer neural network based speech emotion recognition for smart assistance. *CMC-Comput. Mater. Contin.*, 74, 1, 1–18, 2022.

26. Bhola, A. and Singh, S., Visualization and modeling of high dimensional cancerous gene expression dataset. *J. Inf. Knowl. Manag.*, 18, 01, 1950001–22, 2019.

27. Bhola, A. and Singh, S., Gene selection using high dimensional gene expression data: An appraisal. *Curr. Bioinform.*, 13, 3, 225–233, 2018.

28. Rani, S., Gowroju, Kumar, S., IRIS based recognition and spoofing attacks: A review, in: *10th IEEE International Conference on System Modeling &Advancement in Research Trends (SMART)*, December 10-11, 2021.

29. Swathi, A., Kumar, S., Venkata Subbamma., T., Rani, S., Jain, A., Ramakrishna Kumar, M.V.N.M., Emotion classification using feature extraction of facial expression, in: *The International Conference on Technological Advancements in Computational Sciences (ICTACS – 2022)*, pp. 1–6, Tashkent City Uzbekistan, 2022.

# 5

# Applications of Multimodal Biometric Technology

**Shivalika Goyal[1,2] and Amit Laddi[1]***

*[1]Biomedical Applications (BMA), CSIR-CSIO, Chandigarh, India*
*[2]Academy of Scientific and Innovative Research (AcSIR), Ghaziabad,*
*Uttar Pradesh, India*

### Abstract

Multimodal biometric systems (MBS) are an extensive and significant version of unimodal biometric systems (UBS), offering higher data security, safety, recognition, authentication, speed, and reliability. The criteria for making a MBS are vital in designing, handling, and executing an MBS using various fusion technologies between two or more different biometric systems. Components are arranged in such a way in MBS that they follow a designated procedure to communicate the end decision with high precision and information. Several modalities are used in MBS. The two most important are physiological and behavioral, which include Face, Iris, Fingerprint, Palm, GAIT, DNA, Voice, and much more, depending on the sampling methodology. The application of MBS is vast due to its emergence in science as an individual body for research, industrial, and home applications. The future aspects of MBS can lead to new and higher data authentication and implementation scopes.

*Keywords*: Multimodal biometric systems, data security and authentication, components, modalities, applications

## 5.1   Introduction

Multimodal biometric systems (MBS) work on extracting information from two or more biometric input systems.

---

*\*Corresponding author*: amitladdi@csio.res.in

Sandeep Kumar, Deepika Ghai, Arpit Jain, Suman Lata Tripathi and Shilpa Rani (eds.)
*Multimodal Biometric and Machine Learning Technologies: Applications for Computer Vision,*
(85–102) © 2023 Scrivener Publishing LLC

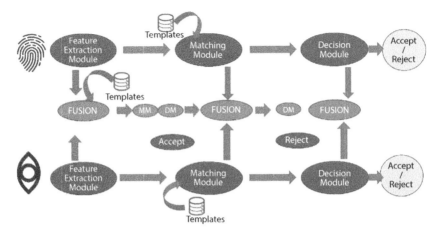

**Figure 5.1** The fusion between iris and thumb print data inputs.

A MBS increases the variety of information taken from users for authentication from the input source. MBS offers higher data precision and more flexibility than a single biometric system. When we talk about unimodal biometric systems (UBS), it has to deal with several challenges like the lack of secrecy, non-generalization of user data samples, the user comfort extent and freeness to handle the system like data spoofing, forging, etc. MBS offers a data security parameter over UBSs [1, 2]. A MBS uses the fusion of combining decisions from every system used in a series and then comes up with a solution/result/conclusion. This is why MBS is more accurate, safe, and conclusive. The working of MBS involves the capturing module, feature recognition and extraction module, comparison and analysis module, and the decision/conclusion module [3–5]. Furthermore, it uses data fusion technology to combine data from two or more different input sources which can be done at any level like during feature extraction, live sample comparison and decision-making module as shown in Figure 5.1.

### 5.1.1   Benchmark for Effective Multimodal Biometric System

The seven essential criteria that we always discuss while implementing an effective MBS [6, 7] are as follows:

    a) **Uniqueness:** It is a primary criterion for making an effective MBS. It ensures that the biometric system can detect a particular user from a group of users or data.

b) **Universality:** It is a secondary criterion for an effective MBS. It determines the need for unique features for each person residing in the world.

c) **Permanence:** It indicates the consistency of personal traits recorded in the database system for a certain period.

d) **Collectability:** It determines the level of easiness at which the data/traits can be obtained or processed further from a wide range of users.

e) **Performance:** It defines the accuracy and effectiveness of the biometric system in terms of fault management, period of checking, and wideness.

f) **Acceptability:** It determines the user's comfort with the biometric system or how easily and speedily the person/user accepts the technology in data capture, accession, sharing, and storage.

g) **Circumvention:** It defines the easiness with which a trait/data/parameter is possibly copied/forged using an outer element or artifact.

## 5.2    Components of MBS

Today's biometric system has become an individual science body incorporated with precision technologies for connecting or identifying personal identities. Biometrics is used for authenticating and authorizing a person [7]. However, these terms are often grouped because they mean different. Let us discuss this with literal examples:

a) **Authentication:** The process of authentication tries to establish the question pre-loaded, "Are you the same identity who you are claiming to be on this system, or Do I know you, or are you already enrolled with me?" This is a one-to-many data matching, comparison, and detection of user's data with the stored database.

b) **Verification:** This is the one-to-one procedure of live sample matching processed by the user with a pre-loaded template in the database. If both data sets match more than 70% credibility, the verification is considered successful [8, 9].

c) **Authorization:** Authorization involves designating access rights to verified persons/users. It tries to find the answer to the question, "Are you legal or qualified to have particular rights to gain access to this data or resource?"

A MBS is divided into four essential components, shown in Figure 5.2 [10].

Let us discuss these essential components in detail for a more comprehensive understanding.

### 5.2.1   Data Store(s)

This component stores and preserves the samples/data collected at the time of enrolment of the user for the system to access. The data sets are recalled during authentication to perform a sample match check whether the user can access the system. An external input device is needed to inject the user data into the database for checking like fingerprint scanner, contactless smart card, etc.

### 5.2.2   Input Interface

This component is termed as the sensing element of a MBS that changes or digitalize the user's biological or behavioral data—e.g., optical sensor for fingerprint scanner, microphone for voice detection, etc.

### 5.2.3   Processing Unit

This component can be termed a microprocessor, digital microprocessor, or a computational device to process the data acquired from the input sensors after their proper digitalization, which involves sample enhancement/optimization, image normalization, feature extraction, and comparison module.

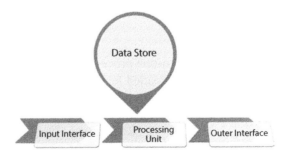

**Figure 5.2** Basic components of MBS.

### 5.2.4   Output Interface

This component of MBS delivers the decision led by the biometric system to enable/disable/lock the user for data/resource access. This interface could be a radio frequency, RFID, Bluetooth, or any other output display device.

## 5.3   Biometrics Modalities

Biometric modality is defined as a category of MBS that depends on the type of data or trait collected from the user/human as an input. Biometrics are gigantically mathematical. Therefore, more data availability promotes uniqueness and reliability, enabling it to use numerous modalities to measure users' features and behavioral patterns [11–13]. These modalities are generally differentiated based on the user's biological or behavioral traits [14, 15]. There are two types of biometric modalities based on fundamental human data factors (i) physiological biometric modalities and (ii) behavioral biometric modalities [12, 13, 16, 17] as shown in Table 5.1. The examples of biometric authenticators are shown in Figure 5.3.

**Table 5.1**  Type of biometric modalities with examples.

| Physiological biometric modality | Behavioral biometric modality |
|---|---|
| Pertains to the shape, size, color, and physical aspects of a human/user body. | Pertains to the change in human/user behavior over a specific period. |
| For Example:<br>Face, Iris, Fingerprint, etc. | For Example:<br>Voice, Gait, etc. |

## 5.4   Applications of Multimodal Biometric Systems

With the advancements in MBS as an individual science body, this technology is significantly incorporated in numerous applications in various sectors. Starting with the use of MBS in the day-to-day life of users, it is implemented substantially on a large scale in almost every digital device/module to authenticate users, data, access, command systems, etc. [11, 18]. Let us discuss the application area of MBS in detail for further understanding.

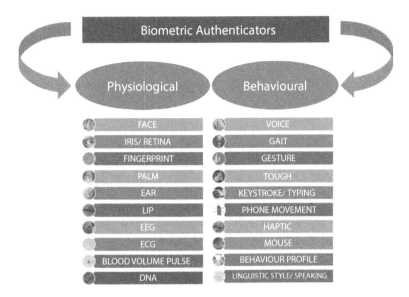

**Figure 5.3** Examples of biometric authenticators used as biometric modalities in MBS.

### 5.4.1  MBS in Forensic Science

Enormously diverse criminal activities attract the use of highly efficient MBS in forensic science to detect illegal and related activities based on their physiological and behavioral activities. Mainly in forensics, physiological data recognition is preferred due to the presentation of facts in technical terms to prove a crime. MBS is an excellent tool in forensics to determine these criminals by the traces they intentionally/unintentionally left at the crime spot or area [19]. Main MBS used in forensics is discussed in Table 5.2.

Besides the physiological modalities of MBS, behavioral modalities, such as GAIT biometrics, odor, ear, dental, keystrokes, cheiloscopy, handwriting, signature, etc. Biometrics are also playing a significant role in Forensics as an effective MBSs. For example, Drs. Michael Nirenberg and Christine Miller in the United States regularly use forensic gait analysis for criminal detection [20, 21].

### 5.4.2  MBS in Government Applications

MBS in government applications is multi-advantageous in the modern world. It is becoming more common regarding governmental data authentication, defence systems, identification systems, public data storage and

**Table 5.2** Different types of biometric authenticators with explanation and examples.

| Authenticator type | Explanation | Example |
|---|---|---|
| **Fingerprint Biometrics** | A pattern of Ridges and Valleys is present on the fingertips' surface. | FBI's Integrated Automated Fingerprint Identification System comprises criminal history, automated fingerprint search capabilities, image storage, etc. |
| **Face Biometrics** | Identifies/Detects a person based on an already existing image or video using facial patterns | INTERPOL's Face Recognition System, which comprises images from around 179 countries modelling, is a distinctive criminal database around the globe. |
| **DNA biometrics** | It involves the identification of DNA pattern chains, which are universally unique in every biological creature. | FBI's Combined DNA Index System helps forensic laboratories deal with crime detection activities at the local, state and governmental levels. |
| **Palm print biometrics** | It identifies the full human hand patterns of ridges and valleys and is more distinctive than fingerprint recognition. | NEC and PRINTRAK developed a High-Definition Recognition system for palm print image capturing for various criminal-related applications. |
| **Iris biometrics** | Recognizes the unique patterns of the iris in the human eye. | UK Federal's Iris Recognition Immigration System for International travellers for their on-spot ID detections. |
| **Voice biometrics** | Identifies the voices by digitalizing sound waves to a significant pattern for human detection. | AGNITIO's Voice ID technology is used for criminal identification and speaker verification in over 35 countries. |

identification systems [22, 23]. Some of the significant examples of MBS in government applications are as follows:

a) Unique Identification Authority of India developed the national identity card AADHAR which maintains the physiological data like fingerprints, iris, and faces of all the residents in India in a single database system from which data is timely recalled on user's and service provider's request to authenticate various operations in telecom services, service subscriptions, Government-Public Internal Authentications between state and central departments and much more [24, 25].

b) In the United States, federal government uses MBS in biometric voter registration systems to conduct forge-free elections and biometric prison management for prisoners' data management like attendance systems, in–out timings from and in the cell, etc. [26, 27].

c) Several countries use biometric border control and military base management systems as a practical MBS tool for better national security, e.g., identifying international travellers at borders and airports, diminishing illegal entries/exits, securing the weapon, and ammunition, documental confidentiality across military operations of a country's defence system [28–31].

d) Ayushman Bharat Digital Mission under the Government of India developed the ABHA system for the public to create an ABHA card comprising an individual's healthcare data like medical conditioning, media claims, etc. [32]. Also, GOI uses biometric authentication systems in e-district digital missions to carry out daily operations of the public using biometric authentication like withdrawal of money using fingerprint authentication, driving license applications, passport application processing, online KYC using fingerprint and face recognition, etc. [33].

### 5.4.3    MBS in Enterprise Solutions and Network Infrastructure

Manually tracking of employee attendance and their in-out timings in the enterprise solutions is complex and time consuming. The biometric authentication system solved this problem by digitalizing the process led by MBSs with the mixed use of iris, fingerprints, faces, and smart cards. Current technologies in public domains are fully designated with MBS tools due to the ease of accessing data, devices, and services [34–36]. According to a survey by VISA, 75% of mobile users prefer fingerprint authentication for unlocking phones and accessing locked apps and services instead of entering manual passwords. To maintain the highest possible security standards by high-tech companies, they need to acquire MBSs in their system to do so like time and attendance, access control, and customer service parameters like customer authentication over IVR, etc. To promote remote workspaces among employees, especially in IT sector companies, MBS is essential in IT techs accessing their last saved work or working remotely around the globe using cloud services [37, 38]. Network security systems use MBS to encrypt the users' data for their reclaimant. In network infrastructure, devices like laptops, Wi-Fi printers, and desktops use MBS to authenticate data between server and client. In the educational sector, teachers' and students' attendance systems are widely used to minimize the cost of card-based attendance, time-saving, effective, accurate attendance, and much more [39–41].

### 5.4.4    MBS in Commercial Applications

To facilitate convenience for the public in operating devices and technology in day-to-day life, MBS became an exciting tool. Smart devices available in the market, like smartphones and intelligent TVs, enabled the use of MBS in public hands as a daily routine. Some examples of commercial applications involve banking, finance, aviation, automobiles, home security, and more [42, 43]. A list of applications is shown in Figure 5.4 for a better understanding of this aspect.

a) **Public Transport:** MBS in public transport plays a significant role in metros and airlines. In metro rails, RFID cards present fare charges and entry openings to prevent non-eligible persons' entry. In aviation, face data are used by immigration authorities to detect passport and visa authenticity [44]. Also, the signature data on passports signify the non-forging and illegal material transport within countries. MBS in aviation is improving the future of air travel by improving the safety, contactless passenger experience, and hassle-free journey with less documentation handling [45–47]. In various countries, especially in London, a CUBIC biometric-based ticketing system is used to travel in public buses without putting yourself in the hassle of booking offline tickets [48–51].

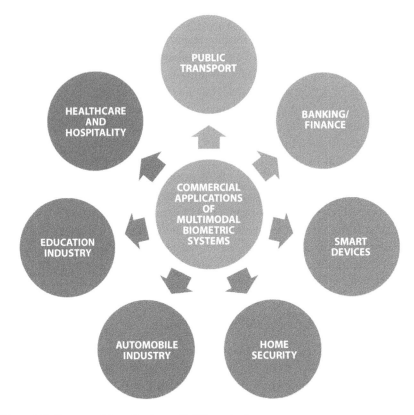

**Figure 5.4** Commercial applications of MBS as a tool.

b) **Banking/Finance:** MBS is a crucial system for almost every banking operation, offline and online. Digital customer onboarding using Social Security Number in the United States, Aadhar KYC in India, etc., are great examples. Modifying or updating customers' data using fingerprint authentication is much-appraised use in the banking sector. The process of point-of-sale verification carries out online fund remittance between two countries by banks, which is also a use case of MBS [48, 49]. Loans, credit cards, account opening, etc., are now possible digitally by using MBS as a tool to recall data saved in government servers. Investments in financial products like the equity market, debt market, real estate funds, etc., are only possible digitally due to the advanced MBS, which carries out Point-of-Sale verification using demographic data [52–55].

c) **Intelligent Devices:** Smart devices like Apple Home Pod, Amazon Alexa, Smartphones, smart TVs, wireless printers, laptops, etc., are all daily-level devices that use the MBS technology to authenticate a user for desired access [51]. Smartphones use the fingerprint sensor, iris detection [52], iris center localization [53], and face recognition for device unlocking and accessing multi-level applications by replacing passwords as a tool. Wireless printers and laptops also use the same MBS to control and gain access to the legit user only. Smart watches detect the pulse rate over the hand to produce data for user's heart rate, oxygen saturation, and stress level, adding a new product to MBS's body. Smart AIs like Apple Home Pod and Amazon Alexa use voice recognition systems to identify and respond to only those voices that were primarily enrolled to use [56–58].

d) **Home Security:** Home security systems are incorporated with MBS to provide better security solutions over conventional security measures for houses. PCZ cameras in houses detect motions which is an example of GAIT biometrics. These cameras can move automatically in the direction of the intruder's movements. Modern door locks are embedded with fingerprint, palm, and iris detection systems to offer better digital security over the classical lock and key method [55]. Smart RFIDs are also being used in corporate colonies for house safety. Also, in the case of money safety, smart safes are in the market, which use fingerprint and retinal biometrics to open and close with strong security and alarm features [59–62].

e) **Automobiles:** Smart vehicles developed by TATA Motors, Kia Motors, BMW, Tesla, etc., highly use MBS technology as a tool in digital access and processing. Modern digital keys replaced conventional car keys, which use RFID to detect their presence near cars for driver authentication. Besides this, intelligent vehicles use camera and infrared to determine objects near or around the car while reversing or parking it. Vehicles developed by Tesla and TATA use fingerprint authentication for engine ignition and shut-off. Innovative vehicles use voice recognition systems like CarPlay to respond to speakers about commands to accept calls, play music, navigation, and much more, which is very helpful during driving as it prevents the manual use of the system leading to zero distraction over road sight [63–66]. Some vehicles have pulse detectors on the steering, which measure the oxygen saturation and fatigue level of a driver while driving and communicate the driver's condition, like stress or intoxication, whether to carry on driving or not, which is very helpful in preventing accidents [58, 59].

f) **Education Sector:** The ease of handling the attendance system of teachers and students is led by the MBS at another level. This removed the card-based or manual attendance of the students in classrooms and helped reduce the time for the attendance takers [67–69]. Also, students can be given access to certain areas of the premises in a controlled manner, like a library, sports complex, gym, canteen, etc. This also removed the risk of losing the students' and teachers' lanyards and ID cards. Entry using MBS structures is safe and quick and cannot be forged like in the manual cases of transferring lanyards from one student to another. Cashless catering systems were implemented in schools, universities, and colleges opened after COVID-19 to deliver contactless services using biometric authentication of face and iris; the significant expenses were further adjusted to their ledger account [60].

g) **Health Care and Hospitality:** Growing advancements in healthcare facilities are being promoted by MBS technology on a broader approach. The data handling, patient management systems, health tracking, and bed/ward allotments are being operated and managed using MBS as a tool. Patient registration in corporate hospitals like CK Birla and Fortis Healthcare is being carried out by fingerprint authentication to recall their demographic, address, and personal data from the database managed by the concerned authorities. Also, biometric authentication is being carried out by updating the health status and claim settlement processes with insurance companies directly by the hospitals [61–63]. Cancer patients are being monitored regarding medicinal acquisition to track which steroid drugs they bought for what reasons. Integrated image processing and sharing systems developed by corporate diagnostics laboratories use a secure channel to share health reports, data, and private images infused with biometric security so that the data transmitted with doctors remain confidential and encrypted among the diagnostics center, the concerned doctor and the patient only [70–72].

In the hospitality sector, hotels use RFID cards as a detection tool for their guests to give them access to the building's lift, pool, gym, and room. Some premium brand hotels introduced the concept of keyless check-in to hotels for their existing loyalty members using fingerprint and mobile devices as a tool. Hotel payments can be automated by authenticating biometric services with payment service providers. Workforce management, time punching of workers, room service fulfillment, etc., are carried out using fingerprint and iris biometrics [73–76].

## 5.5    Conclusion

The emerging growth of MBS as an individual body of science widens the scope for more research and its implementation commercially across the globe. MBSs are more effective, accurate, speedy, and reliable than UBSs. The multimodel approaches used in MBS make it more favorable, safe, and better than UBSs. Fusing two or more sub-biometric systems offers simpler user authentication, which is crucial in data safety. Higher accuracy can be obtained using MBS regarding a person's accurate ethnicity if MBS technology can be significantly fused with the science of genetic algorithm.

## References

1. Ross, A. and Jain, A., Information fusion in biometrics. *Pattern Recognit. Lett.*, 24, 13, 2115–2125, 2003.
2. Sanjekar, P.S. and Patil, J.B., An overview of multimodal biometrics. *Signal Image Process*, 4, 1, 57–64, 2013.
3. Delac, K. and Grgic, M., A survey of biometric recognition methods. *46th International Symposium Electronics in Marine*, pp. 183–194, 2004.
4. Jain, A.K., Hong, L., Pankanti, S., Bolle, R., An identity-authentication system using fingerprints. *Proc. IEEE*, 85, 9, 1365–1388, 1997.
5. Ross, A., Jain, A.K., Qian, JZ., Information fusion in biometrics, in: *Audio- and Video-Based Biometric Person Authentication*, pp. 354–359, Springer, Berlin, 2001.
6. Basha, A.J., Efficient multimodal biometric authentication using fast fingerprint verification and enhanced iris features. *J. Comput. Sci.*, 7, 5, 698–706, 2011.
7. Sivadas, S., A study of multimodal biometric system. *Int. J. Res. Eng Technol.*, 03, 27, 93–98, 2014.

8. Sarhan, S., Alhassan, S., Elmougy, S., Multimodal biometric systems: A comparative study. *Arab. J. Sci. Eng.*, 42, 2, 443–457, 2017.

9. Choras, R.S., Multimodal biometrics for person authentication, in: *Security and Privacy From a Legal, Ethical, and Technical Perspective*, IntechOpen, London, UK, 2020.

10. Sanjekar., P.S. and Patil., J.B., An overview of multimodal biometrics. *Signal Image Process*, 4, 1, 57–64, 2013.

11. Anwar, A.S., Ghany, K.K.A., Elmahdy, H., Human ear recognition using geometrical features extraction. *Procedia Comput. Sci.*, 65, 529–537, 2015.

12. Bibi, K., Naz, S., Rehman, A., Biometric signature authentication using machine learning techniques: Current trends, challenges and opportunities. *Multimed. Tools Appl.*, 79, 1–2, 289–340, 2020.

13. Habeeb, A., Comparison between physiological and behavioral characteristics of biometric systems. *J. Southwest Jiaotong Univ.*, 54, 6, 2019.

14. Biometric modalities, in: *Biometric User Authentication for it Security*, pp. 33–75, Springer-Verlag, New York, 2006.

15. Sasidhar, K., Kakulapati, V.L., Ramakrishna, K., KailasaRao, K., Multimodal biometric systems - study to improve accuracy and performance. *International Journal of Computer Science & Engineering Survey (IJCSES)*, 1, 2, 54–61, 2010.

16. Alay, N. and Al-Baity, H.H., Deep learning approach for multimodal biometric recognition system based on fusion of iris, face, and finger vein traits. *Sensors*, 20, 19, 5523, 2020.

17. Benaliouche, H. and Touahria, M., Comparative study of multimodal biometric recognition by fusion of iris and fingerprint. *Sci. World J.*, 2014, 1–13, 2014.

18. Kakkad, V., Patel, M., Shah, M., Biometric authentication and image encryption for image security in cloud framework. *Multiscale and Multidisciplinary Modeling, Experiments and Design*, 2, 4, 233–248, 2019.

19. Kebande, V.R., A framework for integrating multimodal biometrics with digital forensics. *International Journal of Cyber-Security and Digital Forensics (IJCSDF)*, 4, 4, 498–507, 2015.

20. Saini, M. and Kumar Kapoor, A., Biometrics in forensic identification: Applications and challenges. *J. Forensic Med.*, 1, 2, 1–6, 2016.

21. Jain, A.K. and Ross, A., Bridging the gap: Biometrics to Forensics. *Philos. Trans. R. Soc B: Biol. Sci.*, 370, 1674, 20140254, 2015.

22. Singh, P., Morwal, P., Tripathi, R., Security in e-governance using biometric. *Int. J. Comput. Appl.*, 50, 3, 16–19, 2012.

23. Scott, M., Acton, T., Hughes, M., An assessment of biometric identities as a standard for e-government services. *International Journal of Services and Standards (IJSS)*, 1, 3, 271, 2005.

24. Anand, N., New principles for governing Aadhaar: Improving access and inclusion, privacy, security, and identity management. *Journal of Science Policy & Governance (JSPG)*, 18, 01, 2021.

25. Pali, I., Krishna, L., Chadha, D., Kandar, A., Varshney, G., Shukla, S., A comprehensive survey of aadhar and security issues, in: *Cryptography and Security, Cornell Edu*, New York, arXiv:2007.09409, 2020.
26. Ansolabehere, S. and Konisky, D.M., The introduction of voter registration and its effect on turnout. *Polit. Anal.*, 14, 1, 83–100, 2006.
27. Srikrishnaswetha, K., Kumar, S., Ghai, D., Secured electronic voting machine using biometric technique with unique identity number and I.O.T, in: *Innovations in Electronics and Communication Engineering*, pp. 311–326, Springer, Singapore, 2020.
28. Gold, S., Military biometrics on the frontline. *Biom. Technol. Today*, 2010, 10, 7–9, 2010.
29. Deny, J. and Sivasankari, N., Biometric security in military application. *Procedia Eng.*, 38, 1138–1144, 2012.
30. Khan, N. and Efthymiou, M., The use of biometric technology at airports: The case of customs and border protection (C.B.P.). *Int. J. Inf. Manag. Data Insights*, 1, 2, 100049, 2021.
31. Liu, Y., Scenario study of biometric systems at borders. *Computer Law & Security Review (CLSR)*, 27, 1, 36–44, 2011.
32. Shrisharath, K., Hiremat, S., Nanjesh Kumar, S., Rai, P., Erappa, S., Holla, A., A study on the utilization of Ayushman Bharat Arogya Karnataka (ABArK) among COVID patients admitted in a tertiary care hospital. *Clin. Epidemiol. Glob. Health*, 15, 101015, 2022.
33. Sriee, G.V.,.V. and Maiya, G.R., Coverage, utilization, and impact of Ayushman Bharat scheme among the rural field practice area of Saveetha Medical College and Hospital, Chennai. *J. Family Med. Prim. Care*, 10, 3, 1171, 2021.
34. Diwakar, M., Kumar Patel, P., Gupta, K., Tripathi, A., An impact of biometric system applications services on the biometric service market. *Int. J. Comput. Appl.*, 76, 13, 8–13, 2013.
35. Kloppenburg, S. and van der Ploeg, I., Securing identities: Biometric technologies and the enactment of human bodily differences. *Sci. Cult. (Lond)*, 29, 1, 57–76, 2020.
36. Laddi, A. and Prakash, N.R., Eye gaze tracking based directional control interface for interactive applications. *Multimed. Tools Appl.*, 78, 22, 31215–31230, 2019.
37. Bagga, P., Mitra, A., Das, A.K., Vijayakumar, P., Park, Y., Karuppiah, M., Secure biometric-based access control scheme for future IoT-enabled cloud-assisted video surveillance system. *Comput. Commun.*, 195, 27–39, 2022.
38. Yang, W., Wang, S., Sahri, N.M., Karie, N.M., Ahmed, M., Valli, C., Biometrics for internet-of-things security: A review. *Sensors*, 21, 18, 6163, 2021.
39. Guennouni, S., Mansouri, A., Ahaitouf, A., Biometric systems and their applications, in: *Visual Impairment and Blindness - What We Know and What We Have to Know*, IntechOpen, London, UK, 2020.

40. Selvam, V. and Gurumurthy, S., Design and implementation of biometrics in networks. *J. Technol. Adv. Sci. Res.*, 1, 3, 226–234, 2015.
41. Sanchez-Reillo, R., Heredia-da-Costa, P., Mangold, K., Developing standardized network-based biometric services. *I.E.T. Biom.*, 7, 6, 502–509, 2018.
42. Prabhakar, S. and Bjorn, V., Biometrics in the commercial sector, in: *Handbook of Biometrics*, pp. 479–507, Springer US, Boston, MA, 2008.
43. Hernandez-de-Menendez, M., Morales-Menendez, R., Escobar, C.A., Arinez, J., Biometric applications in education. *International Journal on Interactive Design and Manufacturing (IJIDeM)*, 15, 2–3, 365–380, 2021.
44. Teodorovic, S., The role of biometric applications in air transport security. *Nauka, Bezbednost, Policija*, 21, 2, 139–158, 2016.
45. Khan, N. and Efthymiou, M., The use of biometric technology at airports: The case of customs and border protection (C.B.P.). *Int. J. Inf. Manag. Data Insights*, 1, 2, 100049, 2021.
46. Mahfouz, K., Rameshi, S.M., Rafat, M., Elsayed, M., Sheikh, M., Zidan, H., Route mapping and biometric attendance system in school buses. *2020 Advances in Science and Engineering Technology International Conferences (ASET)*, pp. 1–4, 2020.
47. Balu Kothandaraman, A., Raja, K., Thamaraiselvi, G., Prabha, R., Narasimman, V., Biometrics based bus ticketing system, in: *International Conference on Technological Innovations in Electronics and Management, Aurangabad*, India, 2018.
48. Banga, L. and Pillai, S., Impact of behavioural biometrics on mobile banking system. *J. Phys. Conf. Ser.*, 1964, 6, 062109, 2021.
49. Hosseini, S.S. and Mohammadi, D., Review banking on Biometrics in the world's banks and introducing a biometric model for Iran's banking system. *JBASR*, 2, 9152–9160, 2012.
50. Morake, A., Khoza, L.T., Bokaba, T., Biometric technology in banking institutions: 'The customers' perspectives'. *S.A. Journal of Information Management (SAJIM)*, 23, 1, 12, 2021.
51. Kim, Y.G., Shin, K.Y., Lee, W.O., Park, K.R., Lee, E.C., Oh, C., Lee, H., *Multimodal biometric systems and its application in smart T.V*, pp. 219–226, Springer, Berlin, 2012.
52. Laddi, A. and Prakash, N.R., Comparative analysis of unsupervised eye centre localization approaches. *2015 International Conference on Signal Processing, Computing and Control (ISPCC)*, pp. 190–193, 2015.
53. Laddi, A. and Prakash, N.R., An augmented image gradients based supervised regression technique for iris centre localization. *Multimed. Tools Appl.*, 76, 5, 7129–7139, 2017.
54. Noh, N.S.M., Jaafar, H., Mustafa, W.A., Idrus, S.Z.S., Mazelan, A.H., Smart home with biometric system recognition. *J. Phys. Conf. Ser.*, 1529, 4, 042020, 2020.

55. Saravanan, K., Saranya, C., Saranya, M., A new application of multimodal biometrics in home and office security system. *Cryptog. Security*, arXiv:1210.2971, Cornell Edu, New York, 2012.

56. Manzoor, S.I. and Selwal, A., An analysis of biometric based security systems. *2018 Fifth International Conference on Parallel, Distributed and Grid Computing (PDGC)*, pp. 306–311, 2018.

57. Ćatović, E. and Adamović, S., Application of biometrics in automotive industry - case study based on iris recognition. *Proceedings of the International Scientific Conference - Sinteza 2017*, pp. 44–49, 2017.

58. Villa, M., Gofman, M., Mitra, S., *Survey of biometric techniques for automotive applications*, pp. 475–481, Springer, Cham, 2018.

59. Kiruthiga, N., Latha, L., Thangasamy, S., Real time biometrics based vehicle security system with G.P.S. and GSM technology. *Procedia Comput. Sci.*, 47, 471–479, 2015.

60. Hernandez-de-Menendez, M., Morales-Menendez, R., Escobar, C.A., Arinez, J., Biometric applications in education. *International Journal on Interactive Design and Manufacturing (IJIDeM)*, 15, 2–3, 365–380, 2021.

61. Kumar, S., Rani, S., Jain, A., Verma, C., Raboaca, M.S., Illés, Z., Neagu, B.C., Face spoofing, age, gender and facial expression recognition using advance neural network architecture-based biometric system. *Sens. J.*, 22, 14, 5160–5184, 2022.

62. Kumar, S., Jain, A., Agarwal, A.K., Rani, S., Ghimire, A., Object-based image retrieval using the u-net-based neural network. *Comput. Intell. Neurosci.*, 2021, 1–14, 2021.

63. Fatima, K., Nawaz, S., Mehrban, S., Biometric authentication in health care sector: A survey. *2019 International Conference on Innovative Computing (ICIC)*, pp. 1–10, 2019.

64. Mason, J., Dave, R., Chatterjee, P., Graham-Allen, I., Esterline, A., Roy, K., An investigation of biometric authentication in the healthcare environment. *Array*, 8, 100042, 2020.

65. Nigam, D., Patel, S.N., Raj Vincent, P.M.D., Srinivasan, K., Arunmozhi, S., Biometric authentication for intelligent and privacy-preserving healthcare systems. *J. Healthc. Eng.*, 2022, 1–15, 2022.

66. Mustra, M., Delac, K., Grgic, M., Overview of the DICOM standard. *IEEE*, 1, 39–44, 2008.

67. Bidgood, W.D., Horii, S.C., Prior, F.W., van Syckle, D.E., Understanding and using DICOM, the data interchange standard for biomedical imaging. *Journal American Medical Informatics Association (JAMIA)*, 4, 3, 199–212, 1997.

68. Kumar, S., Rani, S., Laxmi, K.R., *Artificial intelligence and machine learning in 2D/3D medical image processing*, First edition, CRC Press, Boca Raton, C.R.C. Press, 2021, 2020.

69. Ko, C.-H., Tsai, Y.-H., Chen, S.-L., Wang, L.-H., Exploring biometric technology adopted in the hotel processes. *Biotechnology (Faisalabad)*, 13, 4, 165–170, 2014.

70. Abd Al Qawi, A., The possibility of applying biometric safety technology in egyptian hotels: "Evaluating customer experience using the T.A.M. Model. *Journal of Assocciation of Arab Universities for Tourism Hospitality (JAAUTH)*, 14, 1, 113–126, 2017.

71. Prasanna, D.L. and Tripathi, S.L., Machine and deep-learning techniques for text and speech processing, in: *Machine Learning Algorithms for Signal and Image Processing*, IEEE, pp. 115–128, 2023.

72. Lata Tripathi, S., Dhir, K., Ghai, D., Patil, S. (Eds.,), *Health Informatics and Technological Solutions for Coronavirus (COVID-19)*, 1st ed, CRC Press, Florida, 2021, https://doi.org/10.1201/9781003161066.

73. Kumar, S., Haq, M., Jain, A., Jason, C.A., Moparthi, N.R., Mittal, N., Alzamil, Z.S., Multilayer neural network based speech emotion recognition for smart assistance. *CMC-Comput. Mater. Contin.*, 74, 1, 1–18, 2022. Tech Science Press.

74. Bhola, A. and Singh, S., Visualization and modeling of high dimensional cancerous gene expression dataset. *J. Inf. Knowl. Manag.*, 18, 01, 1950001–22, 2019.

75. Bhola, A. and Singh, S., Gene selection using high dimensional gene expression data: An appraisal. *Curr. Bioinform.*, 13, 3, 225–233, 2018.

76. Rani, S., Gowroju, S., Kumar, S., IRIS based recognition and spoofing attacks: A review, in: *10th IEEE International Conference on System Modeling &Advancement in Research Trends (SMART)*, December 10-11, 2021.

# 6

# A Study of Multimodal Colearning, Application in Biometrics and Authentication

Sandhya Avasthi[1*], Tanushree Sanwal[2], Ayushi Prakash[1] and Suman Lata Tripathi[3]

*[1]Department of Computer Science and Engineering, ABES Engineering College, Ghaziabad, India*
*[2]MBA Department, Krishna Group of Institutions, Delhi-NCR, Ghaziabad, India*
*[3]School of Electronics and Electrical Engineering, Lovely Professional University, Jalandhar, India*

## Abstract

"Multimodality" refers to utilizing multiple communication methods to comprehend our environment better and enhance the user's experience. Using multimodal data, we may provide a complete picture of an event or object by including new information and perspectives. Improvements in single-mode apps' performance have been possible thanks to developments in deep learning algorithms, computational infrastructure, and massive data sets. Using many modalities is superior to using a single modality, according to research dating back to 2009. The study explains the limitations of single biometric-based methods in providing security and efficiency. The multimodal architecture is based on different forms of data, such as video, audio, images, and text. Combining these kinds of data is utilized to help people learn and imitate. We provide discussions on various methods to fuse different modalities of data. Recent studies have shown that cutting-edge deep-learning techniques can give even better results in multimodal biometrics and authentication systems on mobile devices. The chapter explains different problems in multimodal colearning, various multimodal fusion methods, existing challenges, and future directions.

*Keywords*: Multimodality, machine learning, multimodal colearning, speech recognition, multimodal biometrics, deep learning, fusion levels

*Corresponding author*: sandhya_avasthi@yahoo.com

Sandeep Kumar, Deepika Ghai, Arpit Jain, Suman Lata Tripathi and Shilpa Rani (eds.)
Multimodal Biometric and Machine Learning Technologies: Applications for Computer Vision,
(103–128) © 2023 Scrivener Publishing LLC

## 6.1    Introduction

From the beginning, human cognitive development depended on multisensory, multimodal perceptions. For instance, a person can learn the meaning of words through visual and acoustic reinforcements along with semantic or syntactic structure. The learning through elements from multisensory experiences can be further applied to a situation where modalities are missing, for example, reading a newspaper [1–3]. A general practice in machine learning is to use unimodal information based on chosen mode after due diligence in researching the domain. However, a better approach would be to apply to education using multimodal information more aligned with human cognitive development. The application of multimodal data for learning can be referred to as multimodal colearning (MCI) in this chapter [4–6]. Naturally, unstructured data from the real world can exist in various modalities, often known as formats, and frequently includes textual and visual material. Researchers in deep learning continue to be motivated by the need to extract valuable patterns from this type of data. The study presented in this chapter investigates multimodal machine learning and colearning and also explores how to develop deep learning models that integrate and mix various forms of visual inputs across different sensory modalities. In addition, it describes multiple approaches and fundamental concepts of deep multimodal learning. According to related surveys [7, 8], general image matching aims to recognize and match the same or similar structure/content from two or more images [9, 10].

The modern world faces difficulties due to a pandemic and numerous other healthcare needs due to its rising life expectancy [11]. As the field of information technology expands exponentially, users' top concerns are security, privacy, and healthcare applications [12, 13]. More inventive patient care is made possible by improved diagnostic technologies, and innovative medical equipment's real-time monitoring of vital signs raises the standard of care. Competent health care aims to inform individuals about their health conditions and treatment options [14–16]. Individuals are better prepared for potential medical emergencies thanks to intelligent healthcare. A remote check-up service is given, which reduces treatment costs and provides medical practitioners with additional options to serve patients in different regions [17]. A robust intelligent healthcare infrastructure is required to ensure patients' access to necessary medical care as smart cities proliferate. Every year, many computer vision researchers work on making systems that let machines act like humans. Using computer vision technology to map their behavior, intelligent devices like mobile phones can find obstacles and track locations [18, 19]. Complex operations can be automated in multimodal applications, including computer vision applications. The main challenge of this research is to extract visual attributes from one or more data streams (also called "modalities") with different shapes and sizes. This is done by learning to combine extracted heterogeneous features and project them into a common representation space. This is called "deep multimodal learning." In many situations, a mix of different cues from different modalities and sensors can give context-relevant information about a single activity [20, 21]. In multimodality, a modality's place in conceptual architecture is determined by the media and the qualities that make it up. Some of these modalities are textual, visual, and auditory. They use specific methods or procedures to encode different kinds of information in a way that makes sense [22].

### 6.1.1    Need for Multimodal Colearning

Multimodal applications incorporate information from several sources at the signal or semantic levels, making them more accurate and dependable than single-modality applications. Applying knowledge gained through one (or more) modalities to tasks involving a different one is the goal of colearning. This typically involves learning a joint representation space, learning external modalities during training, and evaluating the cooperative model's suitability for unimodal tasks. The fusion of multiple data sources is referred to as multimodal fusion [23, 24]. Multimodal systems are those that facilitate communication between users via a variety of channels. An additional definition of multimodality is the capacity of a plan to do automated information processing and to communicate in more than one mode. Six different relationships exist between the modalities: equivalence, transfer, specialization, redundancy, complementarity, and concurrency. "put-that-there" was the first system developed in the 1980s to investigate multimodal systems. This system made inferences about the user's context based on their voice and the cursor's position [25, 26].

As explained, colearning is crucial to maximizing the effectiveness of applications in real-world multimodal. Since currently mobile devices, physiological devices, cameras, medical imaging, and all kinds of sensors are available quickly, multimodal data collection is relatively easy now. Nowadays, multimodal applications range from practical computing, decision-making, control systems, multimedia, autonomous systems, medical devices, military equipment, and satellite systems [27, 28]. The multimodal systems used in these contexts must be dependable and capable of producing accurate predictions in imperfect signals or environmental variation, as shown in Figure 6.1. Doing so will prevent potentially fatal or otherwise disastrous outcomes. Multimodal machine learning aims to develop models capable of processing and connecting input from multiple sources. Multimodal machine learning is not limited to only audiovisual speech recognition applications; it is used in language and computer vision applications, indicating its enormous potential [29, 30].

Using supplementary or auxiliary information, multimodal data enables us to explain things or phenomena from various perspectives or angles. Applications using a single modality have achieved substantially higher performance thanks to developments in deep learning techniques, computer architecture, and massive data sets [31]. Research from 2009 [1] showed that using multiple senses rather than one can improve performance. Recent research has shown that the most recent deep learning methods lead to additional improvements. Consequently, multimodal machine learning and deep learning are becoming increasingly important.

## 6.1.2    Why Multimodal Biometric Systems?

Individual identification is vital to biometric authentication, security management, and video surveillance systems. Primary physical biometrics that identifies people include the face, iris, and fingerprints [16]. However, using any of them effectively in an open environment with a typical surveillance system is complex. Facial biometrics captured at a distance, for instance, are

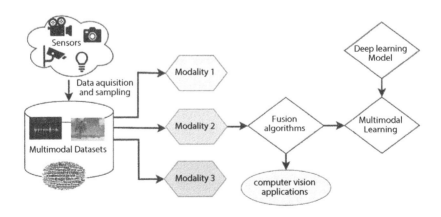

**Figure 6.1** A simple pipeline of a multimodal system.

unsuccessful due to the low quality of the face photos. The only biometrics insensitive to space and the quality of the capturing equipment is a person's gait characteristics, which cannot be imitated easily. However, it imposes certain restrictions on dress, carrying cases, and environmental variables [17]. The recognition efficiency of a unimodal biometric is diminished due to numerous difficulties in acquiring feature patterns. A multimodal biometrics surveillance system allows for more precise information extraction than unimodal systems. Diverse fusion-level techniques are employed for the merging of information from various modalities [32, 33].

Although machine learning (ML) techniques frequently extract biometric features and classify objects from raw data, they could perform better in feature discrimination and selection tasks across multiple application domains. Artificial neural networks (ANN) with several hidden layers are used in deep learning (DL), a recent branch of machine learning, to extract data from the lowest level to the most abstract. DL techniques include flexible feature learning, dependable fault tolerance, and robustness features [18]. In recent years, deep convolutional neural networks (deep CNN) have been used in biometric recognition systems [19].

### 6.1.3   Multimodal Deep Learning

Despite significant advancements, not all facets of human learning have been incorporated into unimodal learning. Multimodal learning enhances comprehension and analysis by actively involving multiple senses in processing information [34–36]. A wide range of media is examined in this paper, including body language, facial expressions, physiological signals, images, videos, text, and audio. Along with a thorough analysis of the foundational approaches, a detailed analysis of recent developments in multimodal deep learning applications over the previous 5 years (2017–2021) has been given. A fine-grained taxonomy of multiple multimodal deep learning approaches is published, focusing on the applications. Finally, the primary concerns for each domain are described separately, along with possible future research directions [20, 21].

This chapter examines multimodal colearning from every conceivable viewpoint, current state, obstacles, data sets, and potential uses. This first effort extends the colearning taxonomy beyond the parallelism of data depicted in Figure 6.2 and into the realm of multimodal colearning [37–39]. We analyzed the preexisting categories, created new ones based on current research and introduced the most up-to-date frameworks that accommodate multimodal colearning and modality circumstances throughout the learning and assessment processes.

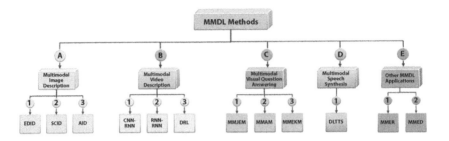

**Figure 6.2** Different applications of multimodal deep learning.

### 6.1.4   Motivation

Recent widespread use of low-cost sensors has led to an explosion of visual data, which has improved the performance of a wide range of computer vision applications (see Figure 6.1). These visual data can be still photos, video sequences, etc., and they can be used to build multimodal models. In contrast to a static image, a video stream contains much meaningful information that considers how successive frames look in space and time. This makes it easy to use and analyze for real-world applications, such as facial expression recognition [22] and video synthesis and description [23]. The term "spatiotemporal concept" refers to analyzing video clips with different lengths in space and time. Multimodal learning analytics combine a video clip's audiovisual and textual features into a single part [40, 41].

The chapter will introduce multimodal colearning, classifying it according to the issues it addresses and the applications it enables. Section 6.1 provides an overview of Multimodal learning, Multimodal Deep Learning, application areas, and motivation for writing this chapter. Section 6.2 gives an outline of Multimodal Deep Learning and its different applications. The Deep Learning Architecture and various techniques are described in Section 6.3. Section 6.4 provides an overview of fusion levels in Multimodal Systems. Section 6.5 gives an outline of a multimodal authentication system in mobile devices. The sixth section discusses challenges, issues, and open problems related to multimodal learning. Concluding remarks and future scope are presented in section seven.

## 6.2   Multimodal Deep Learning Methods and Applications

In the case of single modalities, applications based on text, images, or audio deep learning models have been successfully applied. Many applications use data in

Table 6.1 Description of different multimodal learning applications.

| SN | Application | Full name | Description |
|---|---|---|---|
| 1 | MMDL | Multimodal Deep Learning | It focuses on developing models that combine multiple data modes with varying structures. |
| 2 | EDIT | Encoder-Decoder-Based Image Description | After reading the input photo, a network model that decodes the photo's content into a fixed-length vector. |
| 3 | SCID | Semantic Concept-based Image Description | The concept layer is primarily responsible for resolving the meaning expressed by images via scene, knowledge, and emotion. |
| 4 | AID | Attention-based Image Description | The program was able to generate each word of the caption by paying attention to the area of the image that was the most important. |
| 5 | DRL | Deep Reinforcement Learning | Combines reinforcement learning and deep learning. |
| 6 | MMJEM | Multimedia Joint-embedding Models | Joint embedding aims to develop a model representing different media types in a single format. |
| 7 | MMAM | Multimodal Attention-based Models | fusion of multiple modalities, where each modality has its sequence of feature vectors. |
| 8 | MMEKM | Multimodal External Knowledge-Based Models | Knowledge evaluation and verification can be made more accessible with the help of multi-source knowledge reasoning. |
| 9 | DLTTS | Deep Learning Text to speech | to figure out how to use the audio input to guess what the words and sentences said. |

*(Continued)*

**Table 6.1** Description of different multimodal learning applications. (*Continued*)

| SN | Application | Full name | Description |
|---|---|---|---|
| 10 | MMER | Multimodal Event Recognition | Multimodal social event detection finds events in vast amounts of data, like words, photos, and video clips. |
| 11 | MMED | Multimodal Emotion Detection | Combining different modalities offered an excellent viewpoint and successfully revealed hidden emotions from perceptible sources. |

various forms to improve features, and those applications are based on multimodal deep-learning techniques. Table 6.1 summarizes multiple Multimodal Deep Learning applications, and the detail is provided in subsections.

### 6.2.1   Multimodal Image Description (MMID)

The primary purpose of image description is to produce a textual description of the visual information contained in an input image. Deep learning-era picture descriptions are conducted by combining CV and NLP. This process makes excellent use of both text and image [42, 43]. Figure 6.3 shows the visual description's general structure diagram. There are three types of image description frameworks. They are based on retrieval, templates, and description logic (DL). Two of the first ways to describe an image's visual information are "retrieval" and "template-based." This article has three DL-based approaches to describing pictures: encoder-decoder-based, semantic concept-based, and attention-based. Frameworks based on retrieval, templates, or deep learning can all be used to describe images. One of the oldest ways [25, 26] was to use a template to get visual data from a picture and describe it. This article offers a thorough analysis of DL-based methods for image description. These techniques are further divided into encoder-decoder, semantic concept, and attention-based.

### 6.2.2   Multimodal Video Description (MMVD)

Like image description, video description creates a textual description of what is visible in an input video. This section discusses in depth how DL can be utilized to describe the visual content of videos. When conditions improve in this field, they can be used in various ways. Video stream and text are the two primary modalities utilized in this procedure. This study categorizes video description methods using the following architectural combinations to extract visual features and generate text [27].

The majority of early works on visual description focused on describing still images. Early attempts at providing automated video descriptions relied on a two-stage pipeline that first recognizes semantic visual concepts before stitching them together in a "subject, verb, object" template. Although a template-based solution separates the tasks of idea identification and description development, such templates need to recreate the language richness found in human-generated descriptions of films or situations [44, 45].

### 6.2.3   Multimodal Visual Question Answering (MMVQA)

VQA is a multimodal task that aims to correctly produce a natural language response as output after being presented with an image and a related natural language question. VQA is a new method that interests both the CV and NLP communities. It focuses on creating an artificial intelligence (AI) system that can answer questions in natural language [28]. It involves understanding and connecting the image's content to the question's context. VQA involves a diverse set of CV and NLP sub-problems due to the need to compare the semantics of information present in both modalities (the image and the natural language question related to it) (such as object detection and recognition, scene classification, counting, and so on). This means that it is a problem that can be solved entirely by artificial intelligence. Figure 6.3 displays three examples of images and accompanying questions [46, 47].

**Figure 6.3** Sample examples of images and questions-answer (accessed from https://medium.com/data-science-at-microsoft/visual-question-answering).

### 6.2.4   Multimodal Speech Synthesis (MMSS)

Human behavior is comprised of two forms of communication: writing and speaking. Speech synthesis refers to the complex process of creating natural language spoken by a machine. Speech synthesis, also called TTS, converts text data into standardized, natural speech in real-time. It encompasses numerous academic disciplines, such as computer science, linguistics, digital signal processing, and acoustics. It is a cutting-edge information processing technology [29], especially for modern intelligent speech interaction systems. Early efforts to create speech synthesis technology heavily relied on parametric synthesis methods. Wolfgang von Kempelen, a Hungarian scientist, invented a device that could synthesize simple words in 1971. It uses a series of delicate bellows, springs, bagpipes, and resonance boxes.

Examples of speech synthesis in use today include screen readers, talking toys, talking video games, and human-computer interactive systems. The imitation of human speech is currently TTS systems' main research goal [30]. The effectiveness of the TTS system is assessed in several ways by using the quality of generated speech timing structure, rendering emotions, and pronunciation, quality of each word produced, synthetic speech preferences (listener preference for a better TTS system in terms of voice and signal quality), and human perception factors like comprehensibility [48].

### 6.2.5   Multimodal Event Detection (MMED)

Social event detection is the analysis of actual events in massive amounts of social media data never before seen. Even if the single-media-focused efforts produced satisfactory results, the current environment makes them difficult to manage because social media sites frequently host large amounts of multimodal data. Thanks to the widespread use of media sharing on the Internet, individuals can share their events, activities, and thoughts at any time. Multimodal event detection (MMED) systems attempt to recognize actions and occurrences in various media, including images, videos, audio files, text documents, etc. According to statistics, millions of tweets are sent daily, while more than 30,000 hours of video are uploaded to YouTube every hour. Finding events and activities within this volume of data is a complicated task. It has numerous applications in fields such as disease monitoring, governance, and business, and it enables internet users to comprehend and track global events [31, 32].

Whether or not a message input is part of a social event is determined by event inference, a stage of event discovery. Several works have been inspired by single-modal social event detection works to directly convert non-textual media into textual tags and then use conventional methods for multimodal social event detection. The "media gap"—a situation where descriptions of various media types are inconsistent and cannot be directly measured—between different modalities makes multimodal social event detection difficult. In any event, detection system effectiveness measures how well inference is made. The inference mechanism in such a system is grouped according to social event attributes [49].

### 6.2.6   Multimodal Emotion Recognition

Emotions are one way that people show how they feel. Multimodal Emotion Recognition (MMER) is very important for improving the way people and computers work together. Machine learning aims to let computers learn and recognize new inputs from training data sets. Because of this, it can be used to effectively train computers to detect, analyze, respond to, interpret, and recognize human emotions. So, the main goal of affective computing is to give machines and systems emotional intelligence. It wants to learn about learning, health, education, communication, gaming, a custom user interface, virtual reality, and data retrieval. The AI/ML model prototype extracts emotional information considering different modalities, for instance, image, text, video, body gesture, body position, facial expression and other forms of data. Using facial expressions and EEG (electroencephalogram) signals, the paper [33, 34] developed a fusion method for figuring out how someone is feeling. A neural network classifier can distinguish between happy, neutral, sad, and afraid feelings.

## 6.3   MMDL Application in Biometric Monitoring

Multimodal biometric systems identify and verify individuals based on many physiological features. The system stores a person's fingerprint patterns, face geometry, and iris patterns for user identification. Keeping a person's numerous physiological traits is suitable when it is crucial to preserve sensitive data [50].

### 6.3.1   Biometric Authentication System and Issues

Knowledge-based (based on something the user knows), possession-based (based on something the user possesses), and biometric-based are the three primary methods by which a user can be authenticated and verified (something a user is). IT systems have widely adopted the first two methods, even though they have several well-known drawbacks. Using a person's unique biological and behavioral characteristics for authentication has become increasingly common [35, 36]. Physical characteristics (such as fingerprints and facial features) serve as the basis for physiological factors, while behavioral factors (such as gait analysis and keystroke dynamics) reflect an individual's behavior and personality pattern [37].

The authentication procedure begins with collecting unique biometric features, continues with preprocessing, finds the area of focus, uses feature extraction techniques to pull out the predefined characteristics, and finally uses classification algorithms to reach a verdict [38]. In addition, numerous feature extraction and classifier construction strategies are available. You can classify a biometric system as either unimodal or multimodal based on the number of biometric modalities it supports [51]. Making a unimodal biometric system is less complicated because it only requires one identity and verification method. Problems, such as noisy data, poor recognition performance, less accurate results, and spoofing attacks [35–38], are more likely to occur in a unimodal system where the authentication metric acts as a single point of failure. These unimodal biometric systems rely on data from a single source to authenticate a person. Even though unimodal biometric systems have many benefits, they must overcome many challenges:

a) **Intra-class variation:** The biometric information collected during verification will not be the same as the information used to make a template for a person during enrolment. This is called variation within the same class. A biometric system's false Rejection Rate (FRR) increases when a category has many differences.

b) **Noisy data:** Biometric sensors that are sensitive to noise make it hard to match people because noisy data can lead to a false rejection.

c) **Interclass similarities:** Inter-class similarity is when the space of features for more than one person overlaps. A biometric system's false Acceptance Rate (FAR) increases with many class similarities.

d) **Non-universality:** Some individuals cannot provide the required biometric alone due to illness or disability.

e) **Spoofing** threatens unimodal biometrics because it allows the data to be imitated or forged.

Using a multimodal biometric system based on multiple sources of information for personal authentication is the best way to solve these issues with the unimodal biometric system [52].

### 6.3.2 Multimodal Biometric Authentication System and Benefits

Rather than relying on a single characteristic, a multimodal biometric system uses many or complementary characteristics (such as voice and face features). This makes it considerably more robust and difficult to fool. It has a high identification rate, is less subject to external influences, is more reliable and potent, and is more resistant to spoofing attacks [38]. Since it uses more than two biometric indications for authentication, multimodal biometrics must answer the following questions when merging data from numerous modalities: It is possible to develop a multimodal biometric authentication system by mixing specific parts at specific moments [39]. Choosing which biometric characteristics to combine, such as face and voice, fingerprints, and keystroke dynamics, requires selecting two or more biometric characteristics. How successfully the various biometric components may be integrated depends on when they are fused [53, 34]. This is performed during the pipeline phases of the biometric authentication system. How to unite describes the information's organization. The general multimodal biometrics framework is depicted in Figure 6.4.

A multimodal biometric system will make either a "genuine individual" or "imposter" determination. Fundamentally, the system's accuracy is determined by the genuine acceptance rate (GAR), false rejection rate (FRR), false acceptance rate (FAR), and equal error rate (EER) (ERR). The enrolment phase and the authentication phase are the two primary phases of operation for multimodal biometrics, and each is described as follows:

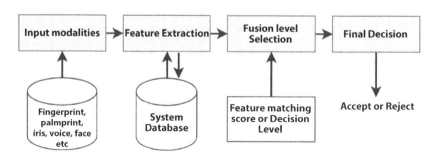

**Figure 6.4** A generic process of multimodal biometric system.

- **Enrolment phase:**
  A user's biometric characteristics are recorded during the enrolment phase and used as a template for that user during the authentication phase by being stored in the system database.
- **Authentication phase:**
  To verify a user's identity, the system takes another look at their unique set of traits. In identification, data is matched to templates for all users in a database called a "one-to-many" match. In verification, data is only matched to the claimed identity template, called a "one-to-one" match [40].

## 6.4    Fusion Levels in Multimodal Biometrics

Technically, multimodal fusion refers to merging data from multiple modalities to predict an end measure, either as a constant value (e.g., sentiment positivity) via regression or as a class (happy vs sad) via classification. Interest in multimodal fusion is sparked by its ability to provide three significant advantages [55]. First, having access to many observational modalities that capture the same phenomenon could aid in developing more accurate forecasts. Combining two or more modalities to complete a task is the first step in creating multimodal systems. Fusion techniques are divided into three categories: early (feature), late (decision), and intermediate (hybrid) fusion, depending on the level of the network at which the representations are fused [56, 57]. There are no hard and fast rules for fusion; instead, it is always different depending on the data, the domain, and the objective. Since early fusion does not consider intra-modality features and late fusion does not consider inter-modality particulars, hybrid fusion is the more popular option.

- **a) Early Fusion:** This merging occurs when the AI model's input data from various sources are combined. Further investigation reveals that the data set is first subjected to the fusion technique before being used as input to the DL algorithm. The fusion process is likely performed on the raw data itself. When raw data undergoes a feature-extraction phase before merging, we say the merging is performed at the feature level.
- **b) Late Fusion:** The AI algorithm is used before fusing. In this case, data are dealt with uniquely and multimodally. This

method looks at the different ways of doing things as separate streams. The possible conditional links between the other modalities are not considered during the learning process. There are a lot of different ways to merge.

c) **Intermediate Fusion:** When the various input data types are combined before and after the relevant AI algorithm is run, it is known as hybrid fusion. This approach may be efficient when combining modalities with similar dimensions or modalities that must be preprocessed before being merged during the training phase.

There are three fusion levels in multimodal biometrics, as described by Jain and Ross [6]: the feature level, the matching score level, and the decision level. It is commonly held that applying the combination scheme as early as possible in the recognition system yields the best results [8, 9]. The following is a breakdown of the three fusion stages:

## 6.4.1   Fusion at Feature Level

Signals from various biometric characteristics are individually processed, and then their feature vectors are fused into a single vector via the feature-level fusion procedure. The feature vectors are combined to create a composite feature vector for classification in the subsequent step [58]. For feature-level fusion to function, redundant features must be eliminated via reduction techniques. Researchers have utilized fusion at the level of features. Figure 6.5 is a demonstration of feature fusion. The primary advantage of feature-level fusion is the discovery of correlated feature values generated by distinct biometric algorithms. This helps identify a small set of significant features that can improve the recognition's accuracy. Typically, reducing the number of dimensions is required to obtain this

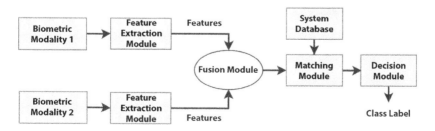

**Figure 6.5** Fusion at the feature level.

set of characteristics. Consequently, feature-level fusion typically requires a large amount of training data.

### 6.4.2   Fusion at Matching Score Level

The feature vectors still need to be put together. Instead, each one is looked at individually to figure out its score [58]. There are many ways to combine match scores, such as logistic regression, highest rank, Borda count and weighted sum, weighted product, Bayes rule, mean fusion, linear discriminant analysis (LDA) fusion, k-nearest neighbour (KNN) fusion, and hidden Markov model (HMM). Normalizing scores from different sources [6] is a critical issue that must be dealt with at the level of Matching scores. The match scores can be normalized with min-max, z-score, median-MAD, double-sigmoidal, tan-h, and piecewise linear. The matching score is the most played fusion level because it is easy. Several researchers [10–12] have used fusion at the Matching score level. Figure 6.6 shows the merging of scores that are the same.

### 6.4.3   Decision-Level Fusion

In this type of fusion, each modality is independently classified, meaning each biometric attribute is captured that follows the extraction of features from that specific trait. Further, these traits are classified as accept or reject based on the extracted features. The final classification relies on the integration of outputs from numerous modalities. The fusion of decision levels is illustrated in Figure 6.7. Fusion was utilized at the level of decision-making [20]. The advantage of this type is that prediction can be possible even if one of the modality data is unavailable.

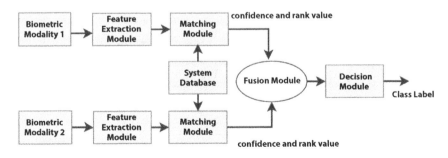

**Figure 6.6** Fusion at matching score level.

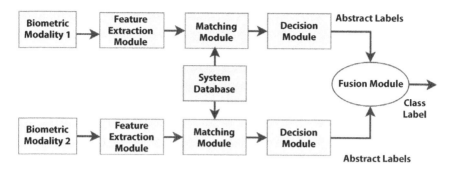

**Figure 6.7**  Fusion at the decision level.

## 6.5 Authentication in Mobile Devices Using Multimodal Biometrics

Implementing secure user authentication for mobile devices to protect users' personal information and data is becoming increasingly vital. Due to their enormous benefits over conventional authentication methods, biometric approaches have gained popularity in academics and business. This section discusses the development of existing biometric identification systems on mobile phones, namely touch-enabled devices, concerning eleven biometric methods. The types of user authentication are physiological and behavioral. In general, physiological biometrics refers to a person's physical characteristics, like their fingerprint, face, iris or retina, or hand or palm, whereas behavioral biometrics refers to their behavioral qualities, like their voice, signature, stride, keystroke dynamics, or touch dynamics.

These techniques use the entry-point authentication model, which can be biometric or based on PINs and passwords. The user only needs to be verified at the beginning of the session. Since attacks can happen after the first authentication, the session authentication paradigm has gotten much bad press. Because of these things, a new method of user authentication based on the "something that the user is" paradigm has been suggested. Continuous authentication (CA) and behavioral biometrics (BB) are used in this method [41, 42]. Mobile device sensors can capture most users' behavior quickly and accurately, allowing behavioral biometric user authentication [43]. Mobile device sensors enrol BB templates, including walking style, gestures, dynamics of keystrokes, hand motions, battery usage, and user profiles. With ongoing authentication, BB can give each user something unique. CA technology adds an extra layer of security on top of the login process by keeping an eye on what users do and frequently re-verifying their identities during a session. CA was first thought about in the early 2000s. Since then, the business and academic worlds have become more interested in this technology. People are becoming more interested in BB and CA technology because sensor costs are expected to decrease, systems are improving, and there is political pressure for stricter security controls. People are eager to use biometric authentication solutions to protect their privacy.

### 6.5.1　Categories of Multimodal Biometrics

Some popular categories of BB and CA are described in this section. Some common biometric patterns are touch gestures, keystrokes dynamics, behavioral profiling, the gait of a person, and hand waving. In addition, we examine how behavioral biometrics are collected and how features are extracted.

- **Walking gait**—Smartphones' accelerometer, gyroscope, and magnetometer sensors allow them to recognize walking patterns. The main advantage of this method is that users' CAs can be deployed without their involvement. The device's orientation moving when walking, uneven ground, potential injuries, footwear, weariness, human features, etc., can all reduce accuracy. The accelerometer records information about people walking normally, slowly, and quickly. The participant's smartphone's orientation in their pocket is estimated using gyroscope data. One can calculate the movement of humans by integrating sensory data from the accelerometer, magnetometer, and gyroscope.

- **Touch gestures**—Recent mobile phones and other intelligent devices are touch-enabled, which means one can draw shapes on the touch screen using one or more strokes. Each stroke is composed of a series of numerical coordinates. The direction and duration of touches, movement velocity, and acceleration are analyzed and measured individually or in combination. They are utilizing a smartphone's touch screen sensor to collect touch data. A gesture output template is generated from input actions using speed, velocity, size, length, and direction variables. These factors vary among users and represent their unique behaviors, making them the foundation of touch gesture authentication systems.

- **Keystroke dynamics**—Keystroke dynamics is recording a user's keyboard inputs on a mobile device and attempting to recognize him by analyzing his tapping patterns. Some studies on keystroke dynamics collect information from specific texts, like writing text messages or entering passwords during a login session. Others obtain data for research purposes without using passwords or particular phrases. The outcomes are precise in both cases.
- **Behavioral profile**—Based on the idea that people use their phones in a certain way when they use apps and digital services, manipulating data from a mobile device can verify an individual's behavior. A profile of a user's behavior could be made based on how he interacts with hosts or a network. In the first scenario, users' connecting patterns to Wi-Fi networks, service providers, etc., are watched. In the second scenario, users' use of apps at different times and places is observed. Data about a device's use can be combined to make user profiles. The paper [45] used the self-created behavioral mobile application Track Maison to find out how people used five social networking sites, such as their location, the length of their sessions, and how often they used them.
- **Hand waving**—People are paying more attention to how a person's wrist moves when using or just holding a mobile phone. This method does not need the user to do anything other than hold the device. There are several ways to use it, such as twisting your wrist, waving fast, waving far, or waving often. Different people can be told apart by how they wave their hands [45].

### 6.5.2    Benefits of Multimodal Biometrics in Mobile Devices

Implementing multimodal biometrics on mobile devices is feasible, as many already support face, voice, and fingerprint recognition. A robust, user-friendly strategy is required for these technologies to be consolidated. In the mobile consumer market segment, multimodal biometrics is a popular authentication method with multiple benefits.

- **Mobile security.** Attackers can take down unimodal biometric systems by spoofing the system's single biometric modality. Attackers must simultaneously impersonate numerous distinct human characteristics to establish identity-based on multiple modalities, which is more complicated.

- **Mobile authentication.** One specific modality can be used to improve the quality issues in other modalities' results. For instance, Proteus evaluates the face-image and voice recording quality and gives more weight to the sample with the highest quality.
- **Accuracy.** When multimodal biometrics are used, they make it much easier to identify a person.
- **Universality.** A multimodal biometric system works for everyone, even if a person is sick or disabled and cannot give one type of biometric. Instead, the system can use a different biometric to verify the person's identity.

## 6.6    Challenges and Open Research Problems

The data is highly diverse, making Multimodal Machine Learning a challenging area of computational study. Understanding natural processes on a deeper level and capturing correspondences between modalities are made possible by learning from multimodal sources. This paper identifies and explores five primary technological obstacles (and sub-challenges) associated with multimodal machine learning. The following five difficulties make up the basis of our taxonomy, which extends beyond the conventional division between early and late fusion.

a) **Representation**-The first challenge in taking advantage of multimodal data is describing and summarizing it to improve the learning process. The variety of multimodal data makes it challenging to create such representations. Language, for instance, frequently reflects symbolic aural and visual modalities, whereas signals do not.

b) **Translation**-The second obstacle is mapping (translating) data from one modality to another. In addition to the diverse data, the relationship between the modalities is frequently vague or subjective. For example, several accurate ways exist to describe an image, yet there may not be a perfect translation.

c) **Alignment**-The second impediment is determining how to map (translate) data from one modality to another. Aside from the heterogeneous data, the relationship between the modalities could be more transparent and subjective. For example, several accurate ways exist to describe an image, but no perfect translation exists.

d) **Fusion**-The fourth issue is combining information from two or more modalities for forecasting. In audiovisual speech recognition, for instance, the speech signal and the visual description of lip motion are merged to predict uttered words. The predictive capacity and noise structure of the information received from many modalities may differ, and at least one may have missing data.

e) **Colearning**-The transfer of information between different modalities is complex, and so is representing multimodal data. Cotraining, conceptual grounding, and zero-shot learning are examples of such algorithms. Colearning studies how information gleaned from one modality may help a computer model created with a different modality. This issue is especially critical when one modality has limited resources (like annotated data).

## 6.7    Conclusion

The way something occurs or is experienced is referred to as its modality. Artificial intelligence must be able to process all of these various types of information concurrently to learn more about the environment around us. The main objective of multimodal machine learning is to utilize data in multiple forms to provide improved results. The newest changes to MMDL and brand-new ideas were covered in this chapter. In addition, the chapter reviews numerous applications using various modalities, including body gestures, facial expressions, physiological signals, images, audio, and video. This review contrasts it with earlier surveys of a similar nature. An overview of Multimodal biometric systems, ideas, and unresolved biometric security issues is given in this chapter. Multimodal biometrics should be the next step for mobile consumer device biometric authentication. Implementing multimodal biometrics on standard mobile devices has been little advancement.

## References

1. Meltzoff, A.N., Origins of the theory of mind, cognition and communication. *J. Commun. Disord.*, 32, 4, 251–269, 1999.

2. Ma, J., Jiang, X., Fan, A., Jiang, J., Yan, J., Image matching from handcrafted to in-depth features: A survey. *Int. J. Comput. Vis.*, 129, 23–79, 2021.

3. Zhou, H., Sattler, T., Jacobs, D.W., Evaluating local features for day-night matching, in: *Proceedings of the European Conference on Computer Vision*, Springer, pp. 724–736, 2016.

4. Luo, Z., Shen, T., Zhou, L., Zhang, J., Yao, Y., Li, S., Fang, T., Quan, L., ContextDesc: Local descriptor augmentation with cross-modality context, in: *Proceedings of the IEEE Conference on Computer Vision and Pattern Recognition*, pp. 2527–2536, 2019.

5. Zhou, H., Ma, J., Tan, C.C., Zhang, Y., Ling, H., Cross-weather image alignment via latent generative model with intensity consistency. *IEEE Trans. Image Process.*, 29, 5216–5228, 2020.

6. Naseer, T., Spinello, L., Burgard, W., Stachniss, C., Robust visual robot localization across seasons using network flows, in: *Proceedings of the AAAI Conference on Artificial Intelligence*, pp. 2564–2570, 2014.

7. Aubry, M., Russell, B.C., Sivic, J., Painting-to-3D model alignment via discriminative visual elements. *ACM Trans. Graph.*, 33, 2, 1–14, 2014.

8. Wei, X., Zhang, T., Li, Y., Zhang, Y., Wu, F., Multimodality cross attention network for image and sentence matching, in: *Proceedings of the IEEE Conference on Computer Vision and Pattern Recognition*, pp. 10941–10950, 2020.

9. Avasthi, S. and Sanwal, T., Biometric authentication techniques: A study on keystroke dynamics. *International Journal of Scientific Engineering Applied Science (IJSEAS)*, 2, 1, 215–221, 2016.

10. Gupta, A. and Avasthi, S., An image-based low-cost method to the OMR process for surveys and research. *International Journal of Scientific Engineering Applied Science (IJSEAS)*, 2, 7, 91–95, 2016.

11. Avasthi, S., Chauhan, R., Acharjya, D.P., Information extraction and sentiment analysis to gain insight into the COVID-19 crisis, in: *International Conference on Innovative Computing and Communications*, pp. 343–353, Springer, Singapore, 2022.

12. Avasthi, S., Chauhan, R., Acharjya, D.P., Topic modeling techniques for text mining over a large-scale scientific and biomedical text corpus. *International Journal of Ambient Computing and Intelligence (IJACI)*, 13, 1, 1–18, 2022.

13. Avasthi, S., Chauhan, R., Acharjya, D.P., Extracting information and inferences from a large text corpus. *Int. J. Inf. Technol.*, 15, 1, 435–445, 2023.

14. Tiulpin, A., Klein, S., Bierma-Zeinstra, S., Thevenot, J., Rahtu, E., Meurs, J.V., Saarakkala, S., Multimodal machine learning-based knee osteoarthritis progression prediction from plain radiographs and clinical data. *Sci. Rep.*, 9, 1, 1–11, 2019.

15. Mullick, T., Radovic, A., Shaaban, S., Doryab, A., Predicting depression in adolescents using mobile and wearable sensors: Multimodal machine learning–Based exploratory study. *JMIR Form. Res.*, 6, 6, e35807, 2022.

16. Buddharpawar, A.S. and Subbaraman, S., Iris recognition based on PCA for person identification. *Int. J. Comput. Appl.*, 975, 8887, 2015.

17. Han, J. and Bhanu, B., Individual recognition using gait energy image. *IEEE Trans. Pattern Anal. Mach. Intell.*, 28, 316–322, 2005.

18. Wang, P., Fan, E., Wang, P., Comparative analysis of image classification algorithms based on traditional machine learning and deep learning. *Pattern Recognit. Lett.*, 141, 61–67, 2021.

19. Boucherit, I., Zmirli, M.O., Hentabli, H., Rosdi, B.A., Finger vein identification using deeply-fused convolutional neural network. *J. King Saud Univ. Comput. Inf. Sci.*, 34, 346–656, 2020.

20. Belo, D., Bento, N., Silva, H., Fred, A., Gamboa, H., ECG biometrics using deep learning and relative score threshold classification. *Sensors*, 20, 15, 4078, 2020.

21. Mekruksavanich, S. and Jitpattanakul, A., Biometric user identification based on human activity recognition using wearable sensors: An experiment using deep learning models. *Electronics*, 10, 3, 308, 2021.

22. Zarbakhsh, P. and Demirel, H., 4D facial expression recognition using multimodal time series analysis of geometric landmark-based deformations. *Vis. Comput.*, 36, 951–965, 2020.

23. Dilawari, A. and Khan, M.U.G., ASoVS: Abstractive summarization of video sequences. *IEEE Access*, 7, 29253–29263, 2019.

24. Summaira, J., Li, X., Shoib, A.M., Li, S., Abdul, J., *Recent advances and trends in multimodal deep learning: A review*, 2021, https://arxiv.org/abs/2105.11087.

25. Avasthi, S., Sanwal, T., Sharma, S., Roy, S., VANETs and the use of IoT: Approaches, applications, and challenges, in: *Revolutionizing Industrial Automation Through the Convergence of Artificial Intelligence and the Internet of Things*, pp. 1–23, 2023.

26. Praharaj, S., Scheffel, M., Drachsler, H., Specht, M., Literature review on Co-located collaboration modelling using multimodal learning analytics—Can we go the whole nine yards? *IEEE Trans. Learn. Technol.*, 14, 3, 367–385, 2021.

27. Rahman, M. M., Abedin, T., Prottoy, K. S., Moshruba, A., Siddiqui, F. H., Video captioning with stacked attention and semantic hard pull. *PeerJ Comput. Sci.*, 7, e664, 2021.

28. Lobry, S., Marcos, D., Murray, J., Tuia, D., RSVQA: Visual question answering for remote sensing data. *IEEE Trans. Geosci. Remote Sens.*, 58, 12, 2020, 2020.

29. Wang, Y., Skerry-Ryan, R.J., Stanton, D., Wu, Y., Weiss, R.J., Jaitly, N., Yang, Z., Xiao, Y., Chen, Z., Bengio, S. *et al.*, *Tacotron: Towards end-to-end speech synthesis*, 2017, https://arxiv.org/abs/1703.10135.

30. Taigman, Y., Wolf, L., Polyak, A., Nachmani, E., *Voiceloop: Voice sitting and synthesis via a phonological loop*, 2018, https://arxiv.org/abs/1707.06588.

31. Huang, S., Huang, D., Zhou, X., Learning multimodal deep representations for crowd anomaly event detection. *Math. Prob. Eng.*, 2018, 1–13, 2018.

32. Koutras, P., Zlatinsi, A., Maragos, P., Exploring cnn-based architectures for multimodal salient event detection in videos, in: *2018 IEEE 13th Image, Video, and Multidimensional Signal Processing Workshop (IVMSP)*, IEEE, 2018.

33. Gibiansky, A., Arik, S., Diamos, G., Miller, J., Peng, K., Ping, W., Raiman, J., Zhou, Y., Deep voice 2: Multi-speaker neural text-to-speech. *Adv. Neural Inf. Process. Syst.*, 30, 2017, 2017.

34. Chauhan, R., Avasthi, S., Alankar, B., Kaur, H., Smart IoT systems: Data analytics, secure smart home, and challenges, in: *Transforming the Internet of Things for Next-Generation Smart Systems*, pp. 100–119, IGI Global, USA, 2021.

35. Al Abdulwahid, A., Clarke, N., Stengel, I., Furnell, S., Reich, C., Continuous and transparent multimodal authentication: Reviewing state of the art. *Cluster Comput.*, 19, 1, 455–474, Mar. 2016.

36. Ayeswarya, S. and Norman, J., A survey on different continuous authentication systems. *Int. J. Biom.*, 11, 1, 67, 2019.

37. Gad, R., El-Fishawy, N., El-Sayed, A., Zorkany, M., Multibiometric systems: A state of the art survey and research directions. *Int. J. Adv. Comput. Sci. Appl.*, 6, 6, 128–138, 2015.

38. Dargan, S. and Kumar, M., A comprehensive survey on the biometric recognition systems based on physiological and behavioural modalities. *Expert Syst. Appl.*, 143, Art. no. 113114, Apr. 2020.

39. Singh, M., Singh, R., Ross, A., A comprehensive overview of biometric fusion. *Inf. Fusion*, 52, 187–205, Dec. 2019.

40. Ross, A. and Jain, A., Information fusion in biometrics. *J. Pattern Recognit. Lett.*, 24, 2115–2125, 2003.

41. Stylios, I.C., Thanou, O., Androulidakis, I., Zaitseva, E., A review of continuous authentication using behavioural biometrics. *Conference: ACM SEEDA-CECNSM*, Kastoria, Greece, 2016.

42. *Biometric authentication: The how and why*, Available: https://about-fraud.com/biometric-authentication, accessed on 21/2/2019.

43. Morency, L.P., Liang, P.P., Zadeh, A., Tutorial on multimodal machine learning, in: *Proceedings of the 2022 Conference of the North American Chapter of the Association for Computational Linguistics: Human Language Technologies: Tutorial Abstracts*, pp. 33–38, 2022, July.

44. Liang, P.P., Zadeh, A., Morency, L.P., *Foundations and recent trends in multimodal machine learning: Principles, challenges, and open questions*, 2022, https://arxiv.org/abs/2209.03430.

45. Stahlschmidt, S.R., Ulfenborg, B., Synnergren, J., Multimodal deep learning for biomedical data fusion: A review. *Brief. Bioinformatics*, 23, 2, bbab569, 2022.

46. Anjomshoa, F., Catalfamo, M., Hecker, D., Helgeland, N., Rasch, A., Kantarci, B., Schuckers, S., Mobile behaviometric framework for sociability assessment and identification of smartphone users, in: *2016 IEEE Symposium on Computers and Communication (ISCC)*, pp. 1084–1089, 2016, June.

47. Kumar, S., Rani, S., Jain, A., Verma, C., Raboaca, M.S., Illés, Z., Neagu, B.C., Face spoofing, age, gender and facial expression recognition using advance neural network architecture-based biometric system. *Sens. J.*, 22, 14, 5160–5184, 2022.

48. Sandeep, K., Jain, A., Agarwal, A.K., Rani, S., Ghimire, A., Object-based image retrieval using the u-net-based neural network. *Comput. Intell. Neurosci.*, 2021, https://www.hindawi.com/journals/cin/2021/4395646/.

49. Kumar, S., Haq, M., Jain, A., Jason, C.A., Moparthi, N.R., Mittal, N., Alzamil, Z.S., Multilayer neural network based speech emotion recognition for smart assistance. *CMC-Comput. Mater. Contin.*, 74, 1, 1–18, 2022. Tech Science Press.

50. Bhola, A. and Singh, S., Visualization and modeling of high dimensional cancerous gene expression dataset. *J. Inf. Knowl. Manag.*, 18, 01, 1950001–22, 2019.

51. Bhola, A. and Singh, S., Gene selection using high dimensional gene expression data: An appraisal. *Curr. Bioinform.*, 13, 3, 225–233, 2018.

52. Rani, S., Gowroju, Kumar, S., IRIS based recognition and spoofing attacks: A review, in: *10th IEEE International Conference on System Modeling & Advancement in Research Trends (SMART)*, December 10-11, 2021.

53. Swathi, A., Kumar, S., Venkata Subbamma., T., Rani, S., Jain, A., Ramakrishna, K. M.V.N.M, Emotion classification using feature extraction of facial expressiona, in: *The International Conference on Technological Advancements in Computational Sciences (ICTACS – 2022)*, Tashkent City Uzbekistan, pp. 1–6, 2022.

54. Rani, S., Lakhwani, K., Kumar, S., Construction and reconstruction of 3D facial and wireframe model using syntactic pattern recognition, in: *Cognitive Behavior & Human Computer Interaction*, pp. 137–156, Scrivener & Willey Publishing House, 2021.

55. Rani, S., Ghai, D., Kumar, S., Kantipudi, M.V.V., Alharbi, A.H., Ullah, M.A., Efficient 3D AlexNet architecture for object recognition using syntactic patterns from medical images. *Comput. Intell. Neurosci.*, 1–19, 2022.

56. Rani, S., Ghai, D., Kumar, S., Reconstruction of simple and complex three dimensional images using pattern recognition algorithm. *J. Inf. Technol. Manag.*, 14, (Special issue: Security and Resource Management challenges for Internet of Things), 235–247, 2022.

57. Bhaiyan, A.J.G., Shukla, R.K., Sengar, A.S., Gupta, A., Jain, A., Kumar, A., Vishnoi, N.K., Face recognition using convolutional neural network in machine learning, in: *2021 10th International Conference on System Modeling & Advancement in Research Trends (SMART)*, pp. 456–461, IEEE, 2021.
58. Bhaiyan, A.J.G., Jain, A., Gupta, A., Sengar, A.S., Shukla, R.K., Jain, A., Application of deep learning for image sequence classification, in: *2021 10th International Conference on System Modeling & Advancement in Research Trends (SMART)*, pp. 280–284, IEEE, 2021.

# 7

# A Structured Review on Virtual Reality Technology Application in the Field of Sports

Harmanpreet Kaur[1]*, Arpit Kulshreshtha[1] and Deepika Ghai[2]

*[1]Department of Physical Education, Lovely Professional University, Phagwara, Punjab, India*
*[2]Department of Electronic and Electrical Engineering, Lovely Professional University, Phagwara, Punjab, India*

## Abstract

Virtual reality (VR) technology is often used by athletes worldwide to help them win more medals in their sport. VR technology must be included in Indian training materials; nevertheless, if Indian athletes are to compete worldwide and accomplish their aims. VR, a widely used technology, is gaining increased attention from the team and individual games since it offers a simple tool for recreating, analyzing, and training circumstances that are occasionally too difficult to play on the field. Previous studies in the area of VR in sports served as the inspiration for the current investigation. The adequate number of interdisciplinary solutions, including VR training approaches, and the absence of applications in the domains of Indian sports. Methods: To conduct a systematic review, all directly relevant studies were categorized according to the names of the authors, the year of publication, and the main goal of the study. This overview of the methodologies used, the findings from VR studies in all sports, and identifying knowledge gaps and open scientific questions were also provided. The various effects of VR technology on sports were then examined. Result: The findings of this study showed the value of VR training for evaluating sports performance accuracy and enhancing player performance. Even though the authors offered a general training curriculum, the accuracy of these approaches was lower than that of the VR training method. Thanks to this technique, players are more equipped to handle the

---

*\*Corresponding author*: harmanpreet.kaur@lpu.co.in

Sandeep Kumar, Deepika Ghai, Arpit Jain, Suman Lata Tripathi and Shilpa Rani (eds.)
*Multimodal Biometric and Machine Learning Technologies: Applications for Computer Vision,*
(129–144) © 2023 Scrivener Publishing LLC

challenges they confront in the competition. VR technology enables researchers to standardize and regulate scenarios while focusing on particular talents and sub-skills. Conclusion: This research chapter also addresses using VR to enhance our understanding of athletic performance.This chapter provides a suitable platform for identifying research gaps in VR technology application approaches in physical education and sport.

*Keywords*: Virtual reality technology (VRT), virtual environment (VE), performance, sports

## 7.1   Introduction

Virtual reality (VR) is interactive, real-time technology. It is a term used to describe 3D computer-generated environments that enable users to inter-act with and experience various realities. There are many different ways that users can interact with computers and the artificial environment [1]. The idea is referred to as "immersive virtual reality." In immersive VR, the user is submerged in a computer-generated, three-dimensional world. The fundamental elements of modern VR are total sensory input and out-put and immersion in a virtual environment. "Virtual reality is a sort of computer technology that first came into widespread use in the 1980s. It consists of computer software, 3D hardware, and various sensor data man-ualsin the virtual world" (Li, Guangxue, 2014).

The world would make considerable use of VR technologies. Nevertheless, the popularity of VR technology has increased due to the recent release of low-cost consumer-grade VR headsets for leisure and gaming [2, 3]. It is clear that VR has found extensive use in various industries, including online gaming, sports, entertainment, education, and construction, and has significant economic value for society. "Virtual reality has shown to be a fantastic tool for various objectives, including entertainment as well as training, rehabilitation, and human behavior."

In contrast to traditional programming instructions, VR is stimulating, and players may have a positive attitude toward using VR in the training process [4, 5]. Immersion and engagement are promoted through the use of VRT, which allows users to manipulate and create objects in a virtual setting. Sunday [20] also mentioned that "By using virtual glasses and gloves with movement trackers, the users can fully immerse themselves in the virtual environments and tools."

By using computers and related technology, users may interact with VR equipment more successfully using this way [6, 7]. Immersion is another essential component of VR technology. Because they are perceptually submerged in the virtual environment, users of immersive VR hardly notice their surroundings. Therefore, when the sensory input from the real world is suppressed, it may seem like a person has physically joined the VE and created an illusion of engagement in the generated world [8]. "Researchers may change the player's viewpoint in the virtual environment in real time by tracking head movements, which improves the player's sense of presence" [4].

Sports and physical education benefit more from VR training using various new, cutting-edge technology tools. Players gain experience playing the game virtually through this novel approach to sports training. As a result, they are better equipped to deal with any challenges that arise during the competition. Their activity dramatically influences the athlete's performance in sports [9, 10]. "To give users the impression that they are exercising in real life, VR sports systems use cutting-edge technology to integrate motion feedback platforms with real sports. These systems are anticipated to benefit users significantly from actual exercise effects through immersion" [6].

Sports use various training techniques to help athletes improve their physical preparedness, skill performances, and teamwork. With new technology, numerous novel training techniques have been developed in the modern era to enhance athletes' performances [11]. The majority of the latest technologies in sports were utilized to study sports performances using biomechanical analysis, but relatively little technology is used in Indian training programs to improve athletes' physical and mental performances. "Virtual reality is a created state shown to the client through programming, causing the client to suspend disbelief and recognize it as a valid domain" [1]. The lack of sports technology tools in India previously prevented players from putting on competent international performances [12]. The players' psychological needs could not be given the trainers' full attention. Creating new training techniques that improve athletes' physical and mental performance uses a wide range of new technology. "Virtual reality (VR) has been incorporated into a variety of industries and has proven to be an effective tool for raising performance standards or learning new skills" [17].

In sports, it combines innovative and cutting-edge technologies but is also extensively employed in physical education and sports. With the help of sensor- and video-based VR training, which allows players to receive customized training regimens tailored to their game in a virtual setting, physical education can become more engaging and active [13–15]. "The one extreme of the continuum is the real world, which includes views of a scene in both direct and indirect ways (through displays)" [7].

VR technology may be used in sports instruction at colleges and universities to help students effectively prevent injuries while training [16–18]. Students can release their hands and feet while practicing and thoroughly demonstrating action technology using VR technology without worrying about unintended accidents [19–21]. "It is crucial to provide a training environment devoid of outside distraction, prevents sports injuries, and fosters a sense of absorption in the sport for the players" [22].

## 7.2   Related Work

This section includes several analyses of earlier research studies on the use of VRT in sports conducted by academics.

- Benoit B., Franck M., and Richard K. investigated real handball goalkeepers' reactions to virtual scenery as in actual games. Human-like figures are typically needed in sports applications to replicate game circumstances, such as duels—virtual training and research on sports. It gives sports scientists a new tool for studying motor control in complicated scenarios involving various characters.
- Jeremy B., Kayur P., and Alexia N. examined that VR opens up new learning opportunities, particularly for teaching people how to do physical movements like those used in physical therapy and exercise. As technology and our knowledge [22] of its interactive features advance, we should experience more learning benefits through VR.
- Robert Riener, Roland Sigrist, and Mathias Wellner explored the level of presence by measuring how the virtual competitors' activities caused the seasoned rowers to behave differently. A more accurate simulation of competition behaviour might strengthen the believability illusion in our virtual environment [23]. One solution is making a virtual trainer that continuously evaluates performance and offers appropriate feedback.
- Richard K., Nicolas V., Sebastien B., Franck M., and Benoit B. presented that athletes' perception-action loop needs to be better understood if performance in sports is to be improved. Three steps are involved in the analysis of sports performance using VR technology. Players must move as realistically as possible for technology to assess sports actions

from a behavioural standpoint to work [24]. By participating in the activity with their players and offering real-time feedback as the game situation develops, they can better assist them in guiding their decision-making.

- Mylene H., Christian C. J., Pierre N., and Annie S. explored whether using VR could assist in identifying attention and restraint problems in adolescent patients [25]. Neuropsychological evaluation using VR showed enhanced sensitivity to the subtle effects of sports concussions compared to the traditional test.
- Guangxue Li investigated the attributes of visual perception, motion perception, auditory perception, tactile perception, and haptic perception, as well as the incorporation of smell sense and taste perception, which are all features of VRT in addition to traditional computer technology [26, 27]. The technical proficiency of athletes among college students and the standard of training is improved by applying this technology in sports training. The utilization of VRT in modern athletic sports is crucial; thus, the technical differences between real athletes and virtual 3D players have been thoroughly investigated.VRT can be improved to a degree, but the standard university sports training model is different and unscientific, and the coach technology level is not the higher practical issue to strengthen the standard of college physical training and students' technical and tactical skills.
- Pedro Kayatt and Ricardo Nakamura examined that the current generation of HMDs' technological advancements is sufficient to overcome various issues previously found in those devices' practical use. HMD improved performance while having no adverse effects on user experience. Other application domains may see the implementation of new experiments.
- Emil M. and Ekaterina P. investigated Sports training environments increasingly utilizing VR. VR allows training in a realistic, safe, and controlled environment, supporting exact performance measurement and user feedback. Compared to the programs listed above, our application's user interface more closely simulates the ski jumping method, making it potentially more effective for training [28]. These features should have been combined with gesture detection for "smart physical training" to the fullest extent possible.

- Anne A. C. and Ineke J.M.V.H. investigated whether fake, modified replays of these events from a first-person perspective in VR can influence one's memory of the physical performance [29]. VR's user-specific views and expansive, three-dimensional range of view naturally provide a strong sense of immersion, making it a tremendously rich form of media. In future studies, it is essential to examine how strongly the feelings of competence and performance motivation are related.

- David L. N., Robyn L. M., and Patrick R. T. introduced the use of VR in sports to more fully comprehend the findings of this research. There are several occasions where researchers employed an approach that was close to the concept of VR sports applications that was put forth. VR could be a valuable supplement to current real-world sports training and participation. Researchers, coaches, and athletes can exploit VR environments to benefit society.

- Jonathan S., Lewis C., Gert j. P. and Leigh E.P. explored the elements to consider when creating a track cycling simulator for the Commonwealth Games velodrome in 2018. VR offers much potential for usage in athletic training. By increasing fidelity and creating sports simulators from diverse sports, it will be simpler to confirm the generalizability of this framework and obtain a more excellent knowledge of the potential of VR technology for performance measurement and advancement.

- Felix H., Jan P. G., Barbara H., and Stefan K. explored augmented feedback automatically generated inside a VR CAVE-based training environment for athletes. Combining more advanced, higher-level features from our pipeline might be one solution. The resulting augmented feedback can only be effective if the classification algorithm performs effectively.

- Kunjal A., Kajal G., Rutvik G., and Manan S. investigated how VR can be used in the classroom, the military, and during athletic training. When using VR for training, focus on the programs misused in study halls with good results. VRT can be helpful in all these disciplines since it makes understanding concepts more straightforward and practical than traditional approaches. It offers a platform for various modeling activities that, in the actual world, carry a risk of life or death. It will be precious to everyone and significantly advance the sports sector.

- Huimin L., Zhiquan W., Christos M., and Dominic K. introduceda VR game program that may be used to create racket sports exercise routines. It evaluated whether participants' performance had improved due to their involvement in VR training sessions. Application for playing VR racquet sports and a way to combine exercise routines. This method allows the user to change the details of the cost terms, and our system will automatically generate an exercise drill that meets the user's specified objectives. Future research may lead to the creation of additional VR training and exercise games.

- Oliver R.L.F., Kirsten S., and Livvie B. introduced VR and technology for coaching, developing skills, and sports. To design and implement appropriate settings for enhancing performance and learning specific skills. Applying such technology has shown positive outcomes in coaching and skill acquisition. Sports-related VR technology study will alter how coaches train their athletes.

- Jian Zhou investigated sports training with VR technology, which can produce more effective training results. It will alter the present single-teacher teaching style, pique students' interest, and enhance the learning environment. VR technology can provide students with theoretical ideas and scientific guidance, so they can study and develop in the game through numerous advanced abstractions.

- Deniz Bedir and Süleyman E. Erhanexamine a comparison of the effects of virtualreality-based imaging (VRBI) and visual motor behavior rehearsal and video modeling (VMBR + VM) training approach on athletes' shot performance and imagery skills. The VRBI program's outcomes were more encouraging regarding performance and visualization skills. The capacity of the athlete to control the process and feel engaged in the surroundings was a significant advantage provided by VR technology.

- Man F., Fan Y., and Rongqi Y. investigated using (VR) technology in professional practice and academic settings for sports rehabilitation. Technology based on VR offers a wealth of materials, an accessible environment to foster diverse thinking, and integrates study and practice. The rehabilitation training industry will undoubtedly undergo a profound revolution, and sports treatment training technology will advance.

- Stefan P., PetriK., Chen C. H., Ana M. W. C., Stirnatis M., Nübel C., and Schlotter L. explored. How much VR training devices can help athletes learn complex sports moves is still being determined. The subjects were instructed to watch the movement on the screen three times in each of the four groups that underwent testing and various interventions for beginners. In particular, VR is an excellent tool for learning sport-specific methods. Integrating external input from the trainer or avatar would be beneficial in conveying the actual value of participants' movement.

- Kun Zhao and Xueying Guo explored the integration of VRT with sports training and the usage of VR in football practice. It is essential to establish a training environment that is free from outside interference and those guards against sports injuries. VR technology has generally advanced football training because of its superiority and high level of simulation. The software platform has been a crucial guide to the players' physical and tactical activity, significantly improving their psychological condition and teamwork during games. Coaches and athletes should be able to receive better training to improve their talents, thanks to the advantages of VR technology. The existing work plan for the VR training program for various sports is shown in Table 7.1.

**Table 7.1** Existing work plan for the VR training program for various sports.

| No. | Author | Year | Objective | Remarks |
| --- | --- | --- | --- | --- |
| 1. | Benoit Bideau, Franck Multon, and Richard Kulpa | 2004 | To presents Goalkeepers in actual handball matches react to the virtual environment. | Human-like figures are typically needed in sports applications to replicate game circumstances, such as duels, virtual training and research on sports. |

*(Continued)*

**Table 7.1** Existing work plan for the VR training program for various sports. (*Continued*)

| No. | Author | Year | Objective | Remarks |
|---|---|---|---|---|
| 2. | Jeremy Bailenson, Kayur Patel, and Alexia Nielsen | 2008 | To measure VR opens up new learning opportunities, particularly for teaching people how to do bodily actions like physical therapy and exercise. | As technology and our knowledge of its interactive features advance, we should experience more learning benefits through VR. |
| 3. | Mathias W., Roland S., and Robert R. | 2010 | To measure the degree to which the activities of the virtual competitors altered the experienced rowers' behaviour. A more accurate simulation of competitive. | Ion behaviour might strengthen the believability illusion in our simulated environment. |
| 4. | Benoit B., Richard K., Nicolas V., Sébastien B., and Franck M. | 2010 | One must better understand players' perspective loop to enhance performance in sports. | Players must move as accurately as possible for technology to assess sports activities from a behavioural standpoint. |
| 5. | Pierre N., Annie S., Mylene H., and Christian C. J. | 2015 | To check whether the VR method may help identify attention and inhibition deficiencies in teenagers. | Compared to the conventional test, neuropsychological evaluation using V.R. demonstrated increased sensitivity to the specific effects of sports concussions. |

(*Continued*)

**Table 7.1** Existing work plan for the VR training program for various sports. (*Continued*)

| No. | Author | Year | Objective | Remarks |
|---|---|---|---|---|
| 6. | Guangxue Li | 2014 | To strengthen the technical competency and level of preparation of college players and to enhance sports training. | The use of advanced technology VR in contemporary athletic sports is significant; as a result, the technical distinctions between real athletes in movement and 3D virtual athletes have been thoroughly examined. |
| 7. | Pedro Kayatt and Ricardo Nakamura | 2015 | The current generation of HMDs' technological advancements is sufficient to overcome various issues previously found in the practical use of those devices. | HMD improved performance while having no adverse effects on user experience. Other application domains may see the implementation of new experiments. |
| 8. | Emil M. Staurset and Ekaterina P. | 2016 | VR is being used more frequently in training settings, including sports. | With support for precise performance evaluation and user feedback, VR offers the chance to practice in a realistic, secure, and regulated environment. |

(*Continued*)

**Table 7.1** Existing work plan for the VR training program for various sports. (*Continued*)

| No. | Author | Year | Objective | Remarks |
|-----|--------|------|-----------|---------|
| 9. | Anne A. C., and Ineke J.M.V. H | 2016 | To propose whether the ability to recall one's physical performance from false, controlled recordings in VR that are shown from a first-person perspective may be altered. | VR's user-specific views and expansive, three-dimensional range of view naturally provide a strong sense of immersion, making it a tremendously rich form of media. |
| 10. | David L. N., Robyn L. M., and Patrick R. T. | 2017 | To create a VR sports application to comprehend this research's findings better. | VR could be a valuable supplement to current real-world sports training and participation. |
| 11. | Jonathan S., Lewis, Gert j. P., and Leigh E.P. | 2018 | The elements to consider when creating a track cycling simulation for the racing track at the 2018 Commonwealth Games. | The use of advanced training through VR for athletes has excellent potential. |
| 12. | Felix H., Jan P. G., Barbara H., Stefan K. | 2018 | Augmented feedback is automatically generated inside a VR CAVE-based training environment for athletes. | Combining more intricate higher-level characteristics from our pipeline could be one way. |

(*Continued*)

**Table 7.1** Existing work plan for the VR training program for various sports. (*Continued*)

| No. | Author | Year | Objective | Remarks |
|---|---|---|---|---|
| 13. | Kunjal A., Kajal G., Rutvik G., and Manan S. | 2019 | The use of VRT in the education field, military training, and sports training is possible. | VRT can be helpful in all these disciplines since it makes understanding concepts more straightforward and more practical than traditional approaches, and it offers a platform for various modellingactivities that, in the actual world, carry a risk of life or death. |
| 14. | Huimin L., Zhiquan W., Christos M., and Dominic K. | 2020 | To analyzea VR game program that may be used to create racket sports exercise routines. | When the user updates the values of the cost terms, our technology will automatically create an exercise drill that satisfies these consumer objectives. |
| 15. | Oliver R.L. F., Kirsten S., and Livvie B. | 2020 | To analyze VR and the use of advanced technology training for coaching, development of skills, and sports performance. | It will alter the present single-teacher teaching style, pique students' interest, and enhance the learning environment. |

(*Continued*)

**Table 7.1** Existing work plan for the VR training program for various sports. (*Continued*)

| No. | Author | Year | Objective | Remarks |
|-----|--------|------|-----------|---------|
| **16.** | Deniz Bedir, and Süleyman E. Erhan | 2021 | To compare (VMBR + VM) and VR-based imaging (VRBI) training methods to determine how they affect athletes' shot performance and imagery abilities. | The athlete's capacity to control the procedure and feel engaged in the surroundings was a significant advantage provided by VR technology. |
| **17.** | Man F., Fan Y., and Rongqi Y. | 2022 | To examinethe use of VR technology in professional practice and academic settings for sports rehabilitation. | Technology based on VR offers a wealth of materials, a comfortable environment to foster diverse thinking, and integrates study and practice. |
| **18.** | Stefan P., Petri K., Chen C. H., Ana M. W. C., Stirnatis M., Nübel C., and Schlotter L. | 2022 | To discuss, it is still being determined how much virtual training devices can help athletes learn complex sports moves. | For beginners, VR is an excellent tool for learning sport-specific methods. |
| **19.** | Kun Z. and Xueying G. | 2022 | To discuss the use of VRT in football practice and the fusion of VRT with sports practice to enhance the skill. | The athletes' psychological state and teamwork have significantly improved thanks to the use of VRT during their physical and tactical practice. |

## 7.3   Conclusion

This chapter examines prior research on how VR training affects athletic performance. Finding research gaps in the area of sports VR training was the main goal of the review. Various scientific articles published between 2004 and 2022 were defined and reviewed to determine the necessity for further research. The study's primary purpose is to analyze and correct the player's performance and evaluate the player's progression. To this end, all structured publications were catalogued by author name, year of publication, and the technique used to recognize the VR training method applied in the sports domain. The critical point to remember is that VR is a useful advanced training tool that makes complex skills easily performed and assesses sports performance.

Therefore, this work effectively evaluated VR training applications and their influence on sports. Future research Recommended that apply VR training programs conducted for assessment in various sports, rehabilitation of injured players, and physical fitness for enhancement of the player's performance.

## References

1. Ahir, K., Govani, K., Gajera, R., Shah, M., Application on virtual reality for enhanced education learning, military training, and sports. *Augment. Hum. Res.*, Switzerland AG, 5, 1–19, 2020, https://doi.org/10.1007/s41133-019-0025-2.

2. Bailenson, J., Patel, K., Nielsen, A., Bajscy, R., Jung, S.H., Kurillo, G., The effect of interactivity on learning physical actions in virtual reality. *Media Psychol.*, 7, 3, 354–376, 2008.

3. Bedir, D. and Erhan, S.E., The effect of virtual reality technology on target-based sports athletes' imagery skills and performance. *Front. Psychol.*, 7, 2073–2078, 2021.

4. Bideau, B., Kulpa, R., Vignais, N., Brault, S., Multon, F., Craig, C., Using virtual reality to analyze sports performance. *IEEE Comput. Graph. Appl.*, 30, 2, 14–21, 2010.

5. Bideau, B., Multon, F., Kulpa, R., Fradet, L., Arnaldi, B., Virtual reality applied to sports: Do handball goalkeepers react realistically to simulated synthetic opponents?, in: *Proceedings of the 2004 ACM SIGGRAPH International Conference on Virtual Reality Continuum and Its Applications in Industry*, vol. 8, pp. 210–216, 2004.

6. Bum, C.H., Mahoney, T.Q., Choi, C., A comparative analysis of satisfaction and sustainable participation in leisure and virtual reality leisure sports. *Sustainability*, 10, 10, 3475–3480, 2018.

7. Capasa, L., Zulauf, K., Wagner, R., Virtual reality experience of mega sports events: A technology acceptance study. *J. Theor. Appl. Electron. Commer. Res.*, 17, 2, 686–703, 2022.

8. Cuperus, A.A. and van der Ham, I.J., Virtual reality replays of sports performance: Effects on memory, feeling of competence, and performance. *Learn. Motiv.*, 56, 48–52, 2016.

9. Fang, M., You, F., Yao, R., Application of virtual reality technology (VR) in practice teaching of sports rehabilitation major. *Journal of Physics: Conference Series (JPCS)*, 1852, 4, 1–7, IOP Publishing, 2021.

10. Farley, O.R., Spencer, K., Baudinet, L., Virtual reality in sports coaching, skill acquisition, and application to surfing: A review. *J. Hum. Sport Exerc.*, University of Alicante, Spain, 16, 4, 454–464, 2020.

11. Hülsmann, F., Göpfert, J.P., Hammer, B., Kopp, S., Botsch, M., Classification of motor errors to provide real-time feedback for sports coaching in virtual reality—A case study in squats and Tai Chi pushes. *Comput. Graph.*, 76, 47–59, 2018.

12. Kayatt, P. and Nakamura, R., Influence of a head-mounted display on user experience and performance in a virtual reality-based sports application, in: *Proceedings of the Latin American Conference on Human-Computer Interaction*, article no. 2, pp. 1–6, 2015.

13. Li, G.X., Research on the application of computer technology in virtual reality in sports. *Adv. Mater. Res.*, 1049, 2024–2027, Trans Tech Publications Ltd. 2014.

14. Liu, H., Wang, Z., Mousas, C., Kao, D., Virtual reality racket sports: Virtual drills for exercise and training, in: *2020 IEEE International Symposium on Mixed and Augmented Reality (ISMAR)*, pp. 566–576, IEEE, Darmstadt, Germany, 2020, https://doi.org/10.1109/ISMAR50242.2020.00084.

15. Neumann, D.L., Moffitt, R.L., Thomas, P.R., Loveday, K., Watling, D.P., Lombard, C.L., Tremeer, M.A., A systematic review of the application of interactive virtual reality to the sport. *Virtual Real.*, 22, 3, 183–198, 2018.

16. Nolin, P., Stipanicic, A., Henry, M., Joyal, C.C., Allain, P., Virtual reality as a screening tool for sports concussion in adolescents. *Brain Injury*, 26, 13–14, 1564–1573, 2012.

17. Pastel, S., Petri, K., Chen, C.H., Wiegand Cáceres, A.M., Stirnatis, M., Nübel, C., Witte, K., Training in virtual reality enables learning of a complex sports movement. *Virtual Real.*, 27, 1–18, 2022.

18. Shepherd, J., Carter, L., Pepping, G.J., Potter, L.E., Towards an operational framework for designing training-based sports virtual reality performance simulators. *Multidiscip. Digital Publ. Inst. Proc.*, 2, 6, 214, 2018.

19. Staurset, E.M. and Prasolova-Førland, E., We are creating an intelligent Virtual Reality simulator for sports training and education, in: *Smart Education and e-Learning*, vol. 2016, pp. 423–433, Springer, Cham, 2016.

20. Sunday, K., Wong, S.Y., Samson, B.O., Sanusi, I.T., Investigating the effect of imikode virtual reality game in enhancing object-oriented programming concepts among university students in Nigeria. *Edu. Inf. Technol.*, 27, 1–27, 2022.

21. Wellner, M., Sigrist, R., Riener, R., Virtual competitors influence rowers. *Presence (Camb)*, 19, 4, 313–330, 2010.

22. Zhao, K. and Guo, X., Analysis of the application of virtual reality technology in football training. *J. Sens.*, 2022, Article ID 1339434, 1–8, 2022.

23. Zhou, J., Virtual reality sports auxiliary training system based on embedded systems and computer technology. *Microprocess Microsyst.*, 82, 307–334, 2nd ed., 2021.

24. Kumar, S., Rani, S., Jain, A., Verma, C., Raboaca, M.S., Illés, Z., Neagu, B.C., Face spoofing, age, gender and facial expression recognition using advance neural network architecture-based biometric system. *Sens. J.*, 22, 14, 5160–5184, 2022.

25. Kumar, S., Jain, A., Agarwal, A.K., Rani, S., Ghimire, A., Object-based image retrieval using the u-net-based neural network. *Comput. Intell. Neurosci.*, 21, 1–14, 2021.

26. Kumar, S., Haq, M., Jain, A., Jason, C.A., Moparthi, N.R., Mittal, N., Alzamil, Z.S., Multilayer neural network based speech emotion recognition for smart assistance. *CMC-Comput. Mater. Contin.*, 74, 1, 1–18, Tech Science Press. 2022.

27. Bhola, A. and Singh, S., Visualization and modeling of high dimensional cancerous gene expression dataset. *J. Inf. Knowl. Manag.*, 18, 01, 1950001–22, 2019.

28. Bhola, A. and Singh, S., Gene selection using high dimensional gene expression data: An appraisal. *Curr. Bioinform.*, 13, 3, 225–233, 2018.

29. Rani, S. and Gowroju, S., IRIS based recognition and spoofing attacks: A review, in: *10th IEEE International Conference on System Modeling &Advancement in Research Trends (SMART)*, December 10-11, 2021.

# 8

# A Systematic and Structured Review of Fuzzy Logic-Based Evaluation in Sports

**Harmanpreet Kaur[1]\*, Sourabh Chhatiye[1] and Jimmy Singla[2]**

*[1]Department of Physical Education, Lovely Professional University, Phagwara, Punjab, India*
*[2]Department of Computer Science and Engineering, Lovely Professional University, Phagwara, Punjab, India*

## Abstract

Fuzzy logic, a subset of logical analysis, enables the implementation of uncertain, dynamic, approximative, ambiguous, ongoing, and more real scenarios that are more like actual physical and psychological thinking. Prior research on intelligent machines (AI) in athletic events, various interdisciplinary approaches, including fuzzy logic methodologies, and a shortage of sports-related implementations inspired the current work. Methods: All relevant studies were categorized according to the names of the authors, the year of publication, the main goal of the investigation, the system input and output variables, and lastly, notes that provided erudite information about the research described in various publications to carry out a systematic review. Following that, several conclusions about fuzzy logic evaluation in sports were analyzed. Results: The findings of this study demonstrated the efficacy of the fuzzy logic approach in evaluating sports performance accuracy. Although the authors used a variety of data mining approaches, these techniques' accuracy was inferior to that of the adaptive neural fuzzy process. The properties of the degree of truth and uncertainty may be identified and represented effectively using this method. Conclusion: This chapter provides an overview of a suitable platform for identifying research gaps and analyzing fuzzy logic approaches in sports and physical education for further investigation.

*\*Corresponding author*: harmanpreet.kaur@lpu.co.in

Sandeep Kumar, Deepika Ghai, Arpit Jain, Suman Lata Tripathi and Shilpa Rani (eds.)
Multimodal Biometric and Machine Learning Technologies: Applications for Computer Vision,
(145–162) © 2023 Scrivener Publishing LLC

*Keywords*: Fuzzy logic, evaluation, structured, sports, artificial intelligence, logical analysis

## 8.1    Introduction

In general, fuzzy logic concerns ambiguous probabilistic reasoning to varying degrees of truthfulness instead of faultless. The several logic systems' fundamental concepts "In general, the fuzzy logic concept involves the idea of a vague rather than exact probabilistic reasoning with different degrees of truth [1–3]. Basic ideas on many-valued logic systems" [11]. Using fuzzy logic approaches in sports is still relatively new yet exciting. However, as seen by the following literature analysis, strategies that utilize the notion of uncertainty have yet to be examined in a lot of strength training. "In the area of sport, the use of fuzzy logic techniques is still a rather new but, at the same time, upcoming field of activity [4, 5]. However, the following literature review shows that uncertainty-based procedures have not yet been investigated in strength training" [11].

The fuzzy method can address problems since it can handle ambiguity, imprecision, unpredictability in data, and evaluation criteria. "Problems can be handled by the fuzzy approach, which can work with uncertainty, imprecision and subjectivity in the data and the evaluation process" [21]. A framework for risk assessment has been developed and put into use that benefits from the fuzzy approach while enhancing the system's flexibility, scalability, and adaptability [6, 7]. "A risk assessment framework was designed and implemented, which takes the advantages of the fuzzy approach, while the flexibility, expandability and the adaptive capacity of the system are improved" [21].

Logic, known as fuzzy logic, transcends the dualism of true and untrue statements. Propositions can be conveyed with a certain amount of ambiguity using fuzzy logic. "Fuzzy logic is a type of logic that goes beyond the dualistic distinction between true and false propositions [8, 9]. Using fuzzy logic, propositions can be represented with a certain degree of vagueness" [9]. A membership function that associates every linguistic answer with a set of characteristics contained in an interval may be used to represent a customer's perception of the level of service provided by a sports facility. Since the concept of "good" might have different connotations for different customers based on their personalities, cultures, and study backgrounds, it is confusing when a client states that a sports facility's service quality is "good." "Using similar reasoning, a customer's perception of quality toward a sports centre service may be represented using a membership function that relates each linguistic response with values enclosed in an [0, 1] interval. For example, when a customer claims that the service quality of a sports centre is "good," this linguistic term has an uncertain meaning because the word "good" can have a heterogeneous meaning for different customers, depending on their personality, culture, or research context [9].

The weighting of the specified parameters was derived using physical fitness and technical skill measures [10]. Using fuzzy sets, the measured data were turned into fuzzy values. Finally, a player rating was compared to sports specialists' viewpoints, verifying the model's reliability. "Measurements of physical fitness and technical skills were used to determine the weighting of the chosen criteria [11, 12]. Then the measured values were converted into fuzzy values using fuzzy sets. Finally, a ranking of players was generated and compared with the opinions of sports experts, which confirmed the model's reliability" [16]. This capability would make it possible to evaluate athletes' performances in critical positions among squads during each game and build a thorough model for analyzing a team's performance over a predetermined time [13, 14]. The COMET technique with either hesitant or intuitionistic fuzzy number expansion may also be used to find the model. "This functionality would help to create a holistic model for evaluating the team's performance over a particular time and allow for the possibility to compare players' performance on specific positions between teams in each match. Besides, the model can also be identified using the COMET method using hesitant or intuitionistic fuzzy set generalization" [16]. A thorough fuzzy evaluation of college students' physical fitness is helpful for acceptable grouping and focused training in a physical education class [15–17]. It is significant and well known for scientifically evaluating students' physical fitness. It has a good reference value for teaching. To increase students' interest in physical activity, mix physical education with competition and fun, and achieve the goal of increasing students' health levels, it is advised to try out the student sports association system or club system at Q University [18–21]. "Fuzzy comprehensive evaluation of college students' physical fitness is also helpful for reasonable grouping and targeted training in a physical education class, which has a good reference value for teaching and is meaningful and popularized for the scientific evaluation of students' physical fitness [22, 23]. It is suggested to try out the student sports association system or club system at Q University to stimulate students' interest in strengthening physical exercise, integrate physical education with competition and entertainment, and strengthen students' physique and improve their health level" [31].

## 8.2   Related Works

This section contains numerous evaluations of prior studies on Fuzzy Logic Based Evaluation in Sports that researchers have done.

- V. Papic, N. Rogulj, and V. Plestina explored a fuzzy rule-based system for scouting and evaluating young athletes. Different motoric abilities tests, morphologic aspect evaluations, and test automation are quantified based on the experience of several people sports professionals and their applicability for a predetermined range of sports. The collected values and the grades for each test's measurable outcomes are entered into the knowledge database. Fuzzy logic is utilized to enhance the flexibility and resilience of the system. The web-based system means online users with valid passwords and usernames can access the built ASP. NET application [24]. The expert system established forecasts acceptance and proposed the best sports for the evaluated individual. Four specialists assessed the system's output results using real-world data.
- Jose A. M, Jae Ko, and Martínez proposed assessed reported quality in the context of fitness and sports services using fuzzy logic, a novel athletic training method. This study demonstrated that fuzzy logic is a valuable technique for increasing the value of customer assessment data [25]. The established approach tackles the drawbacks of third-person research by eliminating categorization and connection bias caused by the association between quantitative and verbal labels. An empirical analysis of customer control samples collected from two clubs shows the advantages of this approach.
- J. Jon Arockiaraj and E. Barathi introduced Deduce to the relationship between anxiety and the motivation of a sportsman using fuzzy logic. Sports include physiological as well as social dimensions. While competing in an event, the sportsman is observed to be full of tension, worry, fear, and stress. Physiological and psychological factors heavily influence the quality of the player's performance. Fuzzy logic can be used to identify a solution to improve their motivation level and overcome their anxiety.

- Mohammad Ebrahim Razaghi investigated, Using fuzzy logic theory, executing knowledge management from the standpoint of employees in Kerman (Iran) province offices of youth and sport. The "research method" is descriptive and application-oriented to analyze a statistical population of a certain number of people by the census. The standard questionnaire developed by Chung et al. is termed a "Data Measurement Tool." The word "outcome" suggests that knowledge management implementation is poor in the offices described and that there is a significant mismatch between the current and anticipated state of factors influencing knowledge management implementation [26].

- Ondrej Hubacek, Jiri Zhanel, and Michal Polach explored tennis players' performance on the TENDIAG1 test battery may be evaluated using fuzzy logic techniques, and the fuzzy approach and the probability approach can be used to analyze tennis players' skill levels. A careful analysis of the data revealed that the fuzzy assessment significantly affects individual tennis players' performance. The total amount is better and more precisely resolved by fuzzy judgment, especially for people with the same evaluation score.

- E. Tóth-Laufer, M. Takács, and I. J. Rudas developed a risk assessment framework to fulfil the physiological parameters, a system for risk assessment was established. This technology is adaptable and provides lots of versatility. A generic, modular system structure connected to a database to specify the attributes of the configurable subsystems is created for ease of extension and transparency.

- Edit Tóth-Laufer developed a risk assessment system based on fuzzy logic that may be tailored to specific needs. The application of the adaptable fuzzy logic-based [27] risk assessment method and value was proved by examining a case study that assesses the level of risk associated with various athletic activities using physiological measures as input parameters.

- Noori and Sadeghi presented an intelligent model for volleyball player talent, identification based on primary and weighting parameters was produced using an analytic network technique of measurement of physical, kinematic, cognitive, biological, and technology elements [28]. The assessments include anthropometrics (length and length of the upper limbs), biomechanics (dexterity and strength), psychology (consciousness and determination), physiology (exceptional stamina and anaerobic), spike, and service (techniques). This talent-discovery process may be a valuable and practical way to choose young people who will grow up to be volleyball stars.

- The results of S. Ribagin and S. Stavrev demonstrate that the measures used for the test battery are incredibly successful in determining the children's initial intellectual and physical development level [29]. It was proposed to apply the inter-criteria analysis technique to data received from college participants in sporting events activities to assess the suitability of the test results.

- Glazkova Svetlana Sergeevna, Babina Yulia Sergeevna, and Babina Yulia Sergeevna created a financial evaluation of corporate fitness and sports programmes. By measuring the effectiveness of the indicators, fuzzy logic was used to analyze the expense of boosting professional sports and exercise science. Businesses may apply the study's findings to professional activities and physical education initiatives.

- Bartłommiej Kizielewicz and Larisa Dobryakova showed that it is possible to construct the appropriate rating even with insufficient data. The resistance of the fuzzy logic technique to the conundrum of the reversed NBA basketball player rankings sets it apart from other approaches.

- Claudio Pinto presented the best of our knowledge; the study's objective is to provide a framework for evaluating sports data (especially for professional sports teams) to develop policy recommendations for enhancing their athletic successes. It uses fuzzy logic and the DEA technique to assess the relative performance of a digital data set of professional soccer teams in uncertainty along two dimensions: efficiency and effectiveness.

- W. Sałabun et al. introduced a multi-criteria model built to evaluate forward players based on their match statistics. Fuzzy triangular numbers, symmetrical and asymmetrical, were used for model identification. The objective outcomes of the COMET model were contrasted with subjective evaluations, such as Balloon D'or and a player worth.

- Z. Xu and Y. Zhang introduced this research examines the outcomes of physical health exams administered to college students using the assessment technique using fuzzy integrals. Few kids have an exception to good balance, while most pupils get passing grades on their physical exams. The fuzzy integral-based fitness rating technique for college students offers generalizability and usefulness [30]. Using the established index system and the complete assessment model, all students in a class or institution may have their overall fitness evaluated extensively.

- Fubin Wang and Qiong Huang analyzed the use of sporting rehabilitation training in physical training and an overview and analysis of sports rehabilitative training's role. It outlines and explains the significance of physical treatment training and gives resources for applying it. The importance and value of physical treatment training in sports conditioning are discussed, as well as an overview of the inpatient rehabilitation training scenario.

- G. Sun, X. Zhang, and Y. Lin developed a method for analyzing the sports culture industry's level of competition and a framework for determining its strengths. According to the evaluation results of the effectiveness of the sports society sector in various locations around China, the assessment approach provided in this work is superior to the old evaluation method. It has helped to promote China's broader sports culture.

- Q. Li, Dayao Zhang, Y. Han, and Y. Xie studied the macro, meso, and micro developing models of regional tourism industry integration in Guangxi are described, along with development countermeasures. Create a fuzzy good assessment model using fuzzy mathematics, then use it to unbiasedly assess the resources for sports tourism in Guangxi Province. In addition to focusing on breakthroughs, expanding the physical and relaxation participation sports tourism sector, and properly laying out and cultivating appealing sports tourism goods, it is intended to develop distinctly helpful sports tourism resources thoroughly.

- A. Scharl, Serge P. von Duvillard, G. Smekal Ralph P. and Arnold Baca Ramon Barón N. Bach, P. Hofmann, and Harald Tschan developed research aimed to assess the precision of predicting the energy output (P) of the maximum lactate stable state (MLSS) on an ergometer using a combination of fuzzy neural logic and regression analysis based

**Table 8.1** Existing work plan for fuzzy logic–based sports evaluation.

| No. | Author | Year | Objective | Input variable | Output | Remarks |
|---|---|---|---|---|---|---|
| 1. | V. Papic, Nenad Rogulj, and V. Plestina | 2009 | A fuzzy expert system for scouting and evaluating young sports prospects is presented. | Motorical, functional and morphological tests | Choosing and determining the best sport for a youngster | All testing revealed that the created system was highly reliable and accurate |
| 2. | J. A. Martinez, Yong Jae Ko, and L. Martínez | 2010 | To assess in the context of sports and fitness, perception services using a unique sports management approach: fuzzy logic. | The perception of quality of sports and fitness services | Reduce the categorization and interaction biases caused by the link between verbal and numerical labels. | This technique is encouraged for use in sport management research. |
| 3. | J. Jon Rockiaraj and E. Barathi | 2014 | To deduce the relationship between anxiety and the motivation of a sportsman using fuzzy logic | Relationship between anxiety and motivation of a sportsman | Fuzzy logic identifies a solution to improve their level of motivation and conquer their degree of anxiety | The players benefit from fuzzy analysis with regret reduction |

*(Continued)*

Table 8.1 Existing work plan for fuzzy logic-based sports evaluation. (*Continued*)

| No. | Author | Year | Objective | Input variable | Output | Remarks |
|---|---|---|---|---|---|---|
| 4. | Mohammad Ebrahim Razaghi | 2014 | To assess the application of knowledge management from the standpoint of personnel in youth and sports agencies. | Evaluating the Implementation of Knowledge Management | Planning is necessary, and practical aspects should be prioritized. | Impacting on knowledge management |
| 5. | Ondrej Hubacek, Jiri Zhanel, and Michal Polach | 2015 | To offer methods for analyzing tennis players' outcomes and comparing tennis players using the TENDIAG1 test battery. | Comparing the levels of tennis players using the fuzzy technique and the probability approach | In the evaluation, I received an equal score. | The application of fuzzy assessment enables a better and more exact determination of the overall level of outcomes. |
| 6. | E. Tóth-Laufer, Márta Takács, and I. J. Rudas | 2015 | To provide a risk assessment framework based on fuzzy logic that may be customized dependent on the situation. | Previous measurements or the patient's medical history | The system's flexibility, expandability, and adaptive capability are enhanced. | These factors are continually monitored in real-time to regulate the individual. |

*(Continued)*

**Table 8.1** Existing work plan for fuzzy logic-based sports evaluation. (*Continued*)

| No. | Author | Year | Objective | Input variable | Output | Remarks |
|---|---|---|---|---|---|---|
| 7. | Edit Tóth-Laufer | 2016 | Built a risk assessment system based on fuzzy logic that may be tailored to diverse requirements depending on the conditions | Measured physiological values | Risk factors can be tweaked, as can their membership functions. | Computes the risk level of numerous sports activities |
| 8. | Mohammad Hossein Noori and Heydar Sadeghi | 2018 | To develop an intelligent algorithm using primary and weighted criteria for recognizing volleyball talent. | Anthropometrical, biomechanical, psychological, physiological, and technical variables | Unmatched, semi-matched, matched, brilliant and rare | A talent identification model might be a reliable tool. |
| 9. | Simeon Ribagin and Spas Stavrev | 2019 | To suggest using the intercriteria analysis approach to information gathered from college students participating in sports. | Male first-year students at UNWE participating in training sessions for basketball and table tennis under the "Physical Culture" subject | Based on intuitionistic fuzzy sets, the analysis provides a way to account for the effects of uncertainty. | The paper outlines a novel approach to handling data gathered from university students participating in sports. |

(*Continued*)

**Table 8.1** Existing work plan for fuzzy logic-based sports evaluation. (*Continued*)

| No. | Author | Year | Objective | Input variable | Output | Remarks |
|---|---|---|---|---|---|---|
| 10. | G. Svetlana Sergeevna, B. Yulia Sergeevna, and B. Yulia Sergeevna | 2019 | To provide an economic evaluation of corporate exercise and physical education | Evaluating cost-effectiveness | Effectiveness estimated using fuzzy logic | Economic effectiveness has evolved |
| 11. | Bartłommiej Kizielewicz, and Larisa Dobryakova | 2020 | For inadequate data, it is still feasible to establish an excellent rating. | COMET is a type of inter judgement approach (MCDA). | Specialists analyzing basketball players | The rating of the provided options has raised no issues using COMET |
| 12. | Claudio Pinto | 2020 | The DEA approach modified to fuzzy logic will be used to assess relative performance in the face of uncertainty along two dimensions; efficiency and effectiveness. | Sports data analysis using fuzzy DEA models | Performances of professional football teams, relative | Propose policy recommendations for improve their athletic performance |

*(Continued)*

**Table 8.1** Existing work plan for fuzzy logic-based sports evaluation. (*Continued*)

| No. | Author | Year | Objective | Input variable | Output | Remarks |
|-----|--------|------|-----------|----------------|--------|---------|
| **13.** | W. Sałabun, Shekhovtsov, Pamučar, J. Wątróbski, B. Kizielewicz, Jakub Wieckowski, Darko Bozanić, Karol Urbaniak and B. Nyczaj | 2020 | A fuzzy-inference system based on fuzzy logic is created to evaluate team sports participants using football data. | Multi-criteria decision-making and analysis techniques | The objective COMET methodology was against subjective rankings like Player Worth and Golden Ball. | The potential to rate players playing as a defender, midfielder, or goalie, among other positions |
| **14.** | Zhenwen Xu, and Yicong Zhang | 2021 | To examine the outcomes of college students' physical health screenings Based on the fuzzy integrals assessment technique | The use of fuzzy integrals has some generalizability and applicability. | Evidence level, Therapeutic studies— investigation of treatment outcomes | The physical health of young people must be actively and scientifically improved |

(*Continued*)

**Table 8.1** Existing work plan for fuzzy logic–based sports evaluation. (*Continued*)

| No. | Author | Year | Objective | Input variable | Output | Remarks |
|---|---|---|---|---|---|---|
| 15. | Fubin Wang and Qiong Huang | 2022 | To examine the usage of physical training for sports rehabilitation and to summarise and analyze the function of exercise, sports, and rehabilitation. | Intelligent, health, monitoring, technology | Finish the extraction of moving targets. | Athletes are healed from sporting injuries via physical rehabilitation. |
| 16. | Guoqiang S., Xinxin Z., and Y. Lin | (2022). | To develop a seven-dimensional sports cultural industry competition | Evaluating strength and a model for assessing the competitiveness | Contributed to the development | Better than the standard, evaluation, method |
| 17. | Smekal, Scharl, and Sevillard, Serge P. Arnold Baca and Roch Pokan Ramon Barón Norbert Bach, Hofmann, and Harald Tschan | 2022 | To determine the accuracy of regression calculations derived from incremental test data using fuzzy neural logic when forecasting the power output (P) of the maximum lactate steady state (MLSS) on a cycle and ergometer. | Regression analysis and neuro-fuzzy logic are precise. | Determining, by advanced human testing, the maximal lactate steady-state output. | Better and more palatable models that may be applied to a broader range of people are needed. |

*(Continued)*

**Table 8.1** Existing work plan for fuzzy logic-based sports evaluation. (*Continued*)

| No. | Author | Year | Objective | Input variable | Output | Remarks |
|---|---|---|---|---|---|---|
| 18. | Zeng and Li | 2022 | Ranking football clubs employing fuzzy set theory and fuzzy clustering analysis | Create a similar fuzzy matrix and a fuzzy equivalence matrix. | Analyze the sensitivity of four parameters. | The research shows that our fuzzy logic technique is dependable and stable when the parameters vary within a specific range. |
| 19. | Xiaojing Song | 2022 | To discuss the use of data mining techniques in managing athletic performance. | Regarding the application of data mining technology | You may receive the guidelines, methodology, and connections between performance. | Promoting decision-making development on a physical level that benefits children |
| 20. | Li, Zhang, Yu Han, and Xie | 2022 | To provide integrated development models for rural sports tourism in Guangxi at the macro, miso, and micro levels and develop countermeasures. | Integrated leisure sports and rural ecological development | Fuzzy comprehensive evaluation model | Develop some alluring sports tourism products. |

on incremental test data. Creating better, more acceptable models that a broader range of individuals can use may be aided by data from various groups.

- W. Zeng and J. Li introduced fuzzy set theory and fuzzy clustering analysis rates football teams. Factors change within a specific range; the study shows that our ranking result is dependable and consistent. Furthermore, our method is generalizable when the number of teams is a positive integer N.
- Xiaojing Song proposed to analyze how data mining techniques are used in sports performance evaluation. The educational system's original data may be converted into important information using the association rules algorithm. The link between performance can be established, improving decision making to benefit the students' physiological body. The existing work plan for fuzzy logic-based sports evaluation is shown in Table 8.1.

## 8.3   Conclusion

This chapter analyzed existing studies on the impact of fuzzy logic based evaluation in sports. The primary purpose of the review was to identify research gaps in the field of fuzzy logic in sports. Therefore, various published scientific articles from 2009 to 2022 were defined and reviewed to establish research needs. To achieve the study's goal, all organized publications were catalogued by author name, year of publication; a technique used for recognition of the fuzzy logic method applying in the sports domain; the key objective of the research, input, and output variables of the system; and closing remarks of the paper. The crucial thing to remember is that fuzzy logic is an appropriate AI technique for describing uncertainty and assessing outstanding results.

Therefore, this work effectively performed a comprehensive evaluation of fuzzy logic applications and influence in the sphere of sports and games. Future research on fuzzy expert systems for fuzzy logic-based assessment in sports and physical fitness for performance evaluation.

## References

1. Arshi, A. and Mahnan, A., Systematic method for assessment and training plan design using three-dimensional models derived from fuzzy logic. *8th Int. Congr. Phys. Educ. Sports Sci.*, 22, 2, 66–70, 2015.

2. Bisso, C.S. and Samanez, C.P., Efficient determination of heliports in Rio de Janeiro for the olympic games and world cup: A fuzzy logic approach. *Int. J. Ind. Eng. (IJIEM)*, 21, 1, 33–44, 2014.

3. Glazkova, S., Babina, Y., Dovgaliuk, I., Economic assessment of the costs of developing corporate sports and physical education based on a fuzzy-multiple approach, in: *4th International Conference on Innovations in Sports, Tourism and Instructional Science*, vol. 6, issue 4, pp. 50–52, Russia, 2019.

4. Hnatchuk, Y., Hnatchuk, A., Pityn, M., Hlukhov, I., Cherednichenko, O., Intelligent decision support agent based on fuzzy logic in athletes' adaptive e-learning systems, in: *2nd International Workshop on Intelligent Information Technologies and Systems of Information Security*, vol. 9, issue 2, pp. 258–265, IntelITSIS, Khmelnytskyi, Ukraine, 2021.

5. Hubáček, O., Zháněl, J., Polách, M., Comparison of probabilistic and fuzzy approaches to evaluating the level of performance preconditions in tennis. *Kinesiologia Slovenica*, 21, 1, 98–202, 2015.

6. Arockiaraj, J.J. and Barathi., E., A comparative study of fuzzy logic towards the motivation and anxiety on a sportsman. *Int. J. Comput. Algorithm (IJCOA)*, 3, 3, 205–207, 2014.

7. Kizielewicz, B. and Dobryakova, L., MCDA-based approach to sports play-ersâ evaluation under incomplete knowledge. *Procedia Comput. Sci.*, 176, 3524–3535, 2020.

8. Li, Q., Zhang, D., Han, Y., Xie, Y., The path evaluation of integrated development of leisure sports and rural ecological environment in Guangxi based on fuzzy comprehensive evaluation model. *Math. Probl. Eng.*, 9, 5, 66–70, 2022.

9. Martínez, J.A., Ko, Y.J., Martínez, L., An application of fuzzy logic to service quality research: A case of fitness service. *J. Sport Manag.*, 24, 5, 502–523, 2010.

10. Noori, M. and Sadeghi, H., Designing an intelligent model in volleyball talent identification via fuzzy logic based on primary and weighted criteria resulted from the analytic hierarchy process. *J. Adv. Sport Technol. (JAST)*, 2, 1, 16–24, 2018.

11. Novatchkov, H. and Baca, A., Fuzzy logic in sports: A review and an illustrative case study in the field of strength training. *Int. J. Comput. Appl.*, 71, 6, 8–14, 2013.

12. Onwuachu, U.C. and Enyindah, P., A Neuro-fuzzy logic model application for predicting the result of a football match. *Eur. J. Electr. Eng. Comput. Sci. (EJECE)*, 6, 1, 60–65, 2022.

13. Pinto, C., *Fuzzy DEA models for sports data analysis: The evaluation of the relative performances of professional (virtual) football teams*, vol. 8, 3, pp. 80–85, Munich Personal RePEc Archive, Munich Germany, 2020.

14. Razaghi, M.E., Evaluating the implementation of knowledge management in offices of youth and sport in Iran: Fuzzy logic method. *Int. J. Sport Manag. Recreat. Tour.*, 16, 56–68, 2014.

15. Ribagin, S. and Stavrev, S., InterCriteria analysis of data from intellectual and physical evaluation tests of students practising sports activities. *NIFS*, 25, 4, 83–89, 2019.

16. Sałabun, W., Shekhovtsov, A., Pamučar, D., Wątróbski, J., Kizielewicz, B., Więckowski, J., Nyczaj, B., The football study case is a fuzzy inference system for player evaluation in multi-player sports. *Symmetry*, 12, 12, 2029– 2033, 2020.

17. Smekal, G., Scharl, A., von Duvillard, S.P., Pokan, R., Baca, A., Baron, R., Bachl, N., Accuracy of neuro-fuzzy logic and regression calculations in determining maximal lactate steady-state power output from incremental tests in humans. *Eur. J. Appl. Physiol.*, 88, 3, 264–274, 2002.

18. Song, X., Discussion concerning the application of data mining technology in sports performance management. *Rev. Bras. Medicina do Esporte*, 28, 460–464, 2022.

19. Sun, G., Zhang, X., Lin, Y., Evaluation model of sports culture industry competitiveness based on fuzzy analysis algorithm. *Math. Prob. Eng.*, 9, 5, 55–58, 2022.

20. Tóth-Laufer, E., *A flexible fuzzy logic-based risk assessment framework*, vol. 6, p. 3, Óbuda University E-Bulletin, Budapest, Baksi UT, 2016.

21. Tóth-Laufer, E., Takács, M., Rudas, I.J., Fuzzy logic-based risk assessment framework to evaluate physiological parameters. *Acta Polytech. Hung.*, 12, 2, 159–178, 2015.

22. Papić, V., Rogulj, N., Pleština., V., Identification of sports talents using a web-oriented expert system with a fuzzy module. *Expert Syst. Appl.*, 36, 5, 8830–8838, 2009.

23. Wang, F. and Huang, Q., Construction and evaluation of sports rehabilitation training model under intelligent health monitoring. *Wireless Commun. Mobile Comput.*, 5, 8, 68–72, 2022.

24. Xu, Z. and Zhang, Y., Analysis of physical health test results of college students using fuzzy logic as an evaluation method. *Rev. Bras. Medicina Do Esporte*, 28, 378–381, 2022.

25. Zeng, W. and Li, J., Fuzzy logic and its application in the football team ranking. *Sci. World J.*, 6, 9, 98–102, 2014.

26. Kumar, S., Rani, S., Jain, A., Verma, C., Raboaca, M.S., Illés, Z., Neagu, B.C., Face spoofing, age, gender and facial expression recognition using advance neural network architecture-based biometric system. *Sens. J.*, 22, 14, 5160–5184, 2022.

27. Kumar, S., Jain, A., Agarwal, A.K., Rani, S., Ghimire, A., Object-based image retrieval using the U-net-based neural network. *Comput. Intell. Neurosci.*, 2021, Article ID 4395646, 1–14, 2021, https://doi.org/10.1155/2021/4395646.

28. Kumar, S., Haq, M., Jain, A., Jason, C.A., Moparthi, N.R., Mittal, N., Alzamil, Z.S., Multilayer neural network based speech emotion recognition for smart assistance. *CMC-Comput. Mater. Contin.*, 74, 1, 1–18, 2022. Tech Science Press.

29. Bhola, A. and Singh, S., Visualization and modeling of high dimensional cancerous gene expression dataset. *J. Inf. Knowl. Manag.*, 18, 01, 1950001–22, 2019.

30. Rani, S. and Gowroju, S., IRIS based recognition and spoofing attacks: A review, in: *10th IEEE International Conference on System Modeling & Advancement in Research Trends (SMART)*, December 10–11, 2021.

31. Xu, Z. and Zhang, Y., Analysis of physical health test results of college students using fuzzy logic as an evaluation method. *Revista Brasileira de Medicina do Esporte*, 28, 378–381, 2022.

# 9

# Machine Learning and Deep Learning for Multimodal Biometrics

Danvir Mandal[1]* and Shyam Sundar Pattnaik[2]

*¹School of Electronics and Electrical Engineering, Lovely Professional University, Phagwara, Punjab, India*
*²National Institute of Technical Teachers Training and Research, Chandigarh, India*

**Abstract**

This chapter presents machine learning and deep learning techniques for multimodal biometrics. Multiple biometrics have been used in this concept to enhance the recognition and authentication accuracy of the person for various applications. Various fusion-based machine learning and deep learning approaches using multimodal biometrics have also been discussed. Many fusion-based machines and deep learning approaches using multimodal biometrics outperformed the unimodal biometrics techniques for classification, recognition, and authentication tasks.

*Keywords*: Machine learning, deep learning, multimodal biometrics, classification, recognition, authentication, verification

## 9.1 Introduction

The revolution in the industry with intelligent devices provided multimodal biometrics-based high-security features. Many classification, recognition, and authentication systems have been proposed and illustrated in recent years using multimodal biometrics. Multiple sensors, along with multimodal biometrics using machine learning, have been employed to enhance the safety of the operators [1]. In Ma *et al.* [2], an identification

---

*Corresponding author*: danvir.mandal@gmail.com

Sandeep Kumar, Deepika Ghai, Arpit Jain, Suman Lata Tripathi and Shilpa Rani (eds.)
Multimodal Biometric and Machine Learning Technologies: Applications for Computer Vision,
(163–172) © 2023 Scrivener Publishing LLC

system using multimodal biometrics like face and ear was developed, adopting a biometric quality assessment (BQA). A quality-aware framework using multiple biometric traits and the number of samples was proposed to enhance the recognition accuracy [3].

A verification system has been developed using face and fingerprint, continuously verifying the logged-in person [4]. Lip movement and voice as multimodal biometrics have also been used for smartphone authentication [5]. The solution for the problem of age and gender classification using ear and face as multimodal biometrics was recently proposed by researchers [6, 7].

Many machine learning and deep learning-based algorithms have been developed in the last few years using multimodal biometrics for recognition, classification, and authentication applications. The concept of biometric fusion was proposed and implemented on multiple machine learning algorithms, and their results are compared and presented in Damousis and Argyropoulos [8].

In Omara *et al.* [9], a multimodal biometric recognition idea based on a hybrid model was proposed and implemented. A semisupervised learning-based framework using serial multimodal biometrics has been illustrated in Zhang *et al.* [10]. Recognition of a person through multimodal biometrics using sparse representation has been proposed and presented in Shekhar *et al.* [11].

Machine learning algorithm-based biometric systems using multimodal electroencephalography (EEG) have also been used with high-accuracy results [12]. A genetic algorithm with a fuzzy approach was employed for recognition application in intelligent cities using enhanced multimodal biometrics [13]. The challenge of brain tumor segmentation and classification utilizing multimodal and machine learning techniques for magnetic resonance imaging [14].

Many deep learning algorithms have also been proposed for recognition and authentication problems using multimodal biometrics. In Medjahed *et al.* [15], score fusion was used for a multimodal biometric system using a deep learning approach for person identification. A deep reinforcement learning approach was proposed and implemented using multimodal biometrics fusion [16]. The recognition problem was illustrated for surveillance videos using transfer learning in deep convolutional neural networks [17]. A recognition system using a fusion of finger vein and finger knuckle print with a deep learning algorithm was proposed, and high-accuracy results were presented in Daas *et al.* [18].

A deep learning approach has been used in recognition problems using multimodal biometrics in facial video with missing modalities [19]. A deep pyramidal approach for recognizing hand veins using multimodal biometrics was proposed and implemented in [20]. Other deep learning-based methods using multimodal biometrics for authentication and recognition problems have been presented in El-Rahiem *et al.*, Tiong *et al.*, Begum and Mustafa, Attia *et al.*, Sharma *et al.*, Alay and Al-Baity, and Wang *et al.* [21–27].

In this work, various machine learning and deep learning-based recognition and authentication problems using multimodal biometrics have been presented and discussed in detail. This work offers a resource for machine and deep learning approaches using multimodal biometrics.

## 9.2 Machine Learning Using Multimodal Biometrics

### 9.2.1 Main Machine Learning Algorithms

The following are the principal machine learning algorithms based on multimodal biometrics presented in Damousis and Argyropoulos [8]:

(i) Artificial neural network (ANN)
(ii) Gaussian mixture model (GMM)
(iii) Support vector machine (SVM)
(iv) Fuzzy expert system (FES)

In SVM implementation, to map the higher dimensional data space with the input data, radial basis kernel function was utilized. The premise space of the FES consisted of three inputs. In FES, trapezoidal membership functions were used to segment each premise input. Four mixture components were utilized in GMM development, and extensive experimentation was conducted to estimate the component weights in GMM. A neural network working in feed-forward mode with three layers was used in the presented work [8]. All the fusion-based machine learning algorithms performed better than those based on unimodal biometrics. This validates the idea that multimodal biometrics effectively improves the performance of recognition and authentication systems.

### 9.2.2 A Hybrid Model

Metric learning can significantly improve recognition and authentication systems. A multimodal biometric-based classification system using learning distance metric (LDM) and kernel SVM has achieved 99.85% accuracy.

This accuracy has been attained using face and ear images. The authentication method in this work was optimized using the LDM along with the directed acyclic graph SVM. The results obtained in this work outdone the previous jobs which used SVM or K-nearest neighbor (KNN) methods [9]. Two data set groups were designed from each dataset to validate the presented system. One group was utilized for training the model, and the other was used for testing. The main objective of the proposed hybrid model was the representation of the ear and faced images and the development of algorithms for the classification of humans.

### 9.2.3    Semisupervised Learning Method

Semisupervised learning approaches have been used with multimodal biometrics employed serially. This approach discussed issues when multimodal biometrics are used parallelly and presented the proposed method's advantages. The proposed system was implemented using two prototypes. One prototype used a fingerprint with face matches, whereas the other used a fingerprint with gait matches. The proposed techniques were better when compared to the parallel fusion system [10].

The presented technique has proposed to use the more convenient traits earlier and those that are less convenient later in the chain. To strengthen the weaker features, the authors proposed using the semisupervised learning approach in the proposed work. The proposed system leads to better performance of the convenience of the user as well as the accuracy of the recognition task.

### 9.2.4    EEG-Based Machine Learning

A multimodal biometric system was used to identify and authenticate the user using a machine learning approach, which merged keystroke dynamics with the EEG. It was the first implementation of its kind, which used keystroke dynamics along with the EEG biometrics. This approach provided additional security for identification and authentication tasks using EEG data and keystroke dynamics [12].

In the case of EEG data alone, the best results were found using the Random Forest classifier. The same results were obtained with and without feature selection in the case of EEG data. With keystroke data alone, the Random Forest classifier demonstrated the best performance again. Regarding keystroke and EEG data, the random forest performed better when all the features were used. However, when feature selection was introduced, linear discriminant analysis (LDA) achieved the best results among all other techniques.

## 9.3 Deep Learning Using Multimodal Biometrics

### 9.3.1 Based on Score Fusion

In this technique, the biometric characteristics of palm prints and the face were fused and utilized for identification tasks using the convolutional neural networks (CNN) and k-nearest neighbors (KNN) method. Data sets with noise were used to validate the performance of the proposed method [15].

### 9.3.2 Deep Learning for Surveillance Videos

Transfer learning and multimodal biometrics were used with deep CNN for recognition problems in surveillance videos. Gait and facial features were fused and used for the learning process. The block diagram of the proposed system is illustrated in Figure 9.1. The classification accuracy obtained in this proposed technique was 97.3% with a 0.004 equal error rate [17].

### 9.3.3 Finger Vein and Knuckle Print-Based Deep Learning Approach

The use of finger vein biometrics and finger knuckle print in recognition tasks using deep learning techniques has been reported in Daas *et al.* [18]. In this approach, different fusion levels were used. Transfer learning was used to extract finger vein features and knuckle print features. The general block diagram of the multimodal recognition system using a fusion of elements in the deep learning method is presented in Figure 9.2.

The fusion in this approach was performed at the feature and score levels. The authors also proposed a unimodal biometric system and presented

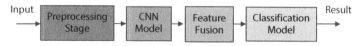

**Figure 9.1** The block diagram of the proposed system in Aung *et al.* [17] with multimodal biometrics.

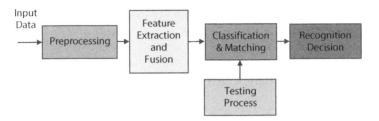

**Figure 9.2** The general block diagram of the multimodal recognition system in Daas *et al.* [18] with the fusion of features.

its performance comparison with a multimodal biometric system. The proposed multimodal biometric recognition system exhibited an accuracy of 99.89% with a 0.05% equal error rate.

### 9.3.4    Facial Video-Based Deep Learning Technique

We know that multiple biometric modalities provide a robust identification system rather than a single biometric modality system. In Maity *et al.* [19], authors proposed a multimodal biometric identification system using several biometric modalities. However, they were taken from a single facial video segment. The primary biometric modalities taken in work were right and left ears, profile face, and frontal face. The authors observed that the system was robust even when a few mentioned modalities were missing in the testing process. The deep neural network used in the presented method was evaluated for different parameters. The maximum number of hidden layers used in this work was seven. However, the authors got the best results when five hidden layers were employed in the deep neural network.

### 9.3.5    Finger Vein and Electrocardiogram-Based Deep Learning Approach

The finger vein and the electrocardiogram (ECG) as multimodal biometrics had been used in an authentication system using a deep fusion approach [21]. The first component of the proposed method was biometric preprocessing. Feature extraction was the next step after the preprocessing of the biometric data. The last step was the authentication of the person. Each biometric was utilized in a preprocessing step by a filtering method and normalization. A deep convolutional neural network extracted the features from multimodal biometrics. For authentication of the person, different classifiers based on machine learning algorithms were used in

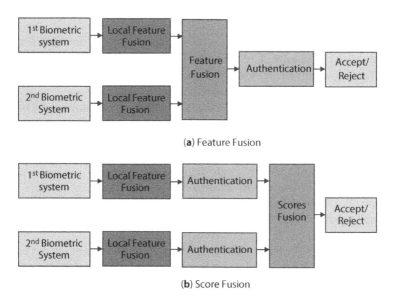

**(a)** Feature Fusion

**(b)** Score Fusion

**Figure 9.3** The basic block diagram of the multimodal biometric authentication system is presented in El-Rahiem *et al.* [21].

the proposed method [21–30]. Feature and score fusion combined the two biometric modalities, i.e., ECG and finger vein. The basic block diagram of the multimodal biometric authentication system presented in El-Rahiem *et al.* [21] is illustrated in Figure 9.3.

The proposed system's feature and score fusion approaches are depicted in parts (a) and part (b) of Figure 9.3, respectively.

## 9.4    Conclusion

This chapter has explored and illustrated many machine learning and deep learning techniques using multimodal biometrics. Main machine learning algorithms, a hybrid model, a semisupervised learning technique, and EEG-based machine learning method using multimodal biometrics are discussed in detail. Further, various multimodal biometric deep learning techniques using score fusion, gait, and facial features in surveillance videos, finger vein and knuckle prints, right and left ears and profile faces, frontal face, and ECG are illustrated in this work. It was observed that the recognition and authentication accuracy was significantly improved by using multimodal biometrics.

# References

1. Abate, A.F., Cimmino, L., Cuomo, I., Nardo, M.D., Murino, T., On the impact of multimodal and multisensor biometrics in smart factories. *IEEE Trans. Industr. Inform.*, 18, 12, 9092–9100, 2022.

2. Ma, Y., Huang, Z., Wang, X., Huang, K., An overview of multimodal biometrics using the face and ear. *Math. Prob. Eng.*, 2020, Article ID 6802905, 17, 2020.

3. Soleymani, S., Dabouei, A., Taherkhani, F., Iranmanesh, S.M., Dawson, J., Nasrabadi, N.M., Quality-aware multimodal biometric recognition. *IEEE Trans. Biom. Behav. Identity Sci.*, 4, 1, 97–116, 2022.

4. Sim, T., Zhang, S., Janakiraman, R., Kumar, S., Continuous verification using multimodal biometrics. *IEEE Trans. Pattern Anal. Mach. Intell.*, 29, 4, 687–700, 2007.

5. Wu, L., Yang, J., Zhou, M., Chen, Y., Wang, Q., LVID: A multimodal biometrics authentication system on smartphones. *IEEE Trans. Inf. Forensics Secur.*, 15, 1572–1585, 2020.

6. Yaman, D., Eyiokur, F.I., Ekenel, H.K., Multimodal soft biometrics: Combining ear and face biometrics for age and gender classification. *Multimed. Tools Appl.*, 81, 22695–22713, 2022.

7. Sarhan, S., Alhassan, S., Elmougy, S., Multimodal biometric systems: A comparative study. *Arab. J. Sci. Eng.*, 42, 443–457, 2017.

8. Damousis, I.G. and Argyropoulos, S., Four machine learning algorithms for biometrics fusion: A comparative study. *Appl. Comput. Intell. Soft Comput.*, 2012, Article ID 242401, 7, 2012.

9. Omara, I., Hagag, A., Chaib, S., Ma, G., El-Samie, F.E.A., Song, E., A hybrid model combining learning distance metric and D.A.G. support vector machine for multimodal biometric recognition. *IEEE Access*, 9, 4784–4796, 2021.

10. Zhang, Q., Yin, Y., Zhan, D.-C., Peng, J., A novel serial multimodal biometrics framework based on semisupervised learning techniques. *IEEE Trans. Inf. Forensics Secur.*, 9, 10, 1681–1694, 2014.

11. Shekhar, S., Patel, V.M., Nasrabadi, N.M., Chellappa, R., Joint sparse representation for robust multimodal biometrics recognition. *IEEE Trans. Pattern Anal. Mach. Intell.*, 36, 1, 113–126, 2014.

12. Rahman, A., Chowdhury, M.E.H., Khandakar, A., Kiranyaz, S., Zaman, K.S., Reaz, M.B., II, Islam, M.T., Ezeddin, M., Kadir, M., A., multimodal E.E.G. and keystroke dynamics based biometric system using machine learning algorithms. *IEEE Access*, 9, 94625–94643, 2021.

13. Rajasekar, V., Predić, B., Saracevic, M., Elhoseny, M., Karabasevic, D., Stanujkic, D., Jayapaul, P., Enhanced multimodal biometric recognition approach for smart cities based on an optimised fuzzy genetic algorithm. *Sci. Rep.*, 12, 622, 2022.

14. Anand, L., Rane, K.P., Bewoor, L.A., Bangare, J.L., Surve, J., Raghunath, M.P., Sankaran, K.S., Osei, B., Development of machine learning and medical enabled multimodal for segmentation and classification of brain tumor using M.R.I. images. *Comput. Intell. Neurosci.*, 2022, Article ID 7797094, 8, 2022.

15. Medjahed, C., Rahmoun, A., Charrier, C., Mezzoudj, F., A deep learning-based multimodal biometric system using score fusion. *IAES Inter. J. Artif. Intell.*, 11, 1, 65–80, 2022.

16. Huang, Q., Multimodal biometrics fusion algorithm using deep reinforcement learning. *Math. Prob. Eng.*, 2022, Article ID 8544591, 9, 2022.

17. Aung, H.M.L., Pluempitiwiriyawej, C., Hamamoto, K., Wangsiripitak, S., Multimodal biometrics recognition using a deep convolutional neural network with transfer learning in surveillance videos. *Computation*, 10, 127, 2022.

18. Daas, S., Yahi, A., Bakir, T., Sedhane, M., Boughazi, M., Bourennane, E.-B., Multimodal biometric recognition systems using deep learning based on the finger vein and finger knuckle print fusion. *I.E.T. Image Process.*, 14, 15, 3859–3868, 2020.

19. Maity, S., Abdel-Mottaleb, M., Asfour, S.S., Multimodal biometrics recognition from facial video with missing modalities using deep learning. *J. Inf. Process. Syst.*, 16, 1, 6–29, 2020.

20. Bhilare, S., Jaiswal, G., Kanhangad, V., Nigam, A., Single-sensor hand-vein multimodal biometric recognition using the multiscale deep pyramidal approach. *Mach. Vision Appl.*, 29, 1269–1286, 2018.

21. El-Rahiem, B.A., El-Samie, F.E.A., Amin, M., Multimodal biometric authentication based on the profound fusion of electrocardiogram (E.C.G.) and finger vein. *Multimed. Syst.*, 28, 1325–1337, 2022.

22. Tiong, L.C.O., Kim, S.T., Ro, Y.M., Implementation of multimodal biometric recognition via multi-feature deep learning networks and feature fusion. *Multimed. Tools Appl.*, 78, 22743–22772, 2019.

23. Begum, N. and Mustafa, A.S., A novel approach for multimodal facial expression recognition using deep learning techniques. *Multimed. Tools Appl.*, 81, 18521–18529, 2022.

24. Attia, A., Mazaa, S., Akhtar, Z., Chahir, Y., Deep learning-driven palmprint and finger knuckle pattern-based multimodal Person recognition system. *Multimed. Tools Appl.*, 81, 10961–10980, 2022.

25. Sharma, A., Jindal, N., Thakur, A., Rana, P.S., Garg, B., Mehta, R., Multimodal biometric for person identification using deep learning approach. *Wireless Pers. Commun.*, 125, 399–419, 2022.

26. Alay, N. and Al-Baity, H.H., Deep learning approach for multimodal biometric recognition system based on fusion of iris, face, and finger vein traits. *Sensors*, 20, 5523, 2020.

27. Wang, Y., Shi, D., Zhou, W., Convolutional neural network approach based on multimodal biometric system with fusion of face and finger vein features. *Sensors*, 22, 6039, 2022.

28. Kumar, K., Sharma, A., Tripathi, S.L., Sensors and their application, in: *Electronic Device and Circuits Design Challenges to Implement Biomedical Applications*, Elsevier, Amsterdam, 2021, https://doi.org/10.1016/B978-0-323-85172-5.00021-6.

29. Prasanna, D.L. and Tripathi, S.L., Machine and deep-learning techniques for text and speech processing, in: *Machine Learning Algorithms for Signal and Image Processing*, pp. 115–128, Wiley, Hoboken, New Jersey, U.S., 2022.

30. Kumar, K., Chaudhury, K., Tripathi, S.L., Future of machine learning (ml) and deep learning (dl) in healthcare monitoring system, in: *Machine Learning Algorithms for Signal and Image Processing*, pp. 293–313, Wiley, Hoboken, New Jersey, U.S., 2022.

# 10

# Machine Learning and Deep Learning: Classification and Regression Problems, Recurrent Neural Networks, Convolutional Neural Networks

**R. K. Jeyachitra[1]\* and Manochandar, S.[2]**

[1]*Department of Electronics and Communication Engineering, National Institute of Technology, Tiruchirappalli, Tamil Nadu, India*
[2]*Department of Master of Business Administration, CARE College of Engineering, Tiruchirappalli, Tamil Nadu, India*

## Abstract

The rapid development of information technology requires intelligent management of systems. Artificial intelligence (AI) is one of the enabling technologies for intelligent systems. Machine learning (ML) and deep learning (DL) are the subsets of AI. This chapter presents the basics of ML and DL techniques. It discusses the various types of ML techniques, such as supervised, unsupervised, reinforcement learning, and semisupervised learning techniques. In addition to the primary and hybrid approaches, some critical systems like multi-task, outline, active, ensemble, meta, concept, multimodal, targeted learnings, and so on are explored. The basics and mathematical derivations of regression analysis are discussed. The linear and nonlinear regressions are also described. Recurrent neural networks (RNN) and convolutional neural networks (CNN) are the most common techniques of DL. The different types and structures of RNNs are explained. Various structures and transfer functions adopted for CNN are presented. This chapter also deals with the real-time applications of ML and DL techniques.

*Keywords:* Machine learning, classification, deep learning, artificial intelligence, regression, transfer learning, recurrent neural networks, convolutional neural networks

*\*Corresponding author*: jeyachitra@nitt.edu

Sandeep Kumar, Deepika Ghai, Arpit Jain, Suman Lata Tripathi and Shilpa Rani (eds.)
*Multimodal Biometric and Machine Learning Technologies: Applications for Computer Vision,*
(173–226) © 2023 Scrivener Publishing LLC

## 10.1   Introduction

In recent years, the world has been moving toward an intelligent system; it makes the prediction and decision-making process inevitable. These processes are highly dependent on the data. Modern technology development and digitalization lead to the generation of an enormous volume of data. Analysis of those data manually and making a decision is the most complicated and automatic process of decision making is a challenging task. Artificial Intelligence (AI) and machine learning are essential components of Data Science. Machine learning (ML) is the subset of (AI). When a machine, instead of a human, does the job, it can do the work intelligently and faster. ML originated in 1950, and Arthur Lee Samuel defined it in 1959. ML is described by Louridas *et al.* [3], which is used to execute the task by learning about the data that can be labeled or unlabeled.

Deep learning (DL) is a subset of a broader family of ML with multiple layers that teach computers to think like humans. In DL, a model learns to perform tasks such as classification, estimation, and prediction from various inputs such as images, texts or sound to achieve higher accuracies. In recent times, DL has improved to the point where it sometimes outperforms human capabilities. DL is a particular category of ML with the differentiating feature that the ML workflow begins with manually extracting the relevant parts from the input datasets [3]. These features are then used to classify the data by building a suitable model.

On the other hand, in DL, the relevant features are extracted automatically. Moreover, the raw data is given in DL to perform the desired task, which is learned automatically. The significant positive note on DL is that its efficiency increases as the volume of the training data increases. The only requirements for DL include large volumes of training data and substantial computing power that hinder the application of the technology more widely. DL is the critical technology behind various applications, such as automatic transmission vehicles, driverless cars, voice-controlled electronics, intelligent home appliances, health care, personalized marketing, financial fraud detection, sentimental analysis, social media, and natural language processing (NLP).

## 10.2   Classification of Machine Learning

This section provides insights into the classification of ML algorithms. The hierarchy of various ML approaches is shown in Figure 10.1, these three ML techniques are primary, hybrid, and other systems. There are three

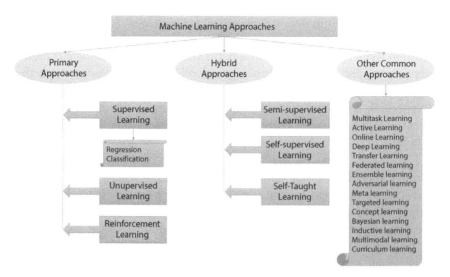

**Figure 10.1** Classification of machine learning.

primary ML approaches, supervised learning, unsupervised learning, and reinforcement learning.

## 10.3   Supervised Learning

Singh *et al.* [1] define supervised learning as used to generate an algorithm that can produce a pattern using the available data to predict the output for future data. The two tasks defined by Mrabet *et al.* [2] can be performed by the supervised learning algorithm, namely regression and classification. The main difference between regression and classification is that the former can predict the numerical output, and the latter can predict the class label for future data from experience. Sarker [39] defines the supervised learning approach as the task-driven approach that builds models or algorithms by learning from the labeled data. In this approach, the dataset contains both the input and output values [3]. The various supervised learning techniques are neural networks (NN), K-nearest neighbor (KNN), decision trees, random forest, support vector machine (SVM), and Naïve Bayes [7].

### 10.3.1   Regression

Mainly regression algorithm is used to predict the value of a particular attribute and is commonly termed statistical regression. Regression is the process of forecasting the variable, which is continuous from the predictor variable [39]. Linear regression, fuzzy classification, Bayesian networks, decision trees, and artificial neural networks (ANN) are the various methods used to apply the principle of regression [3]. Multiple ways to apply the regression code come under specific regression algorithms, such as linear, polynomial, lasso, and ridge regression [39]. The concordance index can be calculated by the rank correlation between observed data and predicted data [40].

Figure 10.2 shows the general block diagram of the regression learner model [38]. The first step of any regression learner model is to select the correct data validated for the applications. The next step is to choose the proper regression algorithm listed above for the data to fit. After selecting the data and choosing the appropriate regression model, the data should be trained using the regression model. The model's performance, such as accuracy, can be assessed from the prepared data. Finally, export the regression model if the algorithm satisfies with greater accuracy.

- Linear regression
  Linear regression, defined by Huang [8], is one of the regression techniques used to fit all the data into a straight line. This technique provides a continuous dependent variable and a continuous or discrete independent variable [39]. Generally, the equation of the line which is used to fit all the data with the standard line equation [8] is $y = mx + c$ where 'm' is the slope, and 'c' is the Intercept.

  Figure 10.3 shows the basic linear regression model developed by the data provided by the database. The data derived from the database contains both the input and output of the model. Build the regression model by calculating the Intercept (c) and Slope (m) from the input-output pair of the data. The linear regression model will be generated using the Intercept and Slope values. Applying the input from the database to the model will produce the output predicted by the model; hence, the output is known as the

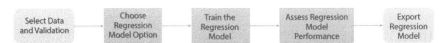

**Figure 10.2** Regression learner model [38].

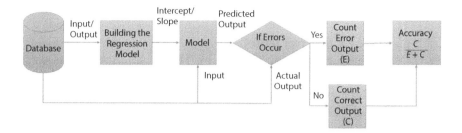

**Figure 10.3**  Linear regression model.

expected output. This predicted output is then compared with the actual output from the database to check the error in the model. Finally, the algorithm calculates the model's efficiency generated by the Intercept and Slope. Figure 10.4 shows the linear regression curve for the model generated by the Intercept and Slope. The dots in the graph are plotted using a scatter plot in which the points (observed value) is obtained from the database. The line (from the predicted value) shown in Figure 10.4 is the line of regression plotted from, giving the linear relationship between the independent variable and the dependent variable.

It is seen from Figure 10.4 that the observed and predicted values are not equal, which leads to the error. Hence, the equation of the line of regression can be precisely written as [39]

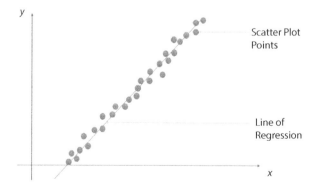

**Figure 10.4**  Linear regression curve.

$$y = mx + c + e \qquad (10.1)$$

where e is the error term.

Linear regression, defined by Hope [42], provides a least-squares solution when fitting a linear set of equations to observations. The underlying assumptions framed by Orbeck [43] for applying the regression analysis method are as follows:

- For every fixed value of $x$, $y$ is normally distributed.
- The relation between $x$ and the mean value of the $y$ is known to be linear. The actual relationship is $y = mx + b$ where $m$ and $b$ are the constants.
- The observations are stochastically independent.

### Discrete form equation

From equation (10.1), we can write for N samples as illustrated by Rubin [44],

$$y_1 + y_2 + \ldots\ldots + y_N = (mx_1 + b) + (mx_2 + b) + \ldots\ldots + (mx_N + b)$$

$$\sum_{i=1}^{N} Y_i = m \sum_{i=1}^{N} X_i + Nb \qquad (10.2)$$

Multiply the equation (10.2) by the term $\sum_{i=1}^{N} X_i$ on both sides,

$$\sum_{i=1}^{N} X_i Y_i = m \sum_{i=1}^{N} X_i^2 + b \sum_{i=1}^{N} X_i \qquad (10.3)$$

## Continuous form equation

Using the definition of the limit of sum [44],

$$\lim_{\substack{N \to \infty \\ \Delta t \to 0}} \Delta t \sum_{i=1}^{N} Y_i = \int_0^t Y \, dt \tag{10.4}$$

$$\lim_{\substack{N \to \infty \\ \Delta t \to 0}} \Delta t \sum_{i=1}^{N} X_i = \int_0^t X \, dt \tag{10.5}$$

$$\lim_{\substack{N \to \infty \\ \Delta t \to 0}} \Delta t \sum_{i=1}^{N} X_i Y_i = \int_0^t XY \, dt \tag{10.6}$$

$$\lim_{\substack{N \to \infty \\ \Delta t \to 0}} \Delta t \sum_{i=1}^{N} X_i^2 = \int_0^t X^2 \, dt \tag{10.7}$$

Now multiply equation (10.2) by $\Delta t$ and apply the limit as $N \to \infty$ and $\Delta t \to 0$, we get

$$\lim_{\substack{N \to \infty \\ \Delta t \to 0}} \Delta t \sum_{i=1}^{N} Y_i = m \lim_{\substack{N \to \infty \\ \Delta t \to 0}} \Delta t \sum_{i=1}^{N} X_i + \lim_{\substack{N \to \infty \\ \Delta t \to 0}} \Delta t N b$$

$$\int_0^t Y \, dt = m \int_0^t X \, dt + bt \tag{10.8}$$

Now multiply equation (10.3) by $\Delta t$ and apply the limit as $N \to \infty$ and $\Delta t \to 0$, we get

$$\lim_{\substack{N \to \infty \\ \Delta t \to 0}} \Delta t \sum_{i=1}^{N} X_i Y_i = m \lim_{\substack{N \to \infty \\ \Delta t \to 0}} \Delta t \sum_{i=1}^{N} X_i^2 + b \lim_{\substack{N \to \infty \\ \Delta t \to 0}} \Delta t \sum_{i=1}^{N} X_i$$

$$\int_0^t XY dt = m \int_0^t X^2 dt + b \int_0^t X dt \tag{10.9}$$

### Slope and intercept of the line

We can rewrite equation (10.8) as

$$bt = \int_0^t Y\, dt - m \int_0^t X\, dt$$

$$b = \frac{\int_0^t Y\, dt - m \int_0^t X\, dt}{t} \tag{10.10}$$

Also, we can rewrite equation (10.9) as

$$m \int_0^t X^2\, dt = \int_0^t XY\, dt - b \int_0^t X\, dt$$

$$m = \frac{\int_0^t XY\, dt - b \int_0^t X\, dt}{\int_0^t X^2\, dt} \tag{10.11}$$

Substitute equation (10.11) with equation (10.10), and we get

$$b = \frac{\int_0^t Ydt - \left[\dfrac{\int_0^t XYdt - b\int_0^t Xdt}{\int_0^t X^2 dt}\right]\int_0^t Xdt}{t}$$

$$bt = \frac{\int_0^t Ydt \int_0^t X^2 dt - \left[\int_0^t XYdt - b\int_0^t Xdt\right]\int_0^t Xdt}{\int_0^t X^2 dt}$$

$$bt\int_0^t X^2 dt = \int_0^t Ydt \int_0^t X^2 dt - \int_0^t XYdt \int_0^t Xdt + b\left[\int_0^t Xdt\right]^2$$

$$bt\int_0^t X^2 dt - b\left[\int_0^t Xdt\right]^2 = \int_0^t Ydt \int_0^t X^2 dt - \int_0^t XYdt \int_0^t Xdt$$

$$b\left\{t\int_0^t X^2 dt - \left[\int_0^t Xdt\right]^2\right\} = \int_0^t Ydt \int_0^t X^2 dt - \int_0^t XYdt \int_0^t Xdt$$

$$b = \frac{\int_0^t Ydt \int_0^t X^2 dt - \int_0^t XYdt \int_0^t Xdt}{t\int_0^t X^2 dt - \left[\int_0^t Xdt\right]^2}$$

$$b = \frac{\int_0^t Ydt \int_0^t X^2 dt - \int_0^t XYdt \int_0^t Xdt}{D} \tag{10.12}$$

where $D = t \int_0^t X^2 dt - \left[ \int_0^t X dt \right]^2$

Similarly, substitute equation (10.10) with equation (10.11), and we get

$$m = \frac{\int_0^t XY dt - \left[ \dfrac{\int_0^t Y dt - m \int_0^t X dt}{t} \right] \int_0^t X dt}{\int_0^t X^2 dt}$$

$$m \int_0^t X^2 dt = \frac{t \int_0^t XY dt - \left[ \int_0^t Y dt - m \int_0^t X dt \right] \int_0^t X dt}{t}$$

$$mt \int_0^t X^2 dt = t \int_0^t XY dt - \int_0^t Y dt \int_0^t X dt + m \left[ \int_0^t X dt \right]^2$$

$$mt \int_0^t X^2 dt - m \left[ \int_0^t X dt \right]^2 = t \int_0^t XY dt - \int_0^t Y dt \int_0^t X dt$$

$$m \left\{ t \int_0^t X^2 dt - \left[ \int_0^t X dt \right]^2 \right\} = t \int_0^t XY dt - \int_0^t Y dt \int_0^t X dt$$

$$m = \frac{t \int_0^t XY dt - \int_0^t Y dt \int_0^t X dt}{t \int_0^t X^2 dt - \left[ \int_0^t X dt \right]^2}$$

$$m = \frac{t \int_0^t XY dt - \int_0^t Y dt \int_0^t X dt}{D} \tag{10.13}$$

where $D = t \int_0^t X^2 dt - \left[ \int_0^t X dt \right]^2$

## Error function

We can rewrite equation (10.13) as

$$mD = t \int_0^t XY \, dt - \int_0^t Y \, dt \int_0^t X \, dt \qquad (10.14)$$

The difference between the LHS and RHS of the equation is given as

$$\varepsilon = mD - t \int_0^t XY \, dt + \int_0^t Y \, dt \int_0^t X \, dt \qquad (10.15)$$

Partially differentiating equation (10.15) concerning , we get

$$\frac{\partial \varepsilon}{\partial m} = D$$

For an arbitrary gain of considerable value [44],

$$\frac{dm}{d\tau} = -k\varepsilon D = -k\varepsilon \frac{\partial \varepsilon}{\partial m} \qquad (10.16)$$

- Multiple Linear Regression
  This can be extended for multiple linear regression illustrated by Sarker [39], which consists of one dependent variable and two or more independent variables. The equation of the line of regression for multiple linear regression can be written as

$$y = m_1 x_1 + m_2 x_2 + m_3 x_3 + \ldots \ldots \ldots + m_n x_n + c + e$$

*Curvilinear Regression*

If a straight line is not fitted for the set of points in the scatter plot due to the nonlinearity relationship between the variables, then it is necessary to find some simple curve which makes the best fit. If we predict from the angle seen from the scatter plot, then the type of regression is called curvilinear regression defined by Hoel [78]. There are various types of curvilinear regression: polynomial and nonpolynomial.

*Polynomial Regression*

Without any theoretical reason, it is necessary to use polynomials for simplicity and flexibility to derive any curve representing the relationship between the variables. This can determine the lower-degree polynomial from the scatter plot, which will best fit the set of points in the scatter plot. To improve the curve found from the scatter plot, a more accurate best-fitting polynomial is found using the method of least squares [78].

Consider the polynomial of degree as shown in the below equation:

$$y = a_0 + a_1 x + a_2 x^2 + \ldots \ldots \ldots + a_k x^k \tag{10.17}$$

*Discrete form equation*

Consider the number of samples as N, then

$$y_1 + y_2 + \ldots \ldots \ldots + y_N$$

$$= a_0 + a_1 (x_1 + x_2 + \ldots \ldots \ldots + x_N) + a_2 (x_1 + x_2 + \ldots \ldots \ldots + x_N)^2$$

$$+ \ldots \ldots \ldots + a_k (x_1 + x_2 + \ldots \ldots \ldots + x_N)^k$$

$$\sum_{i=1}^{N} y_i = a_0 N + a_1 \sum_{i=1}^{N} x_i + a_2 \left( \sum_{i=1}^{N} x_i \right)^2 + \ldots \ldots \ldots + a_k \left( \sum_{i=1}^{N} x_i \right)^k \tag{10.18}$$

Now let us assume the samples are orthogonal to each other; hence the inner product between the samples is zero. Hence, we can rewrite equation (10.18) as

$$\sum_{i=1}^{N} y_i = a_0 N + a_1 \sum_{i=1}^{N} x_i + a_2 \sum_{i=1}^{N} x_i^2 + \ldots\ldots + a_k \sum_{i=1}^{N} x_i^k \quad (10.19a)$$

Multiply the equation (10.19a) by the term $\sum_{i=1}^{N} x_i$, we get,

$$\sum_{i=1}^{N} x_i y_i = a_0 \sum_{i=1}^{N} x_i + a_1 \sum_{i=1}^{N} x_i^2 + a_2 \sum_{i=1}^{N} x_i^3 + \ldots\ldots + a_k \sum_{i=1}^{N} x_i^{k+1}$$

$$(10.19b)$$

Multiply the equation (10.19a) by the term $\sum_{i=1}^{N} x_i^2$, we get,

$$\sum_{i=1}^{N} x_i^2 y_i = a_0 \sum_{i=1}^{N} x_i^2 + a_1 \sum_{i=1}^{N} x_i^3 + a_2 \sum_{i=1}^{N} x_i^4 + \ldots\ldots + a_k \sum_{i=1}^{N} x_i^{k+2}$$

$$(10.19c)$$

Multiply the equation (10.19a) by the term $\sum_{i=1}^{N} x_i^k$, we get,

$$\sum_{i=1}^{N} x_i^k y_i = a_0 \sum_{i=1}^{N} x_i^k + a_1 \sum_{i=1}^{N} x_i^{k+1} + a_2 \sum_{i=1}^{N} x_i^{k+2} + \ldots\ldots + a_k \sum_{i=1}^{N} x_i^{2k}$$

$$(10.19d)$$

### Continuous form equation
Now multiply equation (10.19) by $\Delta t$ and apply the limit as $N \to \infty$ and $\Delta t \to 0$. We get

$$\lim_{\substack{N \to \infty \\ \Delta t \to 0}} \Delta t \sum_{i=1}^{N} y_i = a_0 \lim_{\substack{N \to \infty \\ \Delta t \to 0}} \Delta t N + a_1 \lim_{\substack{N \to \infty \\ \Delta t \to 0}} \Delta t \sum_{i=1}^{N} x_i + a_2 \lim_{\substack{N \to \infty \\ \Delta t \to 0}} \Delta t$$

$$\sum_{i=1}^{N} x_i^2 + \ldots\ldots + a_k \lim_{\substack{N \to \infty \\ \Delta t \to 0}} \Delta t \sum_{i=1}^{N} x_i^k \quad (10.20a)$$

$$\lim_{\substack{N \to \infty \\ \Delta t \to 0}} \Delta t \sum_{i=1}^{N} x_i y_i = a_0 \lim_{\substack{N \to \infty \\ \Delta t \to 0}} \Delta t \sum_{i=1}^{N} x_i + a_1 \lim_{\substack{N \to \infty \\ \Delta t \to 0}} \Delta t \sum_{i=1}^{N} x_i^2 + a_2 \lim_{\substack{N \to \infty \\ \Delta t \to 0}} \Delta t$$

$$\sum_{i=1}^{N} x_i^3 + \ldots\ldots + a_k \lim_{\substack{N \to \infty \\ \Delta t \to 0}} \Delta t \sum_{i=1}^{N} x_i^{k+1} \qquad (10.20b)$$

$$\lim_{\substack{N \to \infty \\ \Delta t \to 0}} \Delta t \sum_{i=1}^{N} x_i^2 y_i = a_0 \lim_{\substack{N \to \infty \\ \Delta t \to 0}} \Delta t \sum_{i=1}^{N} x_i^2 + a_1 \lim_{\substack{N \to \infty \\ \Delta t \to 0}} \Delta t \sum_{i=1}^{N} x_i^3 + a_2 \lim_{\substack{N \to \infty \\ \Delta t \to 0}} \Delta t$$

$$\sum_{i=1}^{N} x_i^4 + \ldots\ldots + a_k \lim_{\substack{N \to \infty \\ \Delta t \to 0}} \Delta t \sum_{i=1}^{N} x_i^{k+2} \qquad (10.20c)$$

$$\lim_{\substack{N \to \infty \\ \Delta t \to 0}} \Delta t \sum_{i=1}^{N} x_i^k y_i = a_0 \lim_{\substack{N \to \infty \\ \Delta t \to 0}} \Delta t \sum_{i=1}^{N} x_i^k + a_1 \lim_{\substack{N \to \infty \\ \Delta t \to 0}} \Delta t \sum_{i=1}^{N} x_i^{k+1} + a_2 \lim_{\substack{N \to \infty \\ \Delta t \to 0}} \Delta t$$

$$\sum_{i=1}^{N} x_i^{k+2} + \ldots\ldots + a_k \lim_{\substack{N \to \infty \\ \Delta t \to 0}} \Delta t \sum_{i=1}^{N} x_i^{2k} \qquad (10.20d)$$

Using the definition of the limit of sum [44], given in equation (10.4) to equation (10.7), equation (10.20) can be rewritten as

$$\int_0^t Y \, dt = a_0 t + a_1 \int_0^t X \, dt + a_2 \int_0^t X^2 \, dt + \ldots\ldots + a_k \int_0^t X^k \, dt$$

$$(10.21a)$$

$$\int_0^t XY\,dt = a_0 \int_0^t X\,dt + a_1 \int_0^t X^2\,dt + a_2 \int_0^t X^3\,dt + \ldots\ldots + a_k \int_0^t X^{k+1}\,dt$$

$$(10.21b)$$

$$\int_0^t X^2Y\,dt = a_0 \int_0^t X^2\,dt + a_1 \int_0^t X^3\,dt + a_2 \int_0^t X^4\,dt + \ldots\ldots + a_k \int_0^t X^{k+2}\,dt$$

$$(10.21c)$$

$$\int_0^t X^kY\,dt = a_0 \int_0^t X^k\,dt + a_1 \int_0^t X^{k+1}\,dt + a_2 \int_0^t X^{k+1}\,dt + \ldots\ldots + a_k \int_0^t X^{2k}\,dt$$

$$(10.21d)$$

Equations (10.19) and (10.20) can be called normal equations [78] in discrete and continuous form, respectively, and this equation can be reduced to two sets of equations each. One pack contains the odd-numbered equation with only the unknowns , and the other includes the even-numbered equations with only the unknowns $a_0, a_2, a_4, \ldots \ldots \ldots, a_{k-1}$, and the other includes the odd-numbered equations with only the unknowns $a_1, a_3, a_5, \ldots \ldots \ldots, a_k$.

- Nonpolynomial Regression
  In the previous section, it is seen about polynomial regression due to a need for knowledge about the nature of the relationship between the variable. But if understanding the heart of the relationship between the variables is known, we can use any form of equation [78].

*Example 1:*
The equation $pv^\gamma$=constant represents the relation between the pressure and volume of an ideal gas which undergoes the adiabatic change. The parameter depends on the particular gas for which an estimate may be obtained from experimental data [78].

***Example 2:***

The function used in studying simple growth phenomena is also an example of non-polynomial regression. Please assume that the growth rate of the population is proportional to its size. In this case, the regression function is a simple exponential function. Let $y$ denote the size of the people at time instant $t$; then the growth rate can be written as

$$\frac{dy}{dt} = cy$$

$$\frac{dy}{y} = c\ dt$$

(10.22)

Integration on both sides of the equation (10.22), we get

$$\log y = ct + k$$

(10.23)

where $k$ is the constant of integration

Let $k = \log b$, then

$$\log y = ct + \log b$$

$$\log y - \log b = ct$$

$$\log\left(\frac{y}{b}\right) = ct$$

(10.24)

$$\frac{y}{b} = e^{ct}$$

$$y = be^{ct}$$

Let us write the set of $n$ points as $(t_1, y_1)$, $(t_2, y_2)$, … … …, $(t_n, y_n)$ represents the size of the growing population at the time $t_1, t_2, $ … … …, $t_n$. Now it is mandatory to estimate the value of $b$ and $c$ using least squares; hence the error value between $y_i$ and $be^{ct_i}$ is to be defined. The least-square error function can be defined as

$$G(b, c) = \sum_{i=1}^{n} [y_i - b\, e^{ct_i}]^2 \qquad (10.25)$$

Take the partial derivative of equation (10.25) with respect to $b$ and equate them to zero. We get the following equation

$$\sum_{i=1}^{n} 2[y_i - b\, e^{ct_i}](-e^{ct_i}) = 0$$

$$\sum_{i=1}^{n} [-y_i e^{ct_i} + b\, e^{2ct_i}] = 0$$

$$-\sum_{i=1}^{n} y_i e^{ct_i} + b\sum_{i=1}^{n} e^{2ct_i} = 0$$

$$b\sum_{i=1}^{n} e^{2ct_i} = \sum_{i=1}^{n} y_i e^{ct_i} \qquad (10.26)$$

Take the partial derivative of equation (10.25) with respect to $c$ and equate them to zero. We get the following equation.

$$\sum_{i=1}^{n} 2[y_i - b\, e^{ct_i}](-bt_i e^{ct_i}) = 0$$

$$\sum_{i=1}^{n} [-bt_i e^{ct_i} y_i + bt_i e^{ct_i} b\, e^{ct_i}] = 0$$

$$-b\sum_{i=1}^{n} t_i e^{ct_i} y_i + b^2 \sum_{i=1}^{n} t_i e^{2ct_i} = 0$$

$$-\sum_{i=1}^{n} t_i e^{ct_i} y_i + b\sum_{i=1}^{n} t_i e^{2ct_i} = 0$$

$$b\sum_{i=1}^{n} t_i e^{2ct_i} = \sum_{i=1}^{n} t_i e^{ct_i} y_i \qquad (10.27)$$

Equations (10.26) and (10.27) can be challenging to solve for the value of $b$ and $c$. To solve these equations, it is necessary to utilise numerical methods, which take much work. This type of problem can be used with the help of linear regression by letting $Y = \log y$ and $a = \log b$. Thus, we can rewrite equation (10.24) as

$$Y = a + ct \tag{10.28}$$

Now the problem can be reduced to the problem of fitting a straight line to a set of points in plane and thus to a simple problem in the least squares. These least square estimates the value of $c$ and $a$, which in turn estimate the value of $c$ and $b$.

## 10.3.2    Fuzzy Classification

Hui-Min Zhang *et al.* [9] explain fuzzy classification algorithms that use fuzzy logic to find the uncertainty and probability. This algorithm can use the undefined membership function, which is used to calculate the membership of a feature. Mostly used fuzzy membership functions, defined by Wing-Kuen Ling, 2007 [10], are the impulsive undefined membership function, triangular unclear membership function, right-sided trapezoidal fuzzy membership function and left-sided fuzzy membership function. This algorithm follows some fuzzy production rules defined by Kasabov [11], such as the simple fuzzy rule, weighted fuzzy production rule and generalized fuzzy production rule.

Figure 10.5 shows the fuzzy classification model proposed by Kasabov [11], which utilizes the fuzzy membership function. The information acquired from the database is applied to the fuzzy membership function with specific rules and interpreted the knowledge to get the desired outcome.

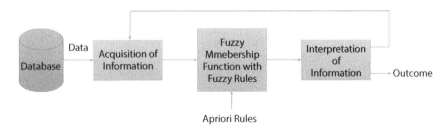

**Figure 10.5** Fuzzy classification model [11].

*Fuzzy Membership Function*

Let us consider a set "A." Set "A" used in the traditional set theory is called a crisp set, a set in which an element is defined as present or absent. At the same time, a fuzzy set is defined as set "A" characterized by a fuzzy membership function $f_A(x) \in [0,1]$.

$$x \in A, \quad if \ f_A(x)=1$$
$$x \notin A, \quad if \ f_A(x)=0 \tag{10.29}$$

As already mentioned, many fuzzy membership functions are used to perform the regression operation. Some of them are listed below with suitable equations defined by Wing-Kuen Ling, 2007 [10]:

Impulsive fuzzy membership function is given as:

$$f_A(x) = \begin{cases} 1, & x = x_0 \\ 0, & otherwise \end{cases} \tag{10.30}$$

Triangular fuzzy membership function is:

$$f_A(x) = \begin{cases} \dfrac{x - x_0}{a_1} + 1, & x_0 - a_1 \leq x \leq x_0 \\ \dfrac{x_0 - x}{a_2} + 1, & x_0 < x \leq x_0 + a_2 \\ 0 & otherwise \end{cases} \tag{10.31}$$

where $a_1, a_2 > 0$.

Right Sided Trapezoidal fuzzy membership function is given as:

$$f_A(x) = \begin{cases} 1, & x \geq x_0 \\ \dfrac{x - x_0}{a_1} + 1, & x_0 - a_1 \leq x < x_0 \\ 0 & otherwise \end{cases} \tag{10.32}$$

where $a_1 > 0$.

Left-sided trapezoidal fuzzy membership function is:

$$f_A(x) = \begin{cases} 1, & x \le x_0 - a_1 \\ \dfrac{x_0 - x}{a_1}, & x_0 - a_1 < x \le x_0 \\ 0 & otherwise \end{cases} \quad (10.33)$$

where $a_1 > 0$.

### Fuzzy Rules
As already mentioned, there are three types of fuzzy rules available, which Nikola K. Kasabov described in 1996 [11] and let us discuss each in detail. Before discussing the fuzzy rules, it is necessary to know the architecture of the fuzzy neural network, which is given in Figure 10.6.

Figure 10.6 shows that DI – Connections connected the rule layer with the condition element layer, whereas CF – Connections made connections to the rule layer with the action element layer [11].

### Simple Fuzzy Rule
The simple fuzzy rule is applied without considering the degree of Importance (DI), Certainty Factor (C.F.), Noise Tolerance (N.T.) coefficients, and Sensitivity Factors (S.F.).

### Weighted Fuzzy Production Rule
The weighted fuzzy production rule is applied with a degree of Importance (DI) and Certainty Factor (C.F.) without considering Noise Tolerance (N.T.) coefficients and Sensitivity Factors (S.F.).

### Generalized Fuzzy Production Rule
The generalized production rule is applied with a degree of importance (DI), certainty factor (CF), noise tolerance (NT) coefficients, and sensitivity factors (SF).

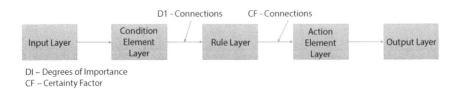

DI – Degrees of Importance
CF – Certainty Factor

**Figure 10.6** Architecture of fuzzy neural network [11].

### 10.3.3    Bayesian Networks

Cao *et al.* [12] describe a Bayesian network as a bi-directional learning system used for the probabilistic relationship among the variables present in the dataset. This network is generally modeled as a graph containing nodes and edges and typically allows to exchange of data between the nodes and utilizes the expectation from the model. The Bayesian network works on the principle of the chain rule theorem [12]. The Bayesian network is a system which it satisfies the two assumptions such as (i) all the predictor variables are conditionally independent given the class variable, and (ii) no hidden variables influence the prediction process. Let us consider two random variables, $C$ and $X$, denoting the class variable and observed attribute value vector, respectively. Now consider the test case , which is to be classified. Then Bayes rule can be applied to compute the probability of each class given the observed attribute value vector [41].

$$p(C = c|X = x) = \frac{p(C = c)p(X = x|C = c)}{p(X = x)} \qquad (10.34)$$

*Essential Connections of Bayesian Networks*
Figure 10.7 shows three essential connections defined by Taroni *et al.* [45], such as serial, diverging, and converging connections of the Bayesian Network. If the first node sends information to the second node, which sends information to the third node and repeats this process, then the connection is said to be serial. When a single node sends data to two or more nodes, the relationship is said to diverge. The link converges when two or more nodes send information to one node. The Bayesian network

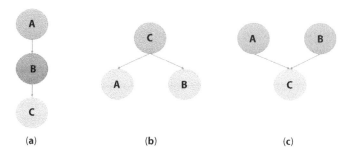

(a)                    (b)                    (c)

**Figure 10.7** Basic connections [45] in Bayesian Networks: (a) serial (b) diverging and (c) converging connection.

follows d-separation properties [45], where $d$ refers to the directional. The d-separation is the graphical criterion that states the condition for stopping the information flow between variables connected through chains.

The d-separated path can be formed in serial and diverging connection if the middle variable is instantiated. The d-separated path can be included in converging if the intermediate variable or one of its families has yet to receive data.

### Chain Rule

According to Bayes's Theorem [45], a joint probability distribution can be represented as the product of conditional probabilities. Let us consider the set of variables $x_1, x_2, \ldots \ldots \ldots, x_n$, then the joint probability density function of $x_1, x_2, \ldots \ldots \ldots, x_n$ is given by

$$p(x_1, x_2, \ldots \ldots \ldots, x_n) = \prod_i P(x_i | parent(x_i)) \qquad (10.35)$$

Now the chain rule [45] can be applied to Figure 10.7.

**Serial:** $p(A, B, C) = p(A)p(B|A)p(C|A, B) = p(A)p(B|A)p(C|B)$
**Diverging:** $p(C, A, B) = p(C)p(A|C)p(B|C)$
**Converging:** $p(A, B, C) = p(A)p(B)p(C|A, B)$

Figure 10.8 shows the various applications of Bayesian networks [46], such as gene regulatory networks, medicine, document verification, system biology, turbo code, spam filter, biomonitoring, image processing, semantic search and information retrieval.

It is used in the Gene Regulatory Network, which is used to imitate the system's performance in which DNA segments in a cell cooperate with another substance in the cell through the product of protein and RNA expression. It can also be used in the medical field to choose the medicine for the disease correctly. In the biomonitoring field, it is used to evaluate the various ingredients in the blood and urine, measure the chemical concentrations in the body, etc. The Bayesian network differentiates the different documents as a separate folders. For example, if the organization conducts any conference in which papers from various domains are received, this algorithm can separate the documents concerning domains. It can also retrieve detailed information from the database, similar to a document classifier. It can also be used as a semantic search in which it searches similar content regarding the content to be searched. It can be

**Figure 10.8** Application of Bayesian networks [46].

used in image processing by treating the image as a two dimensional (2D) signal for conversion operations such as enhancement, restoration, feature extraction, etc. It can be used as a spam filter to filter unwanted messages from the mailbox. It can be used in a turbo code to detect and correct the errors in the received signal received by wireless devices.

### 10.3.4   Decision Trees

Nevada *et al.* [13] illustrated the decision tree algorithm, which converts the dataset into a tree-like structure with two types of nodes: internal and leaf nodes. The internal node in the tree is used to test all the data in the data set, and the leaf node is used to classify the particular data. The various decision tree forms are classification, regression, decision tree forests, and K-means clustering. Figure 10.9 shows the decision tree consisting of the root, internal, and leaf nodes. A decision tree mainly depends on the divide and conquer process to identify the optimal split points within a tree. Qomariyah., N.N *et al.* [47] analysed the ordinal data which can be represented as pairwise comparison with various decision tree algorithms.

### 10.3.5   Artificial Neural Network

A Neural Network (NN) defined by Uhrig, 1995 [14] generally comprises various processing elements as three or more layers: the input layer, the buffer layer and the output layer. Figure 10.10 shows the architecture of ANN comprising three layers: input, buffer, and output layer.

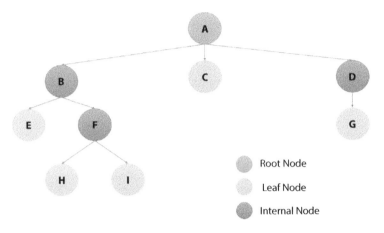

**Figure 10.9** Decision tree.

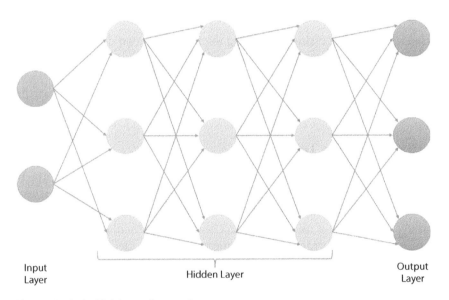

**Figure 10.10** Artificial neural network.

The first layer of the NN is the input layer, and the final layer is called the output layer. The intermediate layer (s) is called the buffer layer, which processes the data from the input layer and sends it to the next middle layer or output layer. Generally, learning and recall are the two main processes of an ANN. The most commonly used learning algorithm in the neural network is Hebbian Learning, Delta rule learning and competitive learning. The recall process occurs without any feedback connection, widely called a feed-forward recall process, from one layer to another. Another recall process is the feedback recall process, in which the output signals are fed back to the input multiple times until convergence criteria are met. These can be used in various applications such as servo control systems, noise filtering, image data compression, etc.

### 10.3.6    Classification

Classification algorithms are used to understand how the various input data fall under particular classes from the available dataset to predict future data. Logistic regression, random forest, SVM, classification trees, etc., are the various methods which employ the classification principle, as given by Louridas *et al.* [3].

- Logistics Regression
  Logistics regression illustrated by Yang *et al.* [15], shown in Figure 10.11, deals with data classification, which utilizes the principle of gradient descent algorithm. The gradient descent algorithm is used to solve for the best possible parameter of the loss function, mainly to minimise the error. This algorithm uses the sigmoid function to make the multivariate linear regression function non-linear [15].
  The sigmoid function is expressed as follows:

$$p = \frac{1}{1 + e^{-(mx+c)}}$$

  Figure 10.12 shows the predicted curve of regression using the logistics regression algorithm. This curve shows the exponentially rising curve, i.e. when the value of the independent variable is near zero; then the dependent variable increases slowly. If the independent variable goes

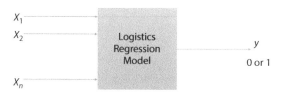

**Figure 10.11** Logistics regression model.

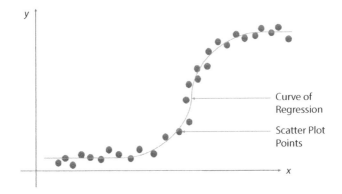

**Figure 10.12** Logistics regression csurve.

beyond zero, the dependent variable increases faster, and if the independent variable moves to infinity, the dependent variable remains constant. Figure 10.13 compares the linear and logistics regression curve in which the former attains the line and the latter reaches the angle.

- Random Forest
  This algorithm, defined by Jaiswal *et al.* [16], can be used in regression and classification problems. The term forest in the name is called a collection of trees, and the random forest is a collection of classification trees, otherwise called decision trees. The decision tree consists of a leaf node and an intermediate node. The former gives the members of the class variable or decision variable, predictor variable or independent variable, and the latter provides the entities of other

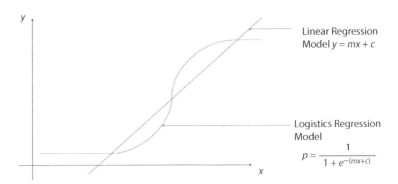

**Figure 10.13** Comparison of linear and logistics regression curve.

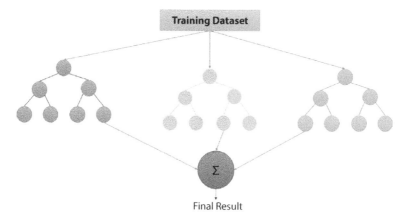

**Figure 10.14** Random forest classifier.

dependent variables. The random forest algorithm is used to build many decision trees and add a new tree at the bottom of the forest. Each tree has its classification, and the forest has to choose the type with the most votes from all the trees available. Figure 10.14 shows the random forest classifier in which many decision trees are formed and adds all the decisions from each tree to obtain the desired result.

- Support Vector Machine
  Like Random Forest, SVM, defined by Ghosh *et al.* [17], is also used in classification and regression problems. SVM is available in two flavours, namely the hyperplane method and kernel function method, where the former is the linear classifier model, and the latter is the non-linear classifier model. SVM is used to investigate data from the dataset and to identify the pattern or decision boundary. It is used in various applications such as filtering spam messages in the inbox, detecting the face from the photograph, identification of biological patterns, etc.

  Figure 10.15 shows the scatterplot for the database and the hyperplane formed by the SVM model using the data available in the database. SVM [48] is said to be a hyperplane classifier in which the class of hyperplanes $wx + b = 0$, $w \in R^n$, $b \in R$ are formed and correspond to the function $f(x) = sign(wx + b)$, which makes the decision. The objective of SVM is to predict the optimal hyperplane, which makes the

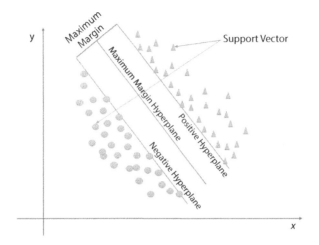

**Figure 10.15** Plot for support vector machine.

separation between two classes to be maximum. The hyperplane can be constructed using the solution of the constraint
quadratic optimization problem. The solution of the equation wx + b = 0, w ∈ $\mathcal{R}^n$, b ∈ $\mathcal{R}$ is given by

$$w = \sum_i v_i x_i \tag{10.36}$$

where $x_i$ is the subset of the training model that remain on the margin.

The optimal hyperplane is orthogonal to the line joining the two classes
and overlaps it halfway. The equation of hyperplane consisting of weight
vector and a threshold such that

$$y_i.(w.x_i + b) > 0 \tag{10.37}$$

Now rescale the weight and threshold such that the points which lie
closest to the hyperplane must satisfy

$$|w.x_i + b| = 1 \tag{10.38}$$

As a result of rescaling, one can get $(w, b)$ of the hyperplane, which satisfies the condition

$$y_i(w.x_i + b) \geq 1 \qquad (10.39)$$

The margin is measured perpendicularly to the hyperplane as

$$Margin = \frac{2}{\|w\|} \qquad (10.40)$$

where $\|w\|$ is the norm of the vector.

As mentioned, the objective is to maximise this margin, so one has to minimise $|w|$ subject to $y_i(w.x_i + b) \geq 1$.

## 10.4   Unsupervised Learning

Unsupervised learning, defined by Mrabet *et al.*, is used to identify the class that the data belongs to or to calculate the input data's numerical value without prior knowledge about the system during the training phase [2]. In this approach, the dataset contains only input value without specifying the solution (output) for the system at the particular input. This learning process includes clustering algorithms, such as K-means clustering, hierarchical clustering, genetic algorithms, Gaussian mixture models, etc. [3]. Unsupervised learning [49] is known as undirected learning. The main objective of this learning approach is to construct the inbuilt pattern within the dataset automatically without any prior knowledge.

- Clustering
  In general, clustering, defined by Rana *et al.* [49], groups similar patterns into a separate cluster. Clustering similar patterns in the dataset lead to reduced processing time and ease of data access. The various clustering algorithms in the literature are K-Means Clustering and Hierarchical Clustering.
- K-Means Clustering
  K-Means Clustering is a clustering process that utilizes the K-Means algorithm where the dataset does not understand the various classes (usually termed an unsupervised algorithm). The basic idea behind the K-Means Clustering, as illustrated by Rana *et al.* [49], is to calculate the Euclidian distance between the $K$ data elements and to move the data elements to the appropriate cluster based on the distance to the centroids. Each class has its centroids, and all the data

elements measure its distance with all the centroids. The data elements are moved to the particular type when the distance between its centroid is less than other centroids.

*Algorithm*
Step 1: Initialise the number of cluster centres (centroids) as c
Step 2: Initialise the centroids for each cluster centres
Step 3: Calculate the Euclidean Distance between each data element and the centroids
Step 4: Move each data element to the centroids whose Euclidean distance is small compared to other centroids
Step 5: The process is repeated until all data elements to the centroids by going to step 3
Step 6: Stop the process when there are no data elements without clustering
The K-Means Algorithm [49] to cluster the data into various clusters without prior knowledge of several groups. This algorithm makes high predictive accuracy, works well with a dataset containing a large number of data and is more sensitive to noise in the dataset.

- Hierarchical Clustering
  The three ways of hierarchical clustering defined by Rana *et al.* [49] are single linkage cluster, complete linkage cluster and average linkage cluster, formed by dividing the distance from one group to the other as the shortest, most significant and average length, respectively. The single linkage cluster formed by the short distance between the sets can be called connectedness or minimum method. The complete linkage cluster formed by the most significant distance between the groups can be called as diameter or maximum method.
  *Algorithm*
  Step 1: Initialise the cluster in which all the data elements from the dataset can be assigned with these initialized clusters. Each data element is considered an initial set, i.e., the number of groups equals to number of data elements, say n.
  Step 2: Initialise the sequence number $S_n$=0.
  Step 3: Determine the pair of clusters which lies very closest to each other and merge them, and this combined cluster can be treated as a new cluster and increment the $S_n$ value.

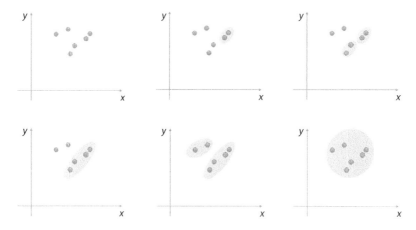

**Figure 10.16** Step-by-step procedure for hierarchical clustering algorithm.

Step 4: Calculate the distance between the new and old existing clusters, merge any two groups with the smallest space, and increment the $S_n$ value.
Step 5: Continue step 4 until $S_n+1=n$.
Step 6: Stop the process if $S_n+1=n$ is reached.

Figure 10.16 shows the step-by-step procedure for Hierarchical Clustering Algorithm in which 6 data points present in the dataset are initialized as six clusters. Then the clusters are grouped based on the minimum distance between the sets; thereby, the number of collections is reduced in the subsequent iterations.

## 10.5   Reinforcement Learning

Reinforcement Learning is one of the ML algorithms defined by Tan *et al.* [4], which is used to learn from others without having any data. The model must give rewards and punishment for the correct or incorrect outcome, respectively. From the rewards and discipline, the model learns and updates the knowledge of the system. This approach can work in a specific or uncertain environment that adjusts and realizes periodically based on the scores obtained as rewards or punishment. It is also defined by Yu *et al.* [5] as the trial-and-error process for learning the environment and trying to increase the reward by taking proper action. In reinforcement learning, defined by Spielberg *et al.* [6], the agent who acts as a controller interacts with an environment by applying some actions. As a result, the agent will

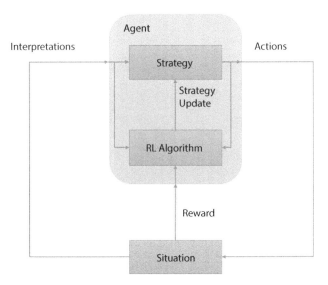

**Figure 10.17** Block diagram of reinforcement algorithm [50].

receive some reward points from the environment in discrete time steps. The reward obtained from the environment is used to ensure the selection of the best and optimal action [2]. Figure 10.17 shows the process of the reinforcement algorithm [50].

The main objective of the reinforcement algorithm is to make an agent, having two components called strategy and learner algorithm, to successfully process the task for any given situation. When the agent applies actions using some strategy to the given situation, the agent receives the interpretation and rewards. Based on the tips, the agent can update the strategic plan.

## 10.6 Hybrid Approach

The hybrid approaches of ML include semisupervised learning, self-supervised learning, and self-taught learning.

### 10.6.1 Semisupervised Learning

The semisupervised algorithm defined by Zeebaree *et al.* [18] is the algorithm which uses both labeled and unlabeled data to train the machine. It exists between the supervised and unsupervised algorithms. Clustering, dimensionality reduction, and classification process can utilize the semisupervised algorithm. This algorithm introduces the model using the labeled data in the managed learning method and compares it with the unsupervised model, which has unlabeled data; hence, the machine collects the features. To ensure the accuracy of the unsupervised algorithm, this algorithm trains the data set with less labeled data to get some information about the dataset and has a more significant amount of unlabeled data. The various methods used in this type of learning are self-training, cotraining, semisupervised SVM, graph-based approaches, and a generative model.

### 10.6.2   Self-Supervised Learning

In self-supervised learning given by Zhao *et al.* [19], the labels are created for the data present in the dataset using the unsupervised model, making the unlabeled data into the labeled data. Now these labeled data can be trained using a supervised learning algorithm. This learning algorithm is mainly used in various applications, such as converting a grayscale image into a color image, puzzle-solving problems, modeling language, etc.

### 10.6.3   Self-Taught Learning

The lack of training data in the supervised algorithm can be solved using a semisupervised learning algorithm in which a smaller number of labeled data and many unlabeled data, which has the same distribution as the labeled data, are used. But getting unlabeled data with the same distribution of labeled data is challenging. The more efficient algorithm proposed by Li *et al.* [20], self-taught learning, is used to avoid restricting the same distribution. This learning process is used to construct higher-level representation from the unlabeled data using a sparse coding mechanism, which is used to model the data set that follows the exponential distribution.

## 10.7   Other Common Approaches

The other common approaches for the ML algorithm are multi-task learning, active learning, outline learning (incremental learning and sequential learning), DL, transfer learning, federated learning, ensemble learning, adversarial learning, meta-learning (metric learning), targeted learning, concept learning, bayesian learning (analytical learning), inductive learning, multimodal learning, and curriculum learning.

### 10.7.1    Multitask Learning

According to Zhang *et al.* [21], the main objective of multitask learning is to use the valuable information available in multiple related tasks. Task clustering, decomposition, low-rank, feature, and task relation learning approaches are the approaches that utilise this multitask learning process. The multitask learning process is used with multiple other learning algorithms, such as active learning, reinforcement learning, unsupervised learning, multiview learning algorithms, etc. This algorithm uses a large volume of data compared to single-task learning.

### 10.7.2    Active Learning

The active learning process can overcome time-consuming problems in various ML algorithms. The main objective of this learning process, illustrated by Calma *et al.* [22], is to perform the sample selection process in which this algorithm selects the sample with the most information for labeling. Thus, this algorithm trains only the pieces chosen from the dataset, reducing the processing time. The three main active learning approaches are stream-based active learning, membership query learning and pool-based active learning.

### 10.7.3    Outline Learning

There are two types of outline learning: incremental learning and sequential learning.

- Incremental Learning Algorithm
  Polikar *et al.* [23] define the incremental learning algorithm as the learning process to select the most useful training data so that the architecture of the classifier has been grown or reduced. One of the most common incremental learning algorithms is Learn++, derived from the AdaBoost (Adaptive Boosting) algorithm. There are two class problems, namely weak learners and robust learners. The former does not utilize the boosting procedure, and the latter uses the boosting system, improving the classification performance. Thus, this algorithm is mainly established to enhance the performance of the weak classifier [23].

- Sequential Learning
  A definition of sequential learning is defined by Kataria *et al.* [24] as the learning process, which is used to analyze and model the system based on time series data representation which may be non-data adaptive (discrete wavelet transform, discrete Fourier transform and random mapping), data-adaptive (adaptive principal component analysis and singular value decomposition), and model-based approach (auto-regressive moving average and Markov chain). The various time series algorithms are the online sequential learning algorithm and the online sequential extreme learning algorithm (various variants of OSELM are Re-OSELM, k-OSELM, and OS-Fuzzy-ELM).

### 10.7.4    Transfer Learning

Zhuang *et al.* [26] define transfer learning as the learning technique in which one transfers knowledge earned from learning to others by sharing process. This is based on the principle of the theory of transfer given by psychologist C.H. Judd. This theorem states that the experience can arise from the learning to transfer, i.e., one should know how the knowledge gained from the learning should be shared. For example, if one organization contains one dataset with a label and another has another data set [26].

### 10.7.5    Federated Learning

Various challenges described by Li *et al.* [27] exist for distributed optimization problems, such as expensive communication, system heterogeneity, statistical heterogeneity, and privacy concern. To solve these challenges, federated learning has been developed. Federated learning is the learning process that remotely trains the statistical model to enable the predictive feature without reducing the user experience. This process involves a single global statistical model developed from tens to millions of devices located in remote positions [27].

### 10.7.6    Ensemble Learning

Huang *et al.* [28] formulate the principle behind ensemble learning: the ensemble (group of learners) has a more robust knowledge than a single learner. The procedure to develop ensemble learning is as follows:

- All the weak component learners (base learner or member learner) should be trained using a proper algorithm.
- Please select the best member learner and combine it to form a strong learner.

The algorithm used for this type of ensemble learning is AdaBoost (Adaptive Boost) and the Bagging algorithm.

### 10.7.7   Adversarial Learning

Tygar, 2011 [29] defined adversarial learning as the learning process in which the algorithm works perfectly even if improperly labeled data occur. One such algorithm which utilizes adversarial learning is the Reject On Negative Impact (RONI) which rejects the training input which will mislead the classifier model [29].

### 10.7.8   Meta-Learning

Meta-learning is defined by Hospedales *et al.* [30] as learning to learn in which it purifies the knowledge gained from various ML algorithms used to improve future learning performance. The three methods to develop the learning process are optimization, black-boxed/model-based, and metric-based/nonparametric [30].

- Metric Learning
  Hospedales *et al.* [30] clearly explain the principle behind this learning process: predicting the label of matching training points by comparing the validation points obtained by the testing process with those received by the training process. This process can be done with the help of matching neural networks, Siamese neural networks, prototypical neural networks, graph neural networks, and related neural networks.

### 10.7.9   Targeted Learning

Targeted learning is defined by Vowels *et al.* [31] as the learning process used to reduce the residual bias by employing a regularise extracted from the influence curve. The three steps involved in targeted learning are as follows:

- With the help of a conditional mean estimator, the conditional mean should be first estimated.
- Second, the propensity score (conditional probability of being assigned treatment) should be estimated using the propensity score estimator.
- Finally, the conditional mean estimator must be updated using the propensity score.

### 10.7.10    Concept Learning

Mirbakhsh *et al.* [32] define concept learning as the learning process in which it sees difficulty arises when different environment works together toward a common goal and learns the knowledge (concept) from that different environment and share that information with the other domain. The main principle behind concept learning is to explore "concept learning and reformation" from the view of an object and a feature.

### 10.7.11    Bayesian Learning

Bayesian learning, defined by Chen, 1969 [33], is the learning process that utilizes the Bayes estimates of the coefficients obtained from the reduced optimal information observed in the learning process. This provides the best and optimal system model from the *a priori* knowledge and needs to improve its weaknesses due to statistics, the complexity of structures, etc. It utilizes the Bayes theorem to overcome the above disadvantages. This can be used in both supervised and unsupervised learning.

- Analytical learning
  The main principle behind analytical learning illustrated by Ibid *et al.* [34] is that it constructs the model for the application program using a set of analytical equations. This model works only if the architecture and application behaviour assumption is matched. It can be used in various applications, such as the computation of stencils and the fast multipole method [34].

### 10.7.12    Inductive Learning

Inductive learning, defined by Dzeroski *et al.* [35], is the learning process of determining the set of relations using logic or purpose in an empirical database. The most common algorithm used in this learning process is the LINUS, which is defined as an inductive logic programming system that induces the virtual relation between positive and negative tuples in the database.

### 10.7.13    Multimodal Learning

As per Zhang *et al.*'s [36] definition of multimodal learning, it is the learning process based on embedding. This process learns from multimodal data instead of from unimodal data to improve the accuracy of the learning process. This can be performed by an unsupervised learning method, supervised learning method, zero-shot learning method, or transformer-based method.

### 10.7.14    Curriculum Learning

Wang *et al.* [37] define curriculum learning as the learning process of training the model from more detailed data to complex data. This replicates the human curriculum in that the learning starts from basics to advanced. Data level generalized curriculum learning is the reweighting target training distribution in T training stages. This learning process is to make better and faster Learning when the target task is challenging to analyze and has a distinct distribution with noisy, uneven quality and heterogeneous data.

## 10.8    DL Techniques

DL is used in various deep neural network applications, consisting of four commonly used architectures: CNN, autoencoder, restricted Boltzmann machine, and long short-term memory (LSTM) [25].

CNN is the most popular architecture for analyzing visual images by recognizing particular features. The commonly used CNN architecture is AlexNet, Inception, ResNet, VGG, and DCGAN [25]. The autoencoder is the technique which uses an unsupervised algorithm to convert the original dataset into a reduced dataset using the dimensionality reduction technique. It consists of an encoder and decoder to generalise the operation of principal component analysis for the dimensionality process [25].

The following architecture, Restricted Boltzmann Machine (RBM), uses unlabeled data for model construction utilizing the unsupervised learning algorithm. This model construction is done by learning the probability distribution of the unlabeled data present in the dataset [25]. The LSTM architecture designs the Recurrent Neural Network (RNN) by retaining the information of the initial state. Hence, this model requires some amount of memory to store that information for the awareness of the state [25]. The most commonly used DL architecture, such as the RNN and the CNN, are explained in the following sections.

## 10.8.1   Recurrent Neural Network (RNN)

RNN [51] creates a cycle by connecting the various nodes on the basics of temporal dynamic behaviour; that is, it allows the output of some nodes to affect the subsequent inputs of some nodes. RNN structure is mainly designed for sequential data. These networks can process variable-length input sequences. They are suitable for handwriting recognition [52] and speech recognition [53]. The detailed architecture of the RNN is represented in Figure 10.18, and the structure of the simple RNN is shown in Figure 10.19.

RNN also refers to networks with infinite impulse response in contrast to CNN with the finite impulse response. Both the finite impulse and the infinite impulse RNNs have stored state in addition that is directly controlled by the neural network. This stored state can be replaced by introducing feedback or time delays using another network or graph. Such states which can be held are called gated states, which form an integral part of LSTMs and gated recurrent units (GRU). "Hidden-to-Hidden," "Hidden-to-Output," and "Input-to-Hidden" are the three types of deep RNN techniques. Compared to CNN, the added advantage of RNN is less feature compatibility and minimized difficulty level of learning. The disadvantages of RNN are its sensitivity towards the gradient exploding and vanishing problem. The angles decay exponentially when the large or small derivatives are reduplicated in the training phase. Also, the sensitivity decays when the network stops thinking about the initial data over the new input data. This problem is overcome by using the LSTM technique [54]. When the new input data is given, the network stops thinking about

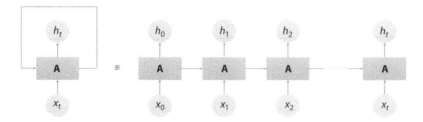

**Figure 10.18** RNN detailed architecture.

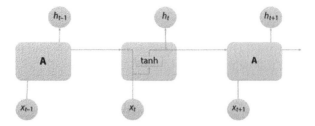

**Figure 10.19** Simple RNN.

the initial ones; this sensitivity decays over time. This issue is rectified by using LSTM. As explained in the later sections, the residual connections in DNN can reduce the vanishing gradient effect.

Four different structures of RNN are used to solve various categories of problems, as depicted in Figure 10.20 They are:

1. *One to One: To solve the problem with one input and output.*
2. *One to Many: To solve the problem with one piece of informa-tion and many results.*
3. *Many to One: To solve the problem with multiple inputs and one output.*
4. *Many to Many: To solve the problem with various inputs and outputs.*

- Long- and Short-Term Memory (LSTM)
  LSTM acts as the memory block, forming the RNN archi-tecture's building blocks. It is used in a network to provide recurrent connections to memory blocks. Each memory block has numerous cells that can hold the network's secular

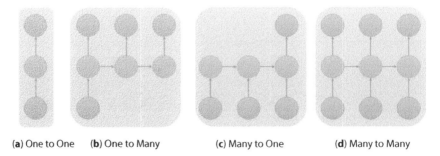

(a) One to One     (b) One to Many        (c) Many to One        (d) Many to Many

**Figure 10.20** Types of the structure of RNN.

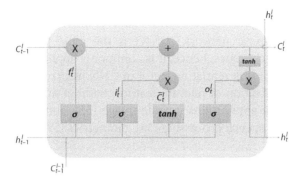

**Figure 10.21** LSTM cell.

states. On the other hand, it also controls the flow of information, which is done by the gated units. The primary role
of LSTMs is to enhance the memory of the RNNs to remember inputs over a long period. The LSTM consists of three
gates: the information, forget and output. The LSTM structure used in RNN is shown in the following Figure 10.21.

• Gated Recurrent Unit (GRU)
  The Gated Recurrent Unit (GRU) is a variation of LSTM.
  GRU consists of two gates one is the update gate, and another
  is the reset gate. The gates are designed to store information
  for a long time without vanishing at a particular time. It is
  mainly used to solve the vanishing gradient problem. The
  GRU architecture is shown in Figure 10.22.

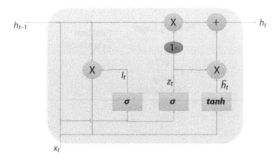

**Figure 10.22** GRU cell.

### 10.8.2   Convolutional Neural Network

Convolutional neural network (CNN) is the most popular algorithm among the DL techniques; hence, it is commonly applied to varied applications. The major differentiating factor of CNN from other methods is its automatic identification of relevant features without human interference. Various real-time applications include image [55], audio [56] and video recognition [57], speech processing [58], biometrics [59], computer vision [60], etc.

The main benefits of CNN are listed below:

1. *The weight-sharing capability of the CNN enables it to reduce the number of trainable parameters, which in turn supports the network's generalization and avoids overfitting.*
2. *The network output can be highly reliant on the features extracted and highly organized by learning the feature extraction and classification layers.*
3. *CNN is used for implementing large-scale networks, which is much easier than other related techniques.*

CNN flowchart is shown below:

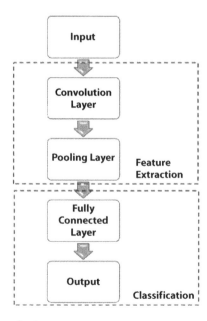

**Figure 10.23**  CNN flow chart.

The architecture of the CNN [61, 62] contains four primary layers, as represented in Figure 10.23, which are briefly explained below:

- Convolutional layer

  The layer of prime importance in the CNN architecture is the convolution layer. It consists of kernels which are nothing but convolutional filters, which are discrete weights in the form of a grid. At the beginning of the training process, the filters are assigned with random values of weights. This is then adjusted in learning significant features by the kernel. The input of the CNN is the visual image which is multi-channelled. The RGB image has three channels, whereas the Grayscale image has a single track. First, the idea is scaled both horizontally and vertically by the kernel. The dot product of the seed and the input image is obtained. This process is carried out until the kernel slides through the entire picture. The feature map of the output is obtained from the dot product values. The application type determines the convolutional filter's padding and stride values. The stride value determines the size of the feature map, where the feature map has less dimension if the stride value is high. The value of padding determines the border information of the input image; by applying it to a pad, the size of the input image becomes small. This is both memories effective and reduces cost since the matrix operation is costlier than the dot product in CNN. Also, the neighbouring layers in CNN do not have allocated weights. Learning a single group of consequences for the entire input reduces the cost and training time as it is not required to learn additional weights. The most common filters used in CNN are as follows: Laplacian filter, Prewitt filters, Sobel filters and so on.

- Pooling Layer

  The primary function of the pooling layer is to reduce the large-size feature maps to small-size feature maps by sub-sampling. It maintains the dominating information at each stage of pooling. The kernel's size and stride are initially assigned before the pooling operation, similar to the convolution layer. Several pooling methods include tree pooling, gated pooling, average pooling, min pooling, max pooling, global average pooling (GAP), and global max pooling. The appropriate pooling type is chosen according to the application. The most frequently used pooling methods are maximum (max), minimum (min), and GAP pooling. In many instances, the performance of the overall CNN depends on the pooling layer, as it plays a significant role in determining whether the input image contains a certain feature and accurately locate the part.

• Activation Function
  The primary function of the activation layer is to map the input to the output. The information is computed using a weighted summation of the bias and the neuron input. This determines if the activation function has to use or not use a neuron for a particular information to generate corresponding output. The non-linear activation function, where the relationship between the input and the result is non-linear, is employed in the CNN after all layers with weights in the architecture. These layers support the CNN architecture to learn more complicated things. As the activation layer uses the method of error backpropagation for training the network, the function needs to decide the most significant features of the input. The most commonly employed activation functions are explained as follows:

  a. *Sigmoid:* The sigmoid activation function gives zero or one output to the input of real numbers. It has an S-shaped function curve and can be mathematically represented as.

$$\sigma(x) = \frac{1}{1+e^{-x}} \qquad (10.41)$$

  b. *Tanh:* The Tanh activation function output is restricted between -1 and 1 for the actual number input.
  c. *ReLU:* ReLU is the most commonly used activation function which converts the absolute value to positive numbers. The mathematical representation of the process is *max(0,x)*.
     The main advantage of using this function is the lesser computational load. The main issue of using this function is when an error backpropagation algorithm with a more significant gradient passes through it, the ReLU updates the weights such that the neuron cannot be

activated again, called the "Dying ReLU" problem. This problem can be overcome using alternatives such as Leaky ReLU, Noisy ReLU, or Parametric Linear Units.

d.  *Leaky ReLU:* The leaky ReLU never ignores the negative input, unlike ReLU, which is instead used for solving the dying ReLU problem. The mathematical representation of the leaky ReLU is *max(0.1x, x).*
    Here, m represents the leak factor mostly set to a minimal value of 0.001.

e.  *Noisy ReLU:* Noisy ReLU employs Gaussian distribution to make ReLU loud.

f.  *Parametric Linear Units:* This function is similar to that of the Leaky ReLU. The only differentiating factor is that the model training process updates the leak factor instead of choosing the minimum fixed value.

- Fully Connected Layer
  The fully connected layer where each neuron is connected to all previous layer neurons marks the end of each CNN architecture. This layer is used as a classifier for the CNN. It is similar to the feed-forward ANN of multi-layer perceptron (MLP). The output of the last convolutional layer or pooling layer is input to the fully connected layer, which is obtained by flattening the feature maps to vectors. The production of the fully connected layer is the final output class or label.

- Loss Functions
  The output layer, which provides the final classification, is the last layer where the loss functions are used to measure the error in prediction. This error helps in optimizing the CNN model learning performance. This error results from the difference between actual and predicted values. The loss functions use the parameter's actual and estimated output as input to calculate the error. Various types of loss functions include softmax, Euclidean and hinge loss functions which are described below:

  a.  *Softmax Loss Function:* Softmax loss function, also called the log-loss function, calculates the CNN performance. It generates the probability distribution in the output layer by employing softmax activations.

    *b.* *Euclidean Loss Function:* Also called the mean square error, the Euclidean loss function is mainly used in regression problems.

    *c.* *Hinge Loss Function:* The hinge loss function is mainly applied to binary classification problems. The process tries to maximise the margin for binary objective classes. It is used primarily for SVMs that focus on max-imum-margin-based classification.

### 10.8.3   Real-Time Applications of DL

The DL techniques have a vast range of real-time applications owing to their efficiency, the feasibility of real-time databases and the computational power of today's world.

*Automatic vehicles:* The recent research in automobile engineering has paved the way for advanced technologies such as driverless cars [63]. DL automatically detects traffic signals [64] and acts accordingly. Also, AI is employed for vehicle collision avoidance [65], an excellent boon for avoiding road accidents.

*Satellite communication:* DL is used for satellite observation and weather prediction [66] and helps monitor the borders for defence [67].

*Medical Research:* Many researchers automatically employ DL techniques to diagnose anomalies and detect diseases [68]. It has also been implemented to monitor sick patients and alert them in case of emergencies [69].

*Industrial Automation:* DL is helping in automating difficult and hazard-ous jobs [70] to avoid human intervention and ensure safety. It also helps detect the safe distance from heavy machinery to prevent accidents [71].

*Electronics:* DL has powered many technologies, such as speech transla-tion [72], that have empowered people to travel beyond boundaries. Home assistance and automation [73] have enabled reduced electricity costs and easier access. For example, managing home devices through voice com-mands [74–76] has made life easier.

*Communication:* Recent trends in DL-based management of wireless [77] and optical [78] communication networks and their performance moni-toring [79–81] has resulted in more efficient and reconfigurable networks for their intelligent management of both user requirements and available resources.

## 10.9    Conclusion

The autonomous and intelligent system needs the process involved in it should be free from human intervention. ML and DL are efficient techniques to make the system smarter. Firstly, this chapter discussed the basics of ML and DL in detail. Then various ML techniques were discussed, supervised, unsupervised, reinforcement learning, and semi-supervised learning techniques. Other vital concepts, such as multitask, ensemble, and multimodal, were presented beside the primary and hybrid approaches. Regression, its analysis and its types are also discussed. Secondly, this chapter focussed on DL techniques and their types. Also, the various activation and loss functions adopted in DL are studied in detail. Finally, the real-time applications of DL in multiple fields have been stated.

## Acknowledgment

The authors gratefully acknowledge the financial support from the Science and Engineering Research Board (SERB), Government of India, Grant No: EEQ/2019/000647.

## References

1. Singh., A., Thakur, N., Sharma, A., A review of supervised machine learning algorithms. *International Conference on Computing for Sustainable Global Development (INDIACom)*, vol. 3, pp. 1310–1315, 2016.
2. El Mrabet., M.A., El Makkaoui., K., Faize, A., Supervised machine learning: A survey. *International Conference on Advanced Communication Technologies and Networking (CommNet)*, pp. 4, 1–10, 2021.
3. Louridas, P. and Ebert, C., Machine learning. *IEEE Softw.*, 33, 110–115, 2016.
4. Tan, Z. and Karakose, M., Optimised deep reinforcement learning approach for dynamic system. *IEEE International Symposium on Systems Engineering (ISSE)*, pp. 1–4, 2020.
5. Yu., T. and Zhen, W.G., A reinforcement learning approach to power system stabiliser, in: *IEEE Power & Energy Society General Meeting*, pp. 1–5, 2009.

6.  Spielberg., S.P.K., Gopaluni, R.B., Loewen., P.D., Deep reinforcement learning approaches for process control. *International Symposium on Advanced Control of Industrial Processes (AdCONIP)*, vol. 6, pp. 201–206, 2017.

7.  Santos., K. J. de O, Menezes., A.G., de Carvalho., A.B., Montesco., C.A.E., Supervised learning in the context of educational data mining to avoid university students' dropouts. *IEEE International Conference on Advanced Learning Technologies (ICALT)*, vol. 19, pp. 207–208, 2019.

8.  Huang., M., Theory and implementation of linear regression. *International Conference on Computer Vision, Image and Deep Learning (CVIDL)*, pp. 210–217, 2020.

9.  Zhang., H.-M., Han, L.-Q., Wang., Z., A fuzzy classification system and its application. *Proceedings of the 2003 International Conference on Machine Learning and Cybernetics*, vol. 4, pp. 2582–2586, 2003.

10. Ling., W.-K., *Non-linear digital filters, analysis and applications*. Academic Press, London, 2007.

11. Kasabov., N.K., Learning fuzzy rules and approximate reasoning in fuzzy neural networks and hybrid systems. *.Fuzzy Sets Syst.*, 82, 135–149, 1996.

12. Cao., Y., Study of the Bayesian networks. *International Conference on E-Health Networking Digital Ecosystems and Technologies (EDT)*, pp. 172–174, 2010.

13. Nevada., A., Ansari, A.N., Patil., S., Sonkamble., B.A., Overview of the use of decision tree algorithms in machine learning. *IEEE Control and System Graduate Research Colloquium*, pp. 37–42, 2011.

14. Uhrig., R.E., Introduction to artificial neural networks. *Proceedings of IECON'95 - Annual Conference on IEEE Industrial Electronics*, vol. 21, pp. 33–37, 1995.

15. Yang., Z. and Li., D., Application of logistic regression with filter in data classification. *Chinese Control Conference (CCC)*, vol. 38, pp. 3755–3759, 2019.

16. Jaiswal., J.K. and Samikannu, R., Application of random forest algorithm on feature subset selection and classification and regression. *World Congress on Computing and Communication Technologies (WCCCT)*, pp. 65–68, 2017.

17. Ghosh., S., Dasgupta., A., Swetapadma., A., A study on support vector machine based linear and non-linear pattern classification. *International Conference on Intelligent Sustainable Systems (ICISS)*, pp. 24–28, 2019.

18. Zeebaree., D.Q., Hasan, D.A., Abdulazeez., A.M., Ahmed., F.Y.H., Hasan, R.T., Machine learning semi-supervised algorithms for gene selection: A review. *IEEE International Conference on System Engineering and Technology (ICSET)*, vol. 11, pp. 165–170, 2021.

19. Zhao, A., Dong, J., Zhou., H., Self-supervised learning from multi-sensor data for sleep recognition. *IEEE Access*, 8, 93907–93921, 2020.

20. Li., S., Li., K., Fu., Y., Self-taught low-rank coding for visual learning. *IEEE Trans. Neural Netw. Learn. Syst.*, 29, 645–656, 2018.

21. Zhang., Y. and Yang., Q., A survey on multi-task learning. *IEEE Trans. Knowl. Data Eng.*, 34, 5586–5609, 2022.

22. Calma., A., Stolz., M., Kottke., D., Tomforde., S., Sick, B., Active learning with realistic data - a case study. *International Joint Conference on Neural Networks (IJCNN)*, pp. 1–8, 2018.
23. Polikar., R., Upda., L., Upda., S.S., Honavar, V., Learn++: An incremental learning algorithm for supervised neural networks. *IEEE Trans. Syst. Man Cybern. Part C Appl. Rev.*, 31, 497–508, 2001.
24. Kataria., R. and Prasad, T., A survey on time series online sequential learning algorithms. *IEEE International Conference on Computational Intelligence and Computing Research (ICCIC)*, pp. 1–4, 2017.
25. Shrestha., A. and Mahmood, A., Review of deep learning algorithms and architectures. *IEEE Access*, 7, 53040–53065, 2019.
26. Zhuang, F. *et al.*, A comprehensive survey on transfer learning. *Proc. IEEE*, 109, 43–76, 2021.
27. Li., T., Sahu, A.K., Talwalkar, A., Smith, V., Federated learning: Challenges, methods, and future directions. *IEEE Signal Process. Mag.*, 37, 50–60, 2020.
28. Huang., F., Xie., G., Xiao., R., Research on ensemble learning. *International Conference on Artificial Intelligence and Computational Intelligence*, pp. 249–252, 2009.
29. Tygar., J.D., Adversarial machine learning. *IEEE Internet Comput.*, 15, 4–6, 2011.
30. Hospedales., T., Antoniou, A., Michelli, P., Storkey, A., Meta-learning in neural networks: A survey. *IEEE Trans. Pattern Anal. Mach. Intell.*, 44, 5149–5169, 2022.
31. Vowels., M.J., Camgoz., N.C., Bowden., R., Targeted VAE: Variational and targeted learning for causal inference. *IEEE International Conference on Smart Data Services (SMDS)*, pp. 132–141, 2021.
32. Mirbakhsh., N., Didandeh., A., Afsharchi., M., Concept learning games: The game of query and response. *IEEE/WIC/ACM International Conference on Web Intelligence and Intelligent Agent Technology*, pp. 234–238, 2010.
33. Chen., C.-H., A Theory of bayesian learning systems. *IEEE Trans. Syst. Sci. Cybern.*, 5, 30–37, 1969.
34. Ibid., H., Meng, S., Dobon., O., Olson., L., Gropp., W., Learning with analytical models. *IEEE International Parallel and Distributed Processing Symposium Workshops (IPDPSW)*, pp. 778–786, 2019.
35. Dzeroski., S. and Lavrac., N., Inductive Learning in deductive databases. *IEEE Trans. Knowl. Data Eng.*, 5, 939–949, 1993.
36. Zhang., C., Yang., Z., He., X., Deng., L., Multimodal intelligence: Representation learning, information fusion, and applications. *IEEE J. Sel. Top. Signal Process.*, 14, 478–493, 2020.
37. Wang., X., Chen, Y., Zhu., W., A survey on curriculum learning. *IEEE Trans. Pattern Anal. Mach. Intell.*, 44, 4555–4576, 2022.
38. https://in.mathworks.in/helps/stats

39. Sarker., I.H., Machine learning: Algorithms, real-world applications and research directions. *SN Comput. Sci.*, 2, 160, 2021.

40. Kurilov., R., Haile-Kains, B., Brors, B., Assessment of modelling strategies for drug response prediction in cell lines and xenografts. *Sci. Rep.*, 10, 2849, 2020.

41. John, G. H. and Langley, P., Estimating continuous distributions in Bayesian classifiers. *Proc. Eleventh Conf. Uncertainty Artif. Intell. (UAI1995)*, arXiv preprint arXiv: 1302.4964, 338–345, 1995, 2013, https://doi.org/10.48550/arXiv.1302.4964.

42. Hope., J.H., A least-squares fitting technique for use with sizeable non-linear plant models. *IEE Colloquium on Model Validation for Control System Design and Simulation*, pp. 4/1–4/2, 1989.

43. Orbeck., T., Discussion of the statistical method used to analyse thermal evaluation data. *E.I. Electrical Insulation Conference Materials and Application*, pp. 111–114, 1962.

44. Rubin., I., Continuous regression techniques using analog computers. *IRE Trans. Electron. Comput.*, 11, 691–699, 1962.

45. Taroni, F., Biedermann, A., Garbolino, P., Aitken, C.G., A general approach to Bayesian networks for the interpretation of evidence. *Forensic Sci. Int.*, 139, 5–16, 2004.

46. https://data-flair.training/blogs/bayesian-network-applications/

47. Qomariyah., N.N., Heriyanni., E., Fajar., A.N., Kazakov., D., Comparative analysis of decision tree algorithm for learning ordinal data expressed as pairwise comparisons. *International Conference on Information and Communication Technology (ICoICT)*, vol. 8, pp. 1–4, 2020.

48. Hearst., M.A., Dumais., S.T., Osuna., E., Platt., J., Scholkopf., B., Support vector machines. *IEEE Intell. Syst. Appl.*, 13, 18–28, 1998.

49. Rana., S. and Garg., R., Application of hierarchical clustering algorithm to evaluate students performance of an institute. *Second International Conference on Computational Intelligence & Communication Technology (CICT)*, pp. 692–697, 2016.

50. https://in.mathworks.com/help/reinforcement-learning/ug/what-is-reinforcement-learning.html

51. Grossberg, S., Recurrent neural networks. *Scholarpedia*, 8, 2, 1888, 2013.

52. Pham, V., Bluche, T., Kermorvant, C., Louradour, J., Dropout improves recurrent neural networks for handwriting recognition. *14th IEEE International Conference on Frontiers in Handwriting Recognition*, pp. 285–290, 2014.

53. Graves, A., Mohamed, A.-R., Hinton, G., Speech recognition with deep recurrent neural networks. *IEEE International Conference on Acoustics, Speech and Signal Processing*, 2013.

54. Salehinejad, H., Sankar, S., Barfett, J., Colak, E., Valaee, S., Recent advances in recurrent neural networks. *arXiv*, 3, 1–21, 2017, preprint arXiv:1801.01078.

55. Liu, Q. *et al.*, A review of image recognition with a deep convolutional neural network, in: *International Conference on Intelligent Computing*, Springer, Cham, 2017.

56. Zhang, S. *et al.*, Multimodal deep convolutional neural network for audio-visual emotion recognition. *Proceedings of the 2016 ACM on International Conference on Multimedia Retrieval*, 2016.

57. Guangle., Y., Tao, L., Jiandan, Z., A review of convolutional-neural-network-based action recognition. *Pattern Recognit. Lett.*, 118, 14–22, 2019.

58. Pandey, A. and Wang., D., A new framework for CNN-based speech enhancement in the time domain. *IEEE/ACM Transactions on Audio, Speech, and Language Processing*, pp. 1179–1188, 2019.

59. Zhang, Y., Huang., Y., Wang., L., Yu., S., A comprehensive study on gait biometrics using a standard CNN-based method. *Pattern. Recognit.*, 93, 228–236, 2019.

60. Khan, S., Rahmani., H., Ali Shah., S.A., Bennamoun., M., A guide to convolutional neural networks for computer vision. Synthesis lectures on computer vision. pp. 1–207, Springer, Morgan & Claypool Publisher, Kentfield, CA, 2018.

61. Jmour, N., Zayen, S., Abdelkrim, A., Convolutional neural networks for image classification. *IEEE International Conference on Advanced Systems and Electric Technologies*, pp. 397–402, 2018.

62. Alzubaidi, L., Zhang., J., Humaidi, A.J., Al-Dujaili, A., Duan, Y., Al-Shamma, O., Santamaría., J., Fadhel, M.A., Al-Amidie, M., Farhan, L., Review of deep learning: Concepts, CNN architectures, challenges, applications, future directions. *J. Big Data*, 8, 1–74, 2021.

63. Ni, J., Chen, Y., Chen, Y., Zhu, J., Ali, D., Cao, W., A survey on theories and applications for self-driving cars based on deep learning methods. *Appl. Sci.*, 10, 2749, 2020.

64. Tabernik, D. and Skočaj, D., Deep learning for large-scale traffic-sign detection and recognition. *IEEE Trans. Intell. Transp. Syst.*, 1, 1427–1440, 2019.

65. Lai, Y.K., Ho, C.Y., Huang, Y.H., Huang, C.W., Kuo, Y.X., Chung, Y.C., Intelligent vehicle collision-avoidance system with deep learning. *IEEE Asia Pacific Conference on Circuits and Systems (APCCAS)*, pp. 123–126, 2018.

66. Ren, X., Li, X., Ren, K., Song, J., Xu, Z., Deng, K., Wang, X., Deep learning-based weather prediction: A survey. *Big Data Res.*, 23, 1–11, 2021.

67. Shi, Y., Sagduyu, Y.E., Erpek, T., Davaslioglu, K., Lu, Z., Li, J.H., Adversarial deep learning for cognitive radio security: Jamming attack and defence strategies. *IEEE International Conference on Communications Workshops (ICC Workshops)*, pp. 1–6, 2018.

68. Li, R., Zhang, W., Suk, H.I., Wang, L., Li, J., Shen, D., Ji, S., Deep learning based imaging data completion for improved brain disease diagnosis, in:

*International Conference on Medical Image Computing and Computer Assisted Intervention*, Vol. 8675, pp. 305–312, Springer, Cham, 2014.

69. Davoudi, A., Malhotra, K.R., Shickel, B., Siegel, S., Williams, S., Ruppert, M., Bihorac, E., Ozrazgat-Baslanti, T., Tighe, P.J., Bihorac, A., Rashidi, P., Intelligent ICU for autonomous patient monitoring using pervasive sensing and deep learning. *Sci. Rep.*, 9, 1, 1–13, 2019.

70. Maschler, B. and Weyrich, M., Deep transfer learning for industrial automation: A review and discussion of new techniques for data-driven machine learning. *IEEE Ind. Electron. Mag.*, 15, 2, 65–75, 2021.

71. Hou, L., Chen, H., Zhang, G., Wang, X., Deep learning-based applications for safety management in the AEC industry: A review. *Appl. Sci.*, 11, 2, 821, 2021.

72. Tan, Y., Design of intelligent speech translation system based on deep learning. *Mobile Inf. Syst.*, 2022, 1–7, 2022.

73. Popa, D., Pop, F., Serbanescu, C., Castiglione, A., Deep learning model for home automation and energy reduction in an innovative home environment platform. *Neural Comput. Appl.*, 31, 5, 1317–1337, 2019.

74. Filipe, L., Peres, R.S., Tavares, R.M., Voice-activated intelligent home controller using machine learning. *IEEE Access*, 9, 66852–66863, 2021.

75. Kumar, K., Chaudhury, K., Tripathi, S.L., Future of machine learning (ML) and deep learning (DL) in healthcare monitoring system, in: *Machine Learning Algorithms for Signal and Image Processing*, pp. 293–313, Wiley-IEEE Press, New Jersey, 2023.

76. Prasanna, D.L. and Tripathi, S.L., Machine and deep-learning techniques for text and speech processing, in: *Machine Learning Algorithms for Signal and Image Processing*, pp. 115–128, Wiley-IEEE Press, New Jersey, 2023.

77. Zappone, A., Di Renzo, M., Debbah, M., Wireless networks design in the era of deep Learning: Model-based, AI-based, or both? *IEEE Trans. Commun.*, 67, 10, 7331–7376, 2019.

78. Karanov, B., Chagnon, M., Thouin, F., Eriksson, T.A., Bülow, H., Lavery, D., Bayvel, P., Schmalen, L., End-to-end deep learning of optical fibre communications. *J. Lightwave Technol.*, 36, 20, 4843–4855, 2018.

79. Sindhumitha, K., Jeyachitra, R.K., Manochandar, S., Joint modulation format recognition and optical performance monitoring for efficient fibre-optic communication links using ensemble deep transfer learning. *Opt. Eng.*, 61, 11, 116103, 2022.

80. Hoel, P.G., *Introduction to mathematical statistics*, Third edition, John Wiley & Sons, Inc, London, 1962.

81. Ghayal, V.S. and Jeyachitra, R.K., Efficient eye diagram analyser for optical modulation format recognition using deep learning technique, in: *Advances in Electrical and Computer Technologies*, pp. 655–666, Springer, Singapore, 2020.

# 11

# Handwriting and Speech-Based Secured Multimodal Biometrics Identification Technique

**Swathi Gowroju[1]\*, V. Swathi[2] and Ankita Tiwari[3]**

*[1]DS Department, Sreyas Institute of Engineering and Technology,
Hyderabad, India*
*[2]CSE Department, Sreyas Institute of Engineering and Technology,
Hyderabad, India*
*[3]Department of Mathematics, Koneru Lakshmaiah Educational Foundation,
Vijayawada, India*

## Abstract

Biometric systems are crucial for security in various industries, especially banking and law enforcement. While unimodal biometric systems have been widely studied, multimodal biometrics is emerging as a critical pattern recognition component. This proposed work focuses on developing a secure authentication procedure that uses voice and signature recognition in a multimodal system for higher accuracy and lower error rates. The proposed remedy is assessed using the Kaggle TensorFlow Speech Recognition Challenge dataset. Our findings and discussions demonstrate that the suggested approach can achieve an accuracy rate of approximately 96.05%, meeting our goal, and low FAR and FRR, enhancing the multimodal authenticity of our system. This study contributes to developing robust and reliable multimodal biometric systems with significant implications for various security applications.

*Keywords*: Multimodal biometrics in biometrics, speech and handwriting profiles, dynamic envelope transformation fusion, feature-level fusion on a score-level, Mel warped cepstral coefficients

*\*Corresponding author*: swathigowroju@sreyas.ac.in

Sandeep Kumar, Deepika Ghai, Arpit Jain, Suman Lata Tripathi and Shilpa Rani (eds.)
*Multimodal Biometric and Machine Learning Technologies: Applications for Computer Vision*,
(227–250) © 2023 Scrivener Publishing LLC

## 11.1   Introduction

The most typical identification method is confirmation, which grants network access to frameworks by coordinating client data and storing that data in an authorized dataset. In terms of usernames and passwords, conventional confirmation frameworks are unquestionably more attackable than biometric validation frameworks. The art of using physical or fundamental characteristics, such as voice, walk, mark, keystroke components, iris, hand vein, face, finger vein, palm print, and fingerprints, to differentiate customers is known as biometric-recognizable evidence [1]. The core characteristics of biometric frameworks are uniqueness (the technology should be distinct for each individual, regardless of whether they are twins), broad-minded, permanence, quantifiability, and usability. The use of biometrics is widespread, but the frameworks are at threat because the environment and their use may affect estimations and need reconciliation, as well as the fact that compromised biometrics cannot be reset. Biometric systems rely on precise knowledge of exceptional biological characteristics [2]. ECG signal, cornea, and distinctive markings are the three biometric traits that many works often attempt to use.

An ECG signal is a signal that the heart transmits electrically. Using sensors linked to a human's chest, it is frequently approximated in an advanced method [3, 4]. Because of its frequent occurrence in biometric determinations, it has recently been used for validation. One benefit of ECG-based verification is aliveness, which differs from other verification methods like finger imprints and secret essential confirmation since living individuals often only employ it. Also, a broader spectrum of persons who cannot provide standard biometrics, such as distinctive markings, iris scans, or palm prints, such as the disabled and the incapacitated, may give an ECG. Moreover, as ECG data may be obtained from several body locations, including the fingertip, it may be relevant for many persons [5, 6]. The white part of the eye, known as the sclera, serves as a sturdy wall again for the look. A coating of biological fluid necessary for smooth eye growth covers the sclera [7, 8]. It is the deepest layer and is ringed by the optic nerve.

Components of the sclera include the episcleral, lying beneath the conjunctiva; the sclera legitimate, a thick white tissue that gives the sclera its white color; and the lamina fusca, a flexible fibre. Each individual has a unique pattern of veins in their sclera, and even identical twins have distinctive vein patterns. This is an evident example that will never change during an individual's lifespan [9, 10]. In a multimodal biometric framework, the sclera alone may distinguish between people. One of the significant developments in biometric verification is unique finger-impression-based confirmation, which is becoming more prevalent in daily life [11, 12]. Creating a framework for acknowledging distinctive markings is crucial and has attracted the attention of many different experts. Worldwide 1:1 synchronization (reassurance) or 1:N authentication (ID) uses fingerprint recognition frameworks.

They can accurately identify individuals for critical certified applications like stock exchange, PC/cell encryption, forensics, and cross-border transit. Specialized finger impression acknowledgement frameworks coordinate fingerprints so that they may be compared to the current fingerprint database [13, 14]. Thus, it can be employed as a security device after that. [15, 16] According to frameworks for finger-impression-based authentication, a finger imprint is a collection of different peaks and valleys on the surface of an image.

The two forms of the biometric framework are the single biometric framework and the multimodal biometric recognition framework [15, 16]. Because unimodal biometric frameworks rely solely on a single physiological characteristic for recognition, they often have concerns with biometric information variability, lack of uniqueness, low recognition accuracy, and parody assaults. Multimodal biometric frameworks are employed to address these issues. The limitations of multimodal biometric frameworks in terms of matching accuracy, difficulty mimicking, comprehensiveness, attainability, and other factors are addressed by multimodal biometric frameworks, which combine many features [17–19]. A multimodal biometric framework improves recognition accuracy, security, and system reliability compared to single-module biometric systems.

Unfortunately, the multimodal biometric framework's biometric modalities' information deterioration taints the outcomes [20–22]. This is because most multimodal techniques now in use also use combined rules that are either inflexible or unable to adequately adapt to the wide range of biometric variables and ecological changes. Unaffected by the degree of combination, element representation and matching processes become infeasible. The subsequent interest is divided between the cost, calculations, and execution of verification. To address these issues, this paper proposes a unique biometric validation framework with the following goals:

- A final "accept" is given if the envelope-based authentications and the Mel-frequency warped cepstral coefficients-based speech fine structure provide "accepts."

- A final "accept" is given if two out of three tries on the two envelope-based authentications result in "accepts."
- A limit of three signatures and name pronunciation tries are permitted.

It is preferred that the biometric measurements utilized for a people identification system are (1) highly individual, (2) simple to produce, (3) time-invariant (no (4) easy for transmission, (4) non-intrusive in the collection, and (4) substantial changes over some time) [1]. On the other hand, certain truly unique biometrics, such as DNA (Deoxyribonucleic Acid) data, may not be admissible or suitable for everyday use owing to ethical or human rights considerations associated with maintaining the record in files. There are frequent trade-offs between dependability, security, overall performance, user-friendliness, system cost, and user acceptance in biometrics-based person identification.

## 11.2   Literature Survey

This study proposes a bimodal identification system that combines voice and signature biometrics, two widely used biometric traits. Compared to standard signature authentication systems [2–5], which require a 2D tablet, a basic visual digitizer, or a specialized writing instrument to collect the characteristics of a handwritten signature, this system uses the sound produced by a rigid-nib pen [6]. This means the system relies solely on analyzing and detecting sound signals, making it more efficient and cost-effective. Handwriting styles, stroke kinds, and dynamics serve as biometric identifiers, and the dynamics of writing motions, such as force, velocity, and acceleration, contribute to the uniqueness of a handwriting style. While topological characteristics may be identified and confirmed using image analysis and pattern recognition, a high-resolution 2D graphic pad or specialized writing equipment [2–5] is required to record nontopological features.

The most common writing devices, such as ballpoint pens, are undoubtedly rigid-nib pens. While using such a tool to write on the sheet or other materials, the nib interacts with the paper's surface roughness and causes vibration, which results in loud noises. These sounds can be used to identify various writers since they are associated with the movements or motions of writing. The convenience of recording sounds with a microphone over assessing writing dynamics using a tablet digitizer makes writing sounds for author identification or verification appealing [15–22].

The effectiveness of the author's sound-based signature approach and related algorithms has been demonstrated. The technique takes advantage of noises produced by friction between stiff pen nibs and sheet surfaces. Studies have shown that as long as the pen's cartridge is firmly and immovably linked to the cylinder, the microphone may be mounted within the pen's cylinder [6]. The pen's cylinder wall transmits sound to the microphone as vibration is brought on by friction on the nib's surface. The envelopes of these written sounds are the main focus of the authentication process. The signal-to-ambient noise ratio does not seem to be an issue with ambient noise up to 65 to 70 dB due to the direct connection technology (A). The spectra of the scribbling sound signals are complex.

The characteristics of handwriting sounds vary depending on the writing tools used, such as pens, paper, writing pads, etc. However, previous studies have shown that the energy is concentrated between 200 and 6,000 hertz, making a sampling frequency of 16,000 Hz appropriate. To avoid distortion, an anti-aliasing filter with a cutoff frequency of around 7,200 Hz is applied before linearly amplifying the microphone signal. The digitized signals are then filtered using a fourth-order bandpass filter with a frequency range of 200 to 6,000 Hz to reduce background noise. This study uses the normalized Hilbert envelope of the writing sounds as the feature space, similar to envelop detection in speech analysis [7]. It is hypothesized that the high-frequency components of handwriting sounds serve as carrier signals.

## 11.3   Proposed Method

The proposed system architecture is described in Figure 11.1. It mainly consists of the following four sections: (1) collecting biometric data, (2) extracting features of biometrics, (3) comparison of the extracted features of both data sets in fusion, (4) classification of class accepts/rejects. The texture characteristics are first retrieved from each subband using a steerable multilevel transform, and then both modalities are independently decomposed into a predetermined number of scales and orientations. Three widely used local descriptors—local directional patterns, binarized quantitative image data, and local phase quantization—are used to determine which local descriptor is the most discriminatory. Lastly, a kNN classifier recognizes persons by fusing the local descriptors from the two modalities at the feature and score levels. The two standard data sets were considered that are the subject of several experiments. The findings show

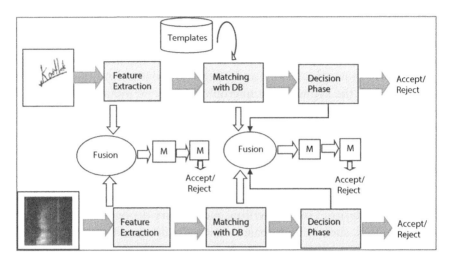

**Figure 11.1** Proposed system architecture.

that the suggested multimodal strategy employing score-level fusion beats feature-level fusion.

The Mel warped cepstral coefficients and the envelope of the prominent names are selected as feature spaces; the latter will authenticate both words and people. The former may tell whether the characters are pronounced correctly. Machine learning establishes terms based on their envelopes in audio signals. Since the envelope technique was previously utilized for signature authentication, this is an easy way to improve the overall system's dependability. In addition, the multilayer feed-forward neural network trained with the backpropagation approach has been effectively implemented in several audio processing and speaker identification applications. The supervised learning technique teaches the ANN to differentiate between envelope data from one speaker uttering a set of words and envelope data from other speakers pronouncing different words. A unique artificial neural network is developed to identify speech envelopes and authenticate the terms. However, the same algorithm and pre-processor are used in signature recognition. Test findings indicate that recognition accuracy greater than 71% is attainable.

Voice recognition in this application is significantly easier than in others because the suggested method is text-dependent and constrained to a small number of syllables, i.e., spoken names. Campbell's tutorial [11] describes the numerous feature spaces proposed for speaker identification. Mel-scale is a non-linear frequency mapping intended to simulate how people perceive pitch. Some authors have also shown that Mel scale warping is effective for automated speaker and voice recognition when paired with other frequency domain analyses. Mel-frequency warped cepstral coefficients (MFCCs) are a frequent feature space for speech and voice recognition with the advantage that no linear prediction approach is required.

The signature's texture and geometric components are generated from photographs of offline signatures. The texture feature represents the image's local information, whereas the geometric element represents the image's global information. The combined feature vector can capture the image's content more precisely and comprehensively. The offline signature image's GLCM may extract detailed data on the orientation, the neighboring interval, and the change in grayscale, which forms the basis for an input image. By merging offline photos with online data for a signature, we intend to provide a more accurate and dependable signature verification. Six columns comprise the online data: X coordinate, Y coordinate, whether or not the stroke begins, whether or not the stroke terminates, and pressure. The two writers' signature information is included in Table 11.1. There is an offline picture and online data for every signature. The online curve in the table was created based on the two complementary signature data. The graph's ordinate indicates the X or Y coordinate change, and the abscissa represents time.

**Table 11.1** Model description using CNN model.

| Layer | Shape | No. of parameters |
|---|---|---|
| Convolution | 32, 32, 16 | 180 |
| Batch normalization | 32, 32, 16 | 64 |
| Activation- ReLu | 32, 32, 16 | 0 |
| Convolution | 32, 32, 16 | 2620 |
| Batch normalization | 32, 32, 16 | 64 |
| Activation | 32, 32, 16 | 0 |
| Max-pooling | 16, 16, 16 | 0 |
| Dropout | 16, 16, 16 | 0 |
| Convolution | 16, 16, 32 | 5640 |
| Batch normalization | 16, 16, 32 | 128 |
| Activation | 16, 16, 32 | 0 |

*(Continued)*

**Table 11.1** Model description using CNN model. (*Continued*)

| Layer | Shape | No. of parameters |
|---|---|---|
| Convolution | 16, 16, 48 | 18572 |
| Batch normalization | 16, 16, 48 | 179 |
| Activation | 16, 16, 48 | 0 |
| Max-pooling | 8, 8, 48 | 0 |
| Dropout | 8, 8, 48 | 0 |
| Convolution | 8, 8, 64 | 26912 |
| Batch normalization | 8, 8, 64 | 256 |
| Activation | 8, 8, 64 | 0 |
| Convolution | 8, 8, 128 | 74556 |
| Batch normalization | 8, 8, 128 | 512 |
| Activation | 8, 8, 128 | 0 |
| Flatten layer | 128 | 0 |
| dropout | 128 | 0 |
| Dense layer | 12 | 1948 |

Let us assume that f (x, y) represents a signature image, that (x1, y1) and (x2, y2) are two points in the picture, that the interval between them is d, that their angle with the horizontal axis of the coordinate system is, and that f (x1, y1) = I and f (x2, y2) = j. A matrix P (i, j) with differ pitches and angles can be created in this fashion. This study examines the grey space at the following coordinates: = 0, 45, 90, 135 for the horizontal, vertical, bottom left to top right, and bottom right to top left. The following diagram illustrates how this study employs the four parameters of contrast, correlation, energy, and homogeneity to depict the matrix scenario.

The dynamic feature's time restriction, movement, and angle variations are more personal styles than static traits. The accuracy and dependability of signature verification may be successfully increased by combining static characteristics with dynamic features. This article uses innovative pen technology to gather offline and online data concurrently before SF-A connects static and dynamic properties. In addition to pressure data, horizontal and vertical coordinates, and other dynamic features, the dynamic features utilized in this work extract four more dynamic characteristics from the live data, including velocity, acceleration, angle, and radius of curvature.

Speech frame MFCCs are turned into a "codebook" using a vector quantization approach for further pattern matching. You may read more about this approach in Swathi *et al.* and Gowroju *et al.* [12, 13]. The test revealed a 91% classification performance. This high rate of recognition is expected. As was previously said, compared to other text-independent tasks, the speaker identification task in this application is relatively easy. In this instance, the system must identify an individual speaking a particular, minimal range of phrases.

## 11.3.1    SVM-Based Implementation

The decision boundary hyperplane computed for the learning sample serves as the decision boundary for the SVM class of generalized linear classifiers, which screen in a supervised learning way. In this study, offline pictures are classified using SVM, and the classification outcomes are obtained using the RBF kernel function. Different quantities of genuine signatures are used in the training phase to train the positive samples. This study introduces the same amount of legitimate signatures from other authors, offering a novel approach to the issue of tiny models. Both the author's genuine signature and counterfeit autographs are included in the test set. The SVM uses the distance between the sample and the hyperplane to classify data while getting the offline verification results. In actual circumstances, a score is used to convey it. We calculate the score and store it as Score1 to serve as the starting point for the succeeding combined characteristics. If the score is less than 0, it is considered a valid signature, and if it is more significant than 0, it is regarded as a forgery.

$$Dec1 = GFScore1(xi) < 0$$
$$Score1(xi) > 0 \quad \text{where } i = 1\ldots1200 \qquad (11.1)$$

## 11.3.2    DTW-Based Implementation

Dynamic Time Warping (DTW) is a well-known optimization problem commonly used for pattern recognition tasks. In this study, DTW is utilized to classify digital signature data. When the test template and reference template match, a time warp function that satisfies certain constraints is solved using DTW to explain the temporal correlation between the two templates. To train the model, diverse genuine signature datasets are used, and their means are used to calculate the Random Variable of the reference template. The degree of similarity between the Gaussian distribution of the test template and this distribution is determined by comparing the two distributions, represented by Score2. Since the number of training samples can vary, the threshold for determining the signature's authenticity can also be adjusted.

$$Dec2 = GFScore2(xi) - threshold < 0$$
$$Score2(xi) - threshold > 0 \quad where\ i = 1...1200 \quad (11.2)$$

### 11.3.3   CNN-Based Method

Audios are transformed into spectrograms using STFT (I used the tutorial's parameters), and then the spectrograms are scaled to 32x32 to condense the feature space before being fed into CNN, as shown in Table 11.1. Standard classifier construction involves 3x3 convolutional kernels, maximum pooling, and a single dense outputting layer.

### 11.3.4   Proposed Model Implementation

The dataset is experimented with the deep speech-2 proposed model by assigning bidirectional weights as shown in Table 11.2:

**Table 11.2** Model description using the proposed model.

| Layer | Shape | No. of parameters |
|---|---|---|
| Convolution | 80, 32 | 180 |
| Batch normalization | 80, 32 | 64 |
| Activation- ReLu | 80, 32 | 0 |
| Convolution | 40, 32 | 2620 |
| Batch normalization | 40, 32 | 64 |
| Activation | 1200 | 0 |
| Bidirectional | 1600 | 11529600 |

(*Continued*)

**Table 11.2** Model description using the proposed model. (*Continued*)

| Layer | Shape | No. of parameters |
|---|---|---|
| Dropout | 1600 | 0 |
| Convolution | 1600 | 5640 |
| Batch normalization | 1600 | 128 |
| Activation | 1600 | 0 |
| Convolution | 1600 | 18572 |
| Batch normalization | 1600 | 179 |
| Activation | 1600 | 0 |
| Bidirectional | 1600 | 0 |
| Dropout | 1600 | 0 |
| Convolution | 1600 | 26912 |
| Batch normalization | 1600 | 256 |
| Activation | 1600 | 0 |
| Convolution | 1600 | 74556 |
| Batch normalization | 1600 | 512 |
| Activation | 1600 | 0 |
| Dense 1 | 1600 | 2561600 |
| Dense 2- ReLu | 1600 | 0 |
| Dense 3 | 29 | 46429 |

## 11.4    Results and Discussion

### 11.4.1    Data Exploitation

A dataset of 64721 wav files with a duration of one second, and these files must be categorized as ("yes, no, up, down, left, right, on, off, stop, go, silent, or unknown]". In terms of these labels, the majority of the files are "unknown." For contemporary voice recognition, the dataset with this

**Table 11.3** Bitrate and length of the dataset.

| Attribute | Bitrate | Length |
|---|---|---|
| Count | 64621 | 64621 |
| Mean | 15000 | 14753.32 |
| Standard deviation | 0 | 851.75 |
| Minimum | 15000 | 5645 |
| Q1 | 15000 | 15000 |
| Q2 | 15000 | 15000 |
| Q3 | 15000 | 15000 |
| Maximum | 15000 | 15000 |

audio duration and the many categories to predict is reasonably primary. SOTA networks can likely categorize it accurately. We are dealing with a genuine issue, though, as the person who assigned me this work stated that a solution using just TensorFlow is preferred. A simple collection of words may be used to voice-control several applications. This indicates that the developed solution will be transferred to another platform that supports TensorFlow. Let's place computational efficiency and prediction speed at the top of our list of goals, as our voice recognition system will be used locally on a webpage or a smartphone device. In this step, we worked with new data to conduct typical tasks like balancing classes, specifying the train-val-test split, creating new silence, and removing unknown labels. Lastly, all the data was transferred into new folders, making it simple to import them into any framework for machine learning. We use the same bitrate, although occasionally, the length is shorter than one second, as shown in Table 11.3.

### 11.4.2   Data Sets Used

The proposed system uses a publicly available dataset from the KaggleTensorFlow Speech Recognition Challenge, which includes a directory of audio tracks and a few informative files. The audio clip's label is the folder name, and the audio clip's subfolders each contain one-second voice command clips. Other labels require prediction. The rest should be regarded as either quiet or the unknown. You may cut up the lengthier

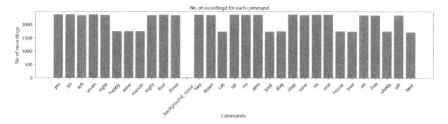

**Figure 11.2** Distribution of data set.

"silent" hooks in the "background noise" folder and use them as training input. The files in the learning audio are not named uniquely among labels, but they are if you take the label folder into account. For instance, the file 00f0204f with no hash 0.wav is in 14 directories. Nonetheless, each folder has a distinct speech command in that file. The unique id of the individual who delivered the voice command appears as the first element in the file names, and the last element indicates repeated orders.

When the subject uses the same term more than once, the command is said to be repeated. The test data does not include a subject id; thus, it is safe to presume that most orders came from subjects not present during training. Sample input signatures and sample frequency distribution is shown in Figure 11.2.

### 11.4.3    Validation and Training

Lists of samples for testing and validation have already been sent to us. Let us see if they are written correctly, considering speakers. That is significant because we should be able to detect instances in which our model inappropriately adapts to the speaker's speech or background noise, as shown in Table 11.4. Except for "unknown," which includes all the other terms we are not required to categorize, classes all have roughly the same number of samples.

### 11.4.4    Results on CNN-Based Methods

The accuracy plots for the model using CNN are shown in Figure 11.3. The confusion matrix is drawn in Figure 11.4. The matrix indicates that "go" and "no| are frequently mislabeled by models. Moreover, the model predicts "unknown" poorly, as it is challenging to train the model to do so in a supervised manner.

**Table 11.4** Count of train validation and test values.

|  | A1 | A2 | A3 | A4 | A5 | A6 | A7 | A8 | A9 | A10 | A11 |
|---|---|---|---|---|---|---|---|---|---|---|---|
| train | 32650 | 1775 | 1564 | 1681 | 1690 | 1453 | 1322 | 1783 | 1642 | 1123 | 1632 |
| validation | 6221 | 346 | 457 | 563 | 123 | 286 | 354 | 562 | 286 | 354 | 276 |
| test | 3568 | 349 | 456 | 456 | 456 | 356 | 451 | 365 | 745 | 367 | 452 |

A1: unknown A2: stop A3: on A4: go A5: yes A6: no A7: right A8: up A9: down A10: left A11: off.

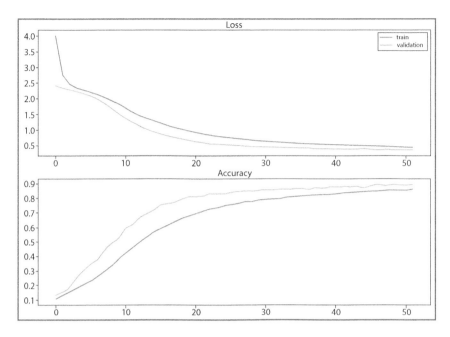

**Figure 11.3** Loss and accuracy plots of training and validation samples of the model for 50 epochs.

The evaluated model has shown a loss of 0.3597 and an accuracy of 0.8794. Even by sight, the spectrograms of the exact words offer similar patterns. While the accuracy of random guessing is 1/12 is nearly 0.083, it provides 0.566 accuracies for the CPU time of 2 min 4 seconds. The performance of this straightforward model may be much enhanced if some effort is spent on feature engineering using signal transformations (with varied values). The validation accuracy is plotted as shown in Figure 11.5.

## 11.4.5    Results of Deep Learning-Based Method

Deep learning is typically done end-to-end, providing sound and receiving text in return. Language and acoustic models are not necessary. Data is transformed into 2D input during preprocessing, such as Fourier - STFT (spectrogram). We can imagine a typical deep language processing model as the sequence-to-sequence one, with convolutional layers starting to catch whole sounds, followed by some recurrent layers, and the layer categorizing the actual phonetic symbols character of the input. This is based on papers published in 2014–2016. A received prediction, such as "c-c-a-a-a—t-t" is converted into the intended word by merging neighbouring letters.

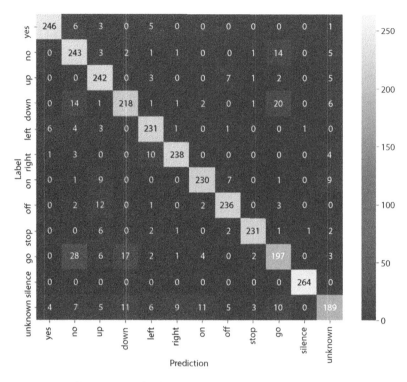

**Figure 11.4** Confusion matrix for the generated model.

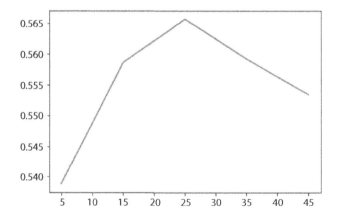

**Figure 11.5** Plot of validation accuracy.

He has also utilized the closest neighbour and threshold-based classifier to identify random forgeries. The results showed a total failure rate of 0.02% and 1.0%, respectively. The author proposed a technique for offline signature recognition [5] in which chain code characteristics by corresponding sequences of line segments with a predetermined length and direction express the border. The database was considering 2400 signature photos. Distance measurements of seven different kinds were employed based on feature vectors created from Eigen-signatures. The Manhattan distance measurement has an accuracy of 96.2%.

On a sheet of paper covered in tiny dots, users of this paper sign their names using an intelligent pen that has a video and pressure sensor. The sign's image and trajectory data may be received instantaneously as it is created. A total of 20 writers' signatures were gathered, with each author receiving 30 genuine autographs and 30 forgeries for a total of 1200 signatures. Finding two to three renters, providing the actual signature, and then performing the forgery following pre-training to achieve the imitation are the steps employed to create the forged signature in this work. The fake signature is accurate and useful. Although the experimental techniques utilized may broadly apply to other languages, the data set presented in this study is only made up of Chinese signatures, as shown in Figures 11.6 and 11.7. With neural networks, there are two major approaches: first, discover and test a large proposed model (and apply transfer learning to fine-tune it); second, create and train a new one of these from the start. Training a Recurrent neural network with CTC loss is an overly complex strategy for a straightforward objective and a tiny dataset. We need the necessary variation in recorded sounds, and the model overfits since some of them only appear in particular combinations. Though, a voice recognition model is optional. We can quickly turn the recordings into equal-sized spectrograms because they are approximately the same length, and since we only need to categorize 13 words, we can train a convolutional classifier to classify the entire word.

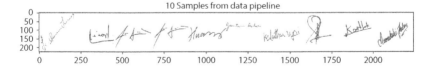

**Figure 11.6** Sample handwriting from CEDAR data set.

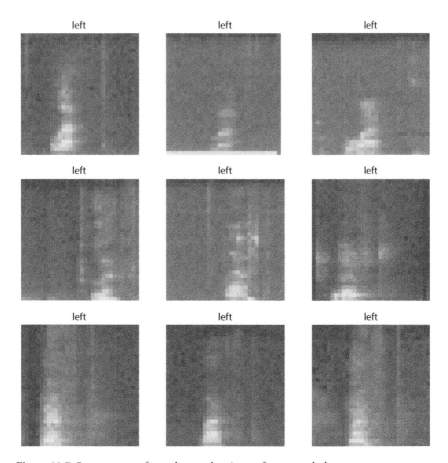

**Figure 11.7** Spectrogram of sample speech snippets from speech dataset.

## 11.4.6    Results of the Proposed Method

The proposed methodology may identify two primary groups of voice recognition methods. The handwritten signature is one of our civilization's first acknowledged forensic and civilian biometric identifying methods. Genuine signatures are often distinguished by human verification. A system for verifying signatures must be able to identify fake signatures while minimizing the rejection of real ones. There are two types of signature verification issues: offline and online. Dynamic information, frequently employed in online signature verification systems, is not used in offline signature verification. In this essay, the issue of offline signature verification is examined. Offline signature verification has been addressed by considering the following forgeries: random forgeries produced without the signer's name or the shape of his signature, simple fakes made with knowledge of the signer's name and the condition of his signature.

Traditional methods for voice recognition include Gaussian mixtures, Hidden Markov models, and other statistical models. Quick and inexpensive; training and running don't need a GPU. Cons: They need meticulous data preparation, the development of features based on signal segmentation, and knowledge of acoustic models. In other words, to utilize them, you need genuinely grasp the field. They also appear erroneous with noisy data comparable to non-deep approaches in computer vision in voice recognition.

Numerous methodologies and techniques have been developed for offline signature verification. Here, we describe some practical methods and ideal approaches. Sabourin's [13] process enables the extraction of broad characteristics of the signature at a low resolution and the extraction of remaining features from distinctive feature regions of the signature at a high resolution [6]. He uses local and global data as a feature vector throughout the verification decision-making process. Sabourin [14] proposed a method that uses local granulometric size distributions. A signature image centred on a grid of rectangular retinas and actuated by regional components of the signature is selected. Using granulometric size distributions, local shape descriptors are generated to quantify the signal activity stimulating each retina.

### 11.4.7   Measure of Accuracy

This experimentation uses a multilingual, text-independent speaker verification system to validate the voice modality. Figure 11.5 illustrates the two essential parts of the speech trait: Acquisition of acoustic features and classification using a Gaussian Mixture Model (GMM). With an average frame duration of 20 milliseconds and a frame advance of 10 milliseconds, the voice signal is analyzed frame by frame [14].

A spectrum with many harmonic series will be dispersed similarly to how the scope circulates. The waveform has repeating temporal patterns. Figure 11.8 illustrates the many procedures required to display the features using Mel frequency cepstral coefficients.

For each frame, a discrete Fourier spectrum is generated using a quick Fourier transform, from which the magnitude-multiplied spectral is computed and then sent through a series of filters. The critical band warping is accomplished by approximating the linear up to 1000 Hz and logarithmic above that frequency Mel-frequency scale. The calculated loss value is 0.0907, while the accuracy value is 0.9811. Figures 11.9 and 11.10 displays the graphs of loss and accuracy for 300 epochs.

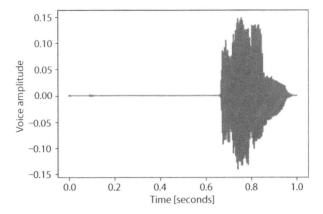

**Figure 11.8** Predicted voice amplitude.

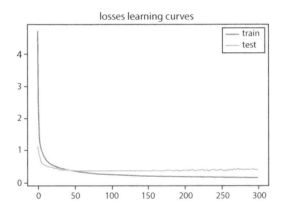

**Figure 11.9** Loss plot of the proposed model.

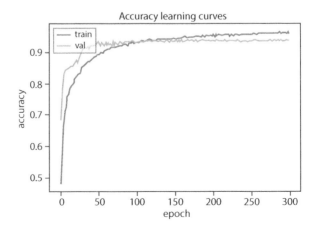

**Figure 11.10** Accuracy of the proposed model.

The model produces representations with semantic meaning after the training phase. By calculating the similarity between two sets of pictures, we can assess how effectively they function. Unlike what we anticipate, pairs of dissimilar photos should have significant gaps. Then, we may choose a level of resemblance over which two images are considered authentic. By selecting this level, the goal is to balance the False Acceptance Rate FAR (which allows for the acceptance of fraudulent signatures) and the False Rejection Rate FRR (legitimate signatures are not accepted). We can calculate the Equal Error Rate, which corresponds to the point at which the FAR and FRR are equal, for the balanced assessment of several models. Two types of data pairings will be built to calculate this measure.

- Pairwise positive (signature and handwriting of the same subject)
- Simple negatives (pair collected from different subjects)
- Harsh refusals (pair from other issues with similarity of matching with the original topic)

The experimental outcomes of the different classes under the local data set, each utilizing an additional feature. The findings of the proposed method using the density plot are shown in Figure 11.11. In this research, merging static and dynamic features through score fusion is superior to utilizing feature validation and logistic regression alone after using various training samples to acquire the results, as shown in Table 11.5.

Acquiring publicly accessible data sets containing offline photographs and accompanying online data is still a significant challenge. However, this

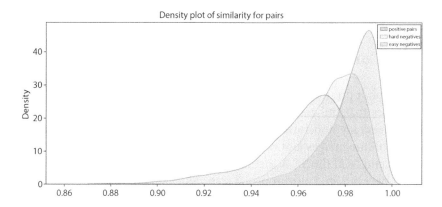

**Figure 11.11** Density plot for similarity of training pairs.

**Table 11.5** Comparison of all methods.

| Algorithm used | False acceptance rate | False reject rate | Average error rate | Accuracy |
|---|---|---|---|---|
| SVM | 18.83% | 13.83% | 14.33% | 83.17% |
| DTW | 13.17% | 11.50% | 13.74% | 86.17% |
| CNN | 13.17% | 10.67% | 9.62% | 89.58% |
| Proposed Work | 3.67% | 5.17% | 6.12% | 96.05% |

chapter aims to accomplish that goal by utilizing 1200 signatures' online and offline data in the studies presented here. The evaluation indicators used in this study include FAR, FRR, AER, and accuracy. FAR represents the proportion of fabricated signatures used for testing determined to be genuine. FRR, on the other hand, represents the proportion of authentic autographs used for testing that were determined to be faked.

The average of FAR and FRR is known as AER, while verification accuracy is determined based on whether the anticipated outcome is consistent. Deep-learning techniques have been successfully used for signature verification, but they require a large amount of data to conduct trials and may need to be more practical. Solving the problem of working with small samples in the real world is crucial for practical applications. Therefore, many researchers have studied minor sample problems and have trained models with between one and ten pieces. In this article, we chose three, five, eight, and ten authentic signature samples for training and performed tests and comparisons on various aspects of 1200 signatures.

## 11.5   Conclusion

This research proposes a safe authentication procedure using multimodal biometrics that utilizes speech and handwriting recognition systems for higher accuracy and lower error rates. We employed intelligent pens to capture offline images and online signatures data, analyzed and extracted features and used the SF-A method for combining static and dynamic elements. We evaluated our proposed technique using an existing storage set and achieved an accuracy rate of 96.05%, along with low FAR and FRR, demonstrating the effectiveness of the proposed solution.

The future scope of this research includes expanding the training dataset to confirm the method's applicability worldwide and examining the verification impact of the suggested technique on other languages. We will make the data sets available to the public so that other academics and institutions may conduct further examinations and comparisons. Additionally, we will investigate signature characteristics in-depth to determine the most illustrative vector of signature traits and continue to explore ways to achieve the best verification effect with minimal training data.

# References

1. Batool, F.E., Khan, M.A., Sharif, M., Javed, K., Nazir, M., Abbasi, A.A., Iqbal, Z., Riaz, N., Offline signature verification system: A novel technique of fusion of GLCM and geometric features using SVM. *Multimed. Tools Appl.*, 84, 312–332, 2020.

2. Alaei, A., Pal, S., Pal, U., Blumenstein, M., An efficient signature verification method based on an interval symbolic representation and a fuzzy similarity measure. *IEEE Trans. Inf. Forensics Secur.*, 12, 2360–2372, 2017.

3. Hadjadj, I., Gattal, A., Djeddi, C., Ayad, M., Siddiqi, I., Abass, F., Offline signature verification using textural descriptors, in: *Proceedings of the Iberian Conference on Pattern Recognition and Image Analysis*, pp. 177–188, Madrid, Spain, 1–4 July 2019.

4. Maergner, P., Pondenkandath, V., Alberti, M., Liwicki, M., Riesen, K., Ingold, R., *Offline signature verification by combining graph edit distance and triplet networks, lecture notes in computer science,* vol. 110, pp. 470–480, Springer International Publishing, 2018.

5. Shen, W. and Tan, T., Automated biometrics-based personal identification. *Proc. Natl. Acad. Sci. U. S. A*, 96, 11065– 11066, 1999.

6. Plamondon, R. and Lorette, G., Automatic signature verification and writer identification – The state of the art. *Pattern Recog.*, 22, 107–131, 1989.

7. Leclerc, F. and Plamondon, R., Automatic signature verification: State of the art 1989-1993. *Int. J. Pattern Recognit. Artif. Intell.*, 8, 643–660, 1994.

8. Rohlík, O., Matoušek, V., Mautner, P., Kempf, J., A new approach to signature verification – Digital data acquisition pen. *Neural Netw. World*, 11-5, 493–501, 2001.

9. Mautner, P., Rohlik, O., Matousek, V., Kempf, J., Fast signature verification without a special tablet. *Proceedings of IWSSIP'02, World Scientific, Manchester*, pp. 496–500, Nov. 2002.

10. Gowroju, S. and Kumar, S., Robust deep learning technique: U-net architecture for pupil segmentation, in: *2020 11th IEEE Annual Information Technology, Electronics and Mobile Communication Conference (IEMCON)*, pp. 0609–0613, IEEE, 2020.

11. Swathi, A.A. and Kumar, S., A smart application to detect pupil for the small dataset with low illumination. *Innovations Syst. Softw. Eng.*, 21, 1–15, 2021.
12. Swathi, A. and Kumar, S., Review on pupil segmentation using CNN-region of interest, in: *Intelligent Communication and Automation Systems*, pp. 157–168, CRC Press, Milton Park, Abingdon, 2021.
13. Gowroju, A. and Kumar, S., Robust pupil segmentation using UNET and morphological image processing, in: *2021 International Mobile, Intelligent, and Ubiquitous Computing Conference (MIUCC)*, IEEE, pp. 105–109, 2021.
14. Gowroju, S.A. and Kumar, S., Review on secure traditional and machine learning algorithms for age prediction using IRIS image. *Multimed. Tools Appl.*, 81, 35503–35531, 2022. https://doi.org/10.1007/s11042-022-13355-4.
15. Kumar, S., Jain, A., Agarwal, A.K., Rani, S., Ghimire, A., Object-based image retrieval using the u-net-based neural network. *Comput. Intell. Neurosci.*, 21, 1–14, 2021.
16. Kumar, S., Rani, S., Jain, A., Verma, C., Raboaca, M.S., Illés, Z., Neagu, B.C., Face spoofing, age, gender and facial expression recognition using advance neural network architecture-based biometric system. *Sens. J.*, 22, 14, 5160–5184, 2022.
17. Kumar, S., Jain, A., Rani, S., Alshazly, H., Idris, S.A., Bourouis, S., Deep neural network based vehicle detection and classification of aerial images. *Intell. Autom. Soft Comput.*, 34, 1, 119–131, 2022.
18. Kumar, S., Jain, A., Shukla, A.P., Singh, S., Raja, R., Rani, S., Harshitha, G., AlZain, M.A., Masud, M., A comparative analysis of machine learning algorithms for detection of organic and non-organic cotton diseases. *Math. Probl. Eng. Hindawi J. Publ.*, 21, 1, 1–18, 2021.
19. Rani, S., Ghai, D., Kumar, S., Kantipudi, M.V.V., Alharbi, A.H., Ullah, M.A., Efficient 3D alexnet architecture for object recognition using syntactic patterns from medical images. *Comput. Intell. Neurosci.*, 22, 1–19, 2022.
20. Choudhary, S., Lakhwani, K., Kumar, S., Three dimensional objects recognition & pattern recognition technique, related challenges: A review. *Multimed. Tools Appl.*, 23, 1, 1–44, 2022.
21. Rani, S., Ghai, D., Kumar, S., Reconstruction of simple and complex three dimensional images using pattern recognition algorithm. *J. Inf. Technol. Manag.*, 14, 235–247, 2022.
22. Rani, S., Ghai, D., Kumar, S., Object detection and recognition using contour based edge detection and fast R-CNN. *Multimed. Tools Appl.*, 22, 2, 1–25, 2022.

# 12

# Convolutional Neural Network Approach for Multimodal Biometric Recognition System for Banking Sector on Fusion of Face and Finger

**Sandeep Kumar[1]\*, Shilpa Choudhary[2], Swathi Gowroju[3] and Abhishek Bhola[4]**

*[1]Department of Computer Science and Engineering, Koneru Lakshmaiah Educational Foundation, Vijayawada, India*
*[2]Department of Computer Science and Engineering, Neil Gogte Institute of Technology, Hyderabad, India*
*Data Science Department, Sreyas Institute of Engineering and Technology, Hyderabad, India*
*[4]Chaudhary Charan Singh Haryana Agricultural University, College of Agriculture, Bawal, Rewari, Haryana, India*

## Abstract

In the last 10 years, fingerprint recognition has become popular because it is now a standard function on most mobile devices, tablets, and PCs. In addition to the security benefits this kind of biometric scanner offers at work, more and more businesses are substituting passwords, ID cards, and door access codes to track attendance and manage their staff. It continues to be plagued by variances, such as print traits, including alignment, edge orientation shift, arches, swirls, and whorls. The face is almost unaffected since it has a solid 3D structure compared to the finger. More application areas can use the face and finger because they can be taken from a distance without being obtrusive. Due to its physiological makeup and placement, the finger may easily replace the face for biometric identification. Combining the face and finger has become famous for nonintrusive multimodal recognition to increase security, durability, and accuracy. A multimodal system achieves a better result than a unimodal system because of the fusion rule.

\*Corresponding author: er.sandeepsahratia@gmail.com

Sandeep Kumar, Deepika Ghai, Arpit Jain, Suman Lata Tripathi and Shilpa Rani (eds.)
*Multimodal Biometric and Machine Learning Technologies: Applications for Computer Vision,*
(251–268) © 2023 Scrivener Publishing LLC

This article describes a machine learning-based multimodal biometrics fusion method. Data pretreatment is accomplished by data transformation. A 2D filter was utilized to examine the texture of local subblocks to extract the phase information of multimodal biometrics data. A proposed algorithm was created for the multimodal integration of biometrics. We evaluated the effectiveness of the suggested approach using the finger and face data sets. Following the findings, the quality of fused images is higher, the accuracy of feature extraction is between 91% and 95%, the average accuracy is 97%, the multimodal biometric impact is positive, and the practicability is reasonable.

*Keywords*: Biometric recognition, face recognition, fingerprint recognition, multimodel system

## 12.1   Introduction

Accurate user recognition systems are now required to control access to current technical resources due to the recent rapidity of their development. The most robust technology currently available is biometric identification technology [1]. Biometrics is the science of verifying a person's identification using partially or entirely automated methods based on behavioural characteristics, like voice or signature, and physical features, such as the face and fingerprint [2, 3]. As biometric data cannot be lost, stolen, or duplicated, it has several benefits over conventional recognition techniques like passwords. Unimodal and multimodal systems for biometric recognition are the two categories. For user identification, the unimodal system only considers one biometric characteristic [4]. Unimodal systems have several drawbacks even if they are reliable and have shown to be better than previously employed conventional approaches. These issues include sensing data noise, nonuniversality, sensitivity to spoofing assaults, and intraclass and interclass similarity issues [5]. In essence, multimodal authentication methods need more than one characteristic to identify people. They are frequently used in real-world settings because they may solve problems with unimodal biometric systems. The information accessible in one of the biometric system's modules can be utilized to combine the many qualities in multimodal biometric systems. Due to their benefits over unimodal systems, multimodal biometric systems have become increasingly popular secure identification techniques [6–8].

Several biometrics researchers have used machine learning techniques to access real-time applications. Before categorizing the raw biometric information, machine learning algorithms must convert the raw data into a suitable format and extract features from it. Also, before feature extraction, machine learning techniques call for a few preprocessing operations [9]. Moreover, certain extraction technologies sometimes need to improve with various biometric kinds or data sets of the same biometrics. Furthermore, they cannot handle biometric picture modifications, such as zooming and rotation.

Convolution Neural Network (CNN) learning has recently significantly influenced and delivered outstanding outcomes in biometrics systems [10, 11]. Several of the drawbacks of conventional approaches, especially those related to feature extraction methods, have been solved by the CNN approach. Biometric image modifications may be handled by CNN-based algorithms, which can also retrieve information from raw data [12–14]. This projected research aims to extensively assess the effectiveness of the convolutional neural network (CNN) algorithm in detecting a person using two biometric qualities, namely a person's face and finger, in light of the excellent performance of CNN techniques in many identification tasks [15–17]. Constructing a CNN model using a human face and finger is the foundation of an efficient multimodal biometric system. These characteristics were picked because the face is distinctive and contains precise recognition data, making it a good choice [18–21]. The second attribute, the finger vein, has been introduced to increase the identification outcome's precision and strengthen the suggested model's security and dependability. The combination of these two forms of biometrics has received minimal investigation so far [22–24]. Few studies have been on a multimodal secured system employing two features. The suggested identification approach is based on end-to-end CNN models that extract characteristics without picture segmentation or detection tools before classifying the subject [25–28].

The article is structured as follows: Multimodal biometric system study is summarized in Section 12.2; the technique is described in Section 12.3; and the experimental findings are in Section 12.4 in great detail. In Section 12.5, the results are discussed and examined. Section 12.6 wraps up the essay and addresses future follow-up research.

## 12.2    Literature Work

Several types of research have been suggested on multimodal biometric systems. This section reviews a recent study that used multimodal biometric systems and conventional and machine-learning techniques, as shown in Table 12.1. Nada Alay *et al.* [1] developed the new multimodal secured system in 2020 due to the growing need worldwide and the widespread usage of biometric identification technology in our day-to-day lives. This research proposes a novel multimodal biometric person identification

**Table 12.1** Existing state-of-art methodology.

| Sr. no. | Author name & year | Proposed work | Database | Remarks |
|---|---|---|---|---|
| 1 | Nada Alay et al. [1], 2020 | ANN | SDUMLA-HMT data set | Accuracy = 97% |
| 2 | Quan Huang [2], 2022 | Reinforcement learning | Casia iris interval v4 and NFBS data sets | Accuracy = 84% & 93% Time = 110ms |
| 3 | Jinfeng Yang et al. [3], 2016 | Gabor Ordinal Measures | FG database | EER = 3.408 Matching Time = 0.257s Recognition Rate = 97.77 |
| 4 | Chuang Lin et al. [4], 2015 | Kernel Locality Preserving Projection | ORL, Yale, AR, and Palmprint databases | Accuracy = 94.44%, 92.9%, 84.5%, and 90.4% |
| 5 | Sumegh Tharewal et al. [5], 2022 | PCA + SVM | Face Recognition Grand Challenge | Accuracy = 89% |
| 6 | Wassim Ghazal et al. [7], 2020 | SD-OCT | Self | Accuracy = 79% |
| 7 | Santosh Kumar Bharti et al. [8], 2020 | Dense Layer + LSTM + SVM | Mustard data set | Accuracy = 67.10% Precision = 73.26% Recall = 66.49% F1-Score = 69.01% |
| 8 | Hyunsoek Choi et al. [9], 2015 | HOG + Viola-Jones | ChaLearn database | EER = 2.41 |

*(Continued)*

**Table 12.1** Existing state-of-art methodology. (*Continued*)

| Sr. no. | Author name & year | Proposed work | Database | Remarks |
|---|---|---|---|---|
| 9 | S.Shunmugam *et al.* [10], 2014 | Viola-Jones | Self | EER = 4.51 |
| 10 | Madhavi Gudavalli *et al.* [11], 2012 | SVM | Self | Accuracy = 90% |
| 11 | JuCheng Yang [12], 2010 | SHT | Self | EER = 6.17 |
| 12 | Kyong I. *et al.* [13], 2005 | PCA + SVM | 2D+3D Face database | Accuracy = 97.5% |
| 13 | Ali Pour Yazdanpanah *et al.* [14], 2010 | Gabor + PCA | ORL, USTB, and CASIA | Accuracy = 95.2%, 97.3%, and 93.22% |
| 14 | Cheng Lu *et al.* [15], 2009 | PCA + LDA + MFA | ORL face and PolyU palmprint database | Recognition Rate = 78.2% & 93.6% Time = 5.41 & 9.65 |
| 15 | Basma Ammour *et al.* [16], 2020 | Log-Gabor filter | ORL + FERET + CASIA | Recognition Rate = 85.62%, 83.57% and 91% |

system based on a neural network-based algorithm for identifying people using their iris, face, and finger vein biometric modalities. The neural networks (NNs) that form the system's structure collect features from pictures and use the softmax classifier to categorize them. Several fusion strategies were used to combine the CNN models to investigate how well they affected recognition performance. These strategies included feature and score-level fusion. By doing many tests on the multimodal biometrics data set SDUMLA-HMT, the performance of the suggested system was empirically assessed. The results showed that utilizing two biometric qualities in biometric identification systems led to accuracy rates of 100% and 99.39%

when employing various score-level and feature-level fusion approaches, respectively. Quan [2] suggested a reinforcement learning-based multimodal biometric fusion technique. The classifier of multiple modal biometrics was built using reinforcement learning, and fractional information was used to perform the fusion of different modal biometrics. The multimodal biometrics fusion algorithm was created, achieving an average feature classification accuracy of 97%, multimodal biometric classification time of 110 ms, sound effects, and great practicability.

This work creates an identifying biometric modalities system that integrates face and finger photos using the CNN model based on findings from prior studies. The most efficient solution was determined using the feature- and score-level fusion with several scoring methodologies.

## 12.3   Proposed Work

In our proposed method, we utilize a multimodal system for authentication that combines face and finger modalities. The proposed method is divided

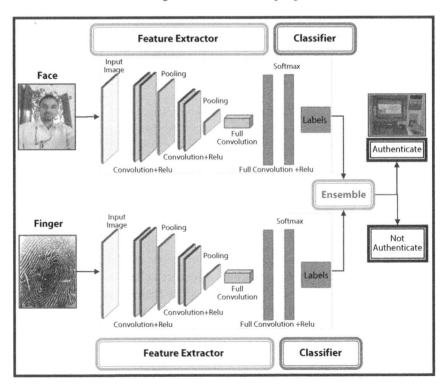

**Figure 12.1** Process of CNN.

into preprocessing, feature extraction, and classification. The architecture of the proposed method is given in Figure 12.1.

## 12.3.1    Pre-Processing

We implement data cleaning and data enhancement techniques to enhance the efficiency of the proposed modal. First, we perform data cleaning by removing any duplicates or outliers in the data. This helps ensure the system is trained on a clean data set and reduces noise's effects. Next, we use data augmentation to increase the data set for training the proposed algorithm. This helps to increase the diversity of the data set and prevent over-fitting of the models. We also use noise reduction techniques to remove any noise or artefacts in the images that could affect the system's accuracy.

## 12.3.2    Feature Extraction

In a multimodal system that uses CNNs for feature extraction, the convolution and ReLU layers are applied to each modality separately. In the proposed approach, we used face and finger modalities; each modality would have its own CNN architecture for feature extraction. Each filter detects a specific feature in the input image, such as edges, corners, or textures. The feature maps represent the activation of each filter at different locations in the input image. In the following step, the output of the convolution layer is subjected to the Leaky ReLU activation function.

Rectified linear unit (ReLU) is a nonlinear activation function commonly used in CNNs, as shown in Figure 12.2. Leaky ReLU sets all negative values to some value and leaves positive values unchanged. This introduces nonlinearity into the CNN architecture, making it more powerful and

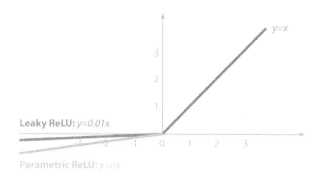

**Figure 12.2** Process of leaky ReLU.

expressive. After the ReLU activation, the feature maps are downsampled using a pooling layer. Max-pooling is a commonly used pooling operation that takes the maximum value in each pooling window. In a multimodal system, classification processes the output feature maps from each modality after concatenating them. The fully connected layer can combine the features from multiple modalities to make a decision or perform a specific task. In conclusion, the convolution and ReLU layers are applied separately to each modality in a multimodal system that uses CNNs for feature extraction. The pooling layer is used to down-sample the feature maps and reduces the spatial dimensionality, as shown in Figure 12.3. The output feature maps from each modality are concatenated and fed into a fully connected layer for classification or further processing.

### 12.3.3   Classification

Convolutional neural networks (CNNs) are used in multimodal systems to extract features, and the results are sent into classification or other processing. Each neuron in the fully connected neural network layer is linked to every neuron in the layer underneath it. The fully connected layer allows the neural network to learn complex, non-linear relationships between the input features and the output classes. In a multimodal system, the output feature maps from each modality are concatenated into a single vector and passed through the FCL. The fully connected layer applies a set of learnable weights and biases to the input vector to generate a set of output activations. The ReLU activation function is commonly used in the fully connected layer to introduce nonlinearity into the model.

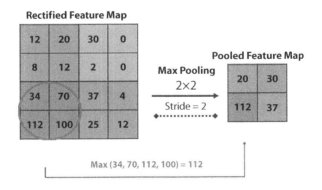

**Figure 12.3** Process of max pooling.

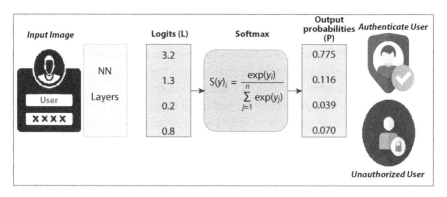

**Figure 12.4** Process of softmax function.

After the fully connected layer, the soft-max layer is used for classification, as shown in Figure 12.4. The soft-max function is an activation function that converts the output activations from the fully connected layer into a set of probability scores for each class. The probabilities sum up to one, ensuring that the outputs can be interpreted as accurate class labels.

During training, the weights and biases in the fully connected layer are updated using back-propagation to minimize the cross-entropy loss. In a multimodal system, the fully connected layer and soft-max layer can combine the features from multiple modalities to make a decision or perform a specific task. For example, in a multimodal authentication system that uses face and finger modalities, the fully connected layer and soft-max layer can combine the features from both modalities to classify whether a person is authorized to access a system. In conclusion, the fully connected and soft-max layers are commonly used for classification in multimodal systems that use CNNs for feature extraction. The fully connected layer applies a set of learnable weights and biases to the concatenated feature vectors from multiple modalities. The soft-max layer converts the output activations into probability scores for each class.

### 12.3.4   Ensemble

Ensemble learning is a machine learning technique that combines multiple models' outputs to improve a system's overall performance. In the context of our multimodal approach, ensemble learning involves combining the outputs of various unimodal models to achieve more accurate and reliable results. There are different ensemble learning methods, but one commonly used approach is "voting." In this approach, each unimodal model makes a prediction, and the final prediction is based on the most common prediction made by the individual models. For example, if three unimodal models predict that a user is authenticated, and one indicates that they are not, the final prediction would be that the user is authenticated. Another approach to ensemble learning is called "stacking." In this approach, the output of each unimodal model is used as an input to a higher-level model that makes the final prediction. The higher-level model can be a simple model, such as logistic regression or a decision tree, or a more complex model, such as a neural network.

Ensemble learning is often used when individual models may have high variance or are prone to overfitting, which can reduce the accuracy and reliability of the overall system. By combining the outputs of multiple models, ensemble learning can reduce the impact of these sources of variability and improve the system's overall performance. In our multimodal approach, we used ensemble understanding to combine the outputs of multiple unimodal models trained on different modalities, such as face and finger data. By using ensemble learning, we achieved more accurate and reliable authentication results, demonstrating the effectiveness of this approach in improving the performance of multimodal systems.

## 12.4   Results and Discussion

### 12.4.1   Data Set Used

- **Face data set:** In this research, we used two standard data sets for face, i.e. LFW and CMU. The Labeled Faces in the Wild (LFW) data set is a popular benchmark data set for face recognition. It contains over 13,000 face images of 5,749 individuals collected from the web. The data set includes variations in pose, expression, illumination, and occlusion. The data set is widely used for evaluating face recognition algorithms and has been used in numerous research studies. The Carnegie Mellon University (CMU) Multi-PIE data set is a face recognition and expression analysis data set. It contains face images of 337 subjects with pose, illumination, expression, and occlusion variations. The data set includes multiple sessions and viewpoints for each subject, making it suitable for multimodal authentication systems. The data set also provides metadata such as pose, illumination, and expression labels, making it ideal for expression recognition tasks. Both data sets are commonly used in computer vision and machine learning for developing and evaluating face recognition and expression analysis algorithms.

- **Finger data set:** Two fingerprint databases, ATVS-FFp and FVC2006, was used to implement the proposed methodology completely. It can recognize 1344 fingerprints and tell if they are fake or authentic. In a proposed multimodal system that uses face and finger modalities for authentication and classification, all four standard databases can be used for training and evaluating the system's face and finger recognition component. Using these data sets can enable the development of a robust and accurate face and finger recognition model that can be combined with the finger modality for multimodal authentication.

## 12.4.2    Evaluation Parameter Used

Accuracy, precision, and recall are standard evaluation metrics used in machine learning for assessing the performance of a classification model, including in multimodal systems that use face and finger modalities for authentication and classification.

Accuracy is a metric that measures the overall performance of the classification model. It is the ratio of correctly predicted samples to the total number of pieces. In a multimodal system, accuracy would measure the percentage of correctly authenticated samples, considering both the face and finger modalities.

Precision is a metric that measures the proportion of accurate positive samples (correctly classified as positive) over the total number of optimistic predictions (true positive + false positive). In a multimodal system, precision would measure the proportion of correctly authenticated samples using both the face and finger modalities over the total number of samples classified as authentic. The recall metric measures the ratio of accurate positive models over the total number of actual positive examples (true positive + false negative). In a multimodal system, the recall would measure the proportion of correctly authenticated samples using the face and finger modalities over the total number of authentic models.

### 12.4.3   Comparison Result

**• Face Data Set Outcomes**
Our research adopted a multimodal approach that leveraged face and finger modalities for authentication and classification. We used several evaluation metrics to assess the performance of our process, including accuracy, precision, recall, and F1-score. We evaluated the performance of our approach using the Labeled Faces in the Wild (LFW) data set and obtained an accuracy of 99.07%, a precision of 97.57%, a recall of 96.35%, and an F1-score of 96.95%, as shown in Table 12.2 and Figure 12.5. These results indicate that our approach achieved high accuracy in authenticating users while maintaining a good balance between precision and recall.

**Table 12.2** Outcomes on face LFW data set, CMU data set.

|  | **LFW data set** | **CMU data set** |
|---|---|---|
| **Accuracy** | 99.07% | 97.38% |
| **Precision** | 97.57% | 96.01% |
| **Recall** | 96.35% | 95.8% |
| **F1-Score** | 96.95% | 95.90% |

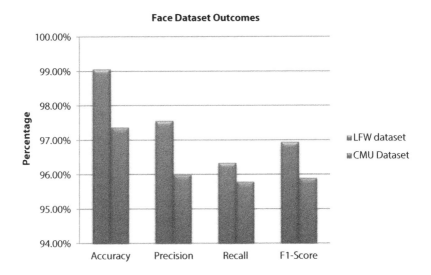

**Figure 12.5** Outcomes on face data set.

Similarly, we evaluated the performance of our approach using the Carnegie Mellon University (CMU) Multi-PIE data set. We obtained an accuracy of 97.38%, a precision of 96.01%, a recall of 95.8%, and an F1-score of 95.90%. These results demonstrate that our multimodal approach achieved high accuracy and maintained a good balance between precision and recall when applied to a different data set. Overall, our results show the effectiveness of our proposed multimodal approach for authentication and classification and suggest that it could be used in various applications that require robust and accurate user identification.

**• Finger Data Set Outcomes**
As part of our evaluation, we also used two finger data sets, namely the ATVS-FFp and FVC2006 data sets. We evaluated our multimodal approach on mentioned data sets. On the ATVS-FFp data set, our multimodal approach achieved an accuracy of 99.18%, a precision of 97.31%, a recall of 96.88%, and an F1-score of 97.09%, as shown in Table 12.3 and Figure 12.6. These results demonstrate that our approach was highly influential in authenticating users based on face data, achieving high accuracy while maintaining a good balance between precision and recall. Similarly, on the FVC2006 data set, our approach achieved an accuracy of 98.08%, a precision of 96.19%, a recall of 95.47%, and an F1-score of 95.83%.

These results indicate that our approach effectively authenticates users on this data set, achieving high accuracy and maintaining a good balance between precision and recall. Our evaluation of the face data sets revealed that they are more effective and adaptable for authentication and classification, showing their potential for various real-world uses. In our research, we explored unimodal and multimodal authentication and classification approaches. We trained and tested our models using face or finger data

**Table 12.3** Outcomes on finger ATVS-FFp data set, FVC2006 data set.

|  | ATVS-FFp data set | FVC2006 data set |
|---|---|---|
| **Accuracy** | 98.18% | 98.08% |
| **Precision** | 97.31% | 96.19% |
| **Recall** | 96.88% | 95.47% |
| **F1-Score** | 97.09% | 95.83% |

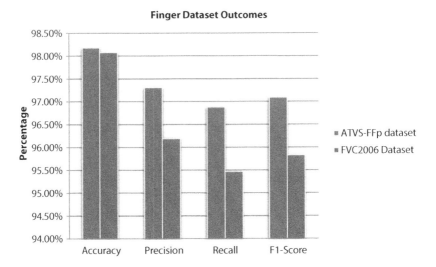

**Figure 12.6** Outcomes on finger data set.

separately for the unimodal approach. On the face data, our unimodal system achieved an accuracy of 98.22%.

Similarly, on the finger data, our unimodal policy attained an accuracy of 98.13%. These results indicate that face and finger data can be adequate for user authentication when used in isolation. However, to improve our approach's overall performance and reliability, we also explored an ensemble learning approach that combined the outputs of our unimodal models. Using this approach, we achieved an accuracy of 98.08% as shown in Table 12.4. Although the accuracy achieved using the ensemble learning approach is slightly lower than that achieved using the unimodal process on face data, it provides a more robust and reliable method for user authentication.

**Table 12.4** Average accuracy on a unimodal and multimodal biometric system.

| | Traits | Accuracy |
|---|---|---|
| **Unimodal biometric** | Face | 98.22% |
| | Finger | 98.13% |
| **Multimodal biometric** | Ensemble $\{f=\max(x_1,x_2,x_3,....x_n)\}$ $F=\max(97.38, 98.08)$ | 98.08% |

By combining the outputs of multiple models trained on different modalities, we can reduce the impact of noise and other sources of variability that may affect individual modalities, leading to more accurate and reliable authentication results. Overall, our results demonstrate the potential of multimodal approaches and highlight the importance of considering ensemble learning methods for improving the accuracy and robustness of authentication and classification systems.

## 12.5   Conclusion

In conclusion, a unique, secured, multimodal paradigm for user identification has been developed. The suggested system used the CNN algorithm and ensemble methods to authenticate the user based on features of their face and fingers. A multimodal identification biometric system with two components, the finger trait, has also received relatively little research, as was already indicated. The suggested model identified each characteristic using two CNNs. The model's performance was assessed using openly accessible benchmark data sets. The experimental findings proved the remarkable performance of the CNN algorithms. It also demonstrated that utilizing two biometric features rather than one can improve the performance of identification systems.

For additional study, the researchers want to create CNNs for more than three biometric modules. The authors also intend to examine how deep learning methods affect recognition qualities, etc.

## References

1. Alay, N. and Al-Baity, H.H., Deep learning approach for multimodal biometric recognition system based on a fusion of iris, face, and finger vein traits. *Sensors*, 20, 19, 5523, 2020.
2. Huang, Q., Multimodal biometrics fusion algorithm using deep reinforcement learning. *Math. Probl. Eng.*, 22, 1, 1–9, 2022.
3. Yang, J., Zhong, Z., Jia, G., Li, Y., Spatial circular granulation method based on multimodal finger feature. *J. Electr. Comput. Eng.*, 16, 1, 1–7, 2016.
4. Lin, C., Jiang, J., Zhao, X., Pang, M., Ma, Y., Supervised kernel optimized locality preserving projection with its application to face recognition and palm biometrics. *Math. Prob. Eng.*, 15, 1, 1–10, 2015.
5. Tharewal, S., Malche, T., Tiwari, P.K., Jabarulla, M.Y., Alnuaim, A.A., Mostafa, A.M., Ullah, M.A., Score-level fusion of 3D face and 3D ear for multimodal biometric human recognition. *Comput. Intell. Neurosci.*, 22, 1, 1–9, 2022.

6. Ma, Y., Huang, Z., Wang, X., Huang, K., An overview of multimodal biometrics using the face and ear. *Math. Probl. Eng.*, 20, 1, 1–17, 2020.

7. Ghazal, W., Georgeon, C., Grieve, K., Bouheraoua, N., Borderie, V., Multimodal imaging features of Schnyder corneal dystrophy. *J. Ophthalmol.*, 20, 1, 1–10, 2020.

8. Bharti, S.K., Gupta, R.K., Shukla, P.K., Hatamleh, W.A., Tarazi, H., Nuagah, S.J., Multimodal sarcasm detection: A deep learning approach. *Wirel. Commun. Mob. Comput.*, 22, 1, 1–10, 2022.

9. Choi, H. and Park, H., A multimodal user authentication system using faces and gestures. *BioMed. Res. Int.*, 15, 1, 1–8, 2015.

10. Shunmugam, S. and Selvakumar, R.K., Electronic transaction authentication—A survey on multimodal biometrics, in: *2014 IEEE International Conference on Computational Intelligence and Computing Research*, pp. 1–4, 2014.

11. Gudavalli, M., Viswanadha Raju, S., Vinaya Babu, A., Srinivasa Kumar, D., Multimodal biometrics–sources, architecture, and fusion techniques: An overview, in: *International Symposium on Biometrics and Security Technologies*, pp. 27–34, 2012.

12. Yang, J., Biometrics verification techniques combing with digital signature for a multimodal biometrics payment system, in: *IEEE International Conference on Management of e-Commerce and e-Government*, pp. 405–410, 2010.

13. Chang, K., II, Bowyer, K.W., Flynn, P.J., An evaluation of multimodal 2D+ 3D face biometrics. *IEEE Trans. Pattern Anal. Mach. Intell.*, 27, 4, 619–624, 2005.

14. Pour, Y.A., Faez, K., Amirfattahi, R., Multimodal biometric system using face, ear and gait biometrics, in: *10th IEEE International Conference on Information Science, Signal Processing and their Applications (ISSPA 2010)*, pp. 251–254, 2010.

15. Lu, C., Liu, D., Wang, J., Wang, S., Multimodal biometrics recognition by dimensionality reduction method, in: *Second IEEE International Symposium on Electronic Commerce and Security*, pp. 113–116, 2009.

16. Ammour, B., Boubchir, L., Bouden, T., Ramdani, M., Face–Iris multimodal biometric identification system. *Electronics*, 9, 1, 85–91, 2020.

17. Kumar, S., Jain, A., Agarwal, A.K., Rani, S., Ghimire, A., Object-based image retrieval using the u-net-based neural network. *Comput. Intell. Neurosci.*, 21, 1–14, 2021.

18. Kumar, S., Rani, S., Jain, A., Verma, C., Raboaca, M.S., Illés, Z., Neagu, B.C., Face spoofing, age, gender and facial expression recognition using advance neural network architecture-based biometric system. *Sens. J.*, 22, 14, 5160–5184, 2022.

19. Rani, S., Gowroju, S., Kumar, S., IRIS based recognition and spoofing attacks: A review, in: *2021 10th International Conference on System Modeling & Advancement in Research Trends (SMART)*, IEEE, pp. 2–6, 2021.

20. Kumar, S., Singh, S., Kumar, J., Prasad, K.M.V.V., Age and gender classification using seg-net based architecture and machine learning. *Multimed. Tools Appl.*, 22, 3, 1–18, 2022.

21. Kumar, S., Singh, S., Kumar, J., Face spoofing detection using improved SegNet architecture with blur estimation technique. *Int. J. Biom. Indersci. Publ.*, 13, 2-3, 131–149, 2021.

22. Rani, S., Kumar, S., Ghai, D., Prasad, K.M.V.V., Automatic detection of brain tumor from CT and MRI images using wireframe model and 3D Alex-Net, in: *2022 International Conference on Decision Aid Sciences and Applications (DASA)*, pp. 1132–1138, 2022.

23. Rani, S., Lakhwani, K., Kumar, S., Three-dimensional wireframe model of medical and complex images using cellular logic array processing techniques, in: *International Conference on Soft Computing and Pattern Recognition*, Springer, Cham, pp. 196–207, 2020.

24. Rani, S., Ghai, D., Kumar, S., *Reconstruction of a wireframe model of complex images using syntactic pattern recognition*, pp. 8–13, IET, Bahrain, 2021.

25. Shilpa, R., Ghai, D., Kumar, S., Kantipudi, M.V.V., Alharbi, A.H., Ullah, M.A., Efficient 3D AlexNet architecture for object recognition using syntactic patterns from medical images. *Comput. Intell. Neurosci.*, 22, 1–19, 2022.

26. Sandeep, K., Singh, S., Kumar, J., Face spoofing detection using improved SegNet architecture with blur estimation technique. *Int. J. Biom. Indersci. Publ.*, 13, 2-3, 131–149, 2021.

27. Kumar, S., Mathew, S., Anumula, N., Chandra, K.S., Portable camera-based assistive device for real-time text recognition on various products and speech using android for blind people, in: *Innovations in Electronics and Communication Engineering, Lecture Notes in Networks Systems*, pp. 437–448, 2020.

28. Gowroju, S. and Kumar, S., Robust pupil segmentation using UNET and morphological image processing, in: *2021 International Mobile, Intelligent, and Ubiquitous Computing Conference (MIUCC)*, pp. 105–109, IEEE, 2021.

# 13

# Secured Automated Certificate Creation Based on Multimodal Biometric Verification

**Shilpa Choudhary[1]\*, Sandeep Kumar[2], Monali Gulhane[3] and Munish Kumar[4]**

[1]*Department of Computer Science and Engineering (AI&ML), Neil Gogte Institute of Technology, Hyderabad, India*
[2]*Department of Computer Science and Engineering, Koneru Lakshmaiah Educational Foundation, Vijayawada, India*
[3]*Department of Computer Science and Engineering, Symbiosis Institute of Technology (SIT) Nagpur, Symbiosis International (Deemed University) (SIU), Pune, Maharashtra, India*
[4]*Department of E&CE, Maa Saraswati Institute of Engineering and Technology, Kalanaur, India*

## Abstract

Multimodal biometric verification in the secured automated certificate creation system is crucial to its security and accuracy. The system can verify the user's identity with high accuracy and reliability by utilizing multiple biometric characteristics, such as facial, fingerprint, and voice recognition. Each biometric element provides a unique identifier that is difficult to replicate or fake, reducing the risk of fraud or impersonation in the certificate creation process. One of the main steps in this system is the collection of candidate face images and fingerprints in a secure format, such as tif, jpg, or png. The collected images are then used as a base to create unique certificates for each candidate using software that retains the underlying characteristics of the image. Data are stored in xls and xlsx formats to ensure the accuracy and security of the certificate creation process. MS Excel is used as it offers mathematical and statistical tools that can be utilized for internal computation and analysis of data within the file. This approach helps automate the certificate creation process, ensuring high accuracy, security, and data integrity. Overall,

---

*\*Corresponding author*: shilpachoudhary1987@gmail.com

Sandeep Kumar, Deepika Ghai, Arpit Jain, Suman Lata Tripathi and Shilpa Rani (eds.)
*Multimodal Biometric and Machine Learning Technologies: Applications for Computer Vision,*
(269–282) © 2023 Scrivener Publishing LLC

this system provides a more efficient and reliable certificate creation solution that reduces administrators' workload and minimizes the potential for errors.

*Keywords*: Face recognition, Haar features, finger recognition, chaff features, excel

## 13.1    Introduction

With the increasing importance of personal identification in computer-based applications, biometric techniques have become increasingly popular, especially in embedded system applications. However, centralized cloud environments have several drawbacks, such as data security, system management, and lost storage and computing opportunities in personal portable devices. Security is a significant concern, particularly with biometrics, as it is sensitive data, and privacy laws govern its use [1]. A multimodal authentication system that utilizes encrypted biometrics for automated certificate production was developed to address these challenges [2]. The method leverages various physical and behavioral characteristics, such as facial features, fingerprints, iris, and voice patterns, to identify individuals uniquely. This approach is familiar as it has been used for thousands of years, with the science of identifying people based on anatomical and behavioral characteristics, also known as Bertillonage, invented by French police officer Alphonse Bertillon in the late 19th century [1, 3]. Facial recognition technology uses mathematical models to identify unique features, such as the distance between the eyes, nose, and mouth. Similarly, fingerprint recognition technology identifies unique patterns on fingertips, such as ridges and valleys, while voice recognition technology analyzes pitch, tone, and accent to identify individuals uniquely. Combining these biometric characteristics, the Secured Automated Certificate Creation system ensures highly secure and accurate verification, crucial in automated certificate production [4].

Biometric qualities, such as facial features, fingerprints, and iris patterns, are physical characteristics used to identify a person as shown in Figure 13.1. Biometric-based authentication methods are preferred over traditional authentication systems because they are automated and offer higher security [5]. Conventional authentication methods rely on something you have, such as a smart card or something you know, like a password, which can be lost, stolen, or forgotten. Biometric systems that recognize people are widely used in various applications, including access control, time and attendance management, and identity verification. These systems operate

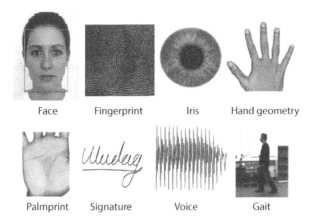

| Face | Fingerprint | Iris | Hand geometry |

| Palmprint | Signature | Voice | Gait |

**Figure 13.1** Various biometric traits.

in two modes: identification, which uses one-to-one matching, and verification, which uses one-to-many matching [6, 7]. In identification mode, the system compares the biometric characteristic of an individual against a database of known biometric data to determine their identity.

In verification mode, the system compares an individual's biometric data against their stored data to authenticate their identity. The proposed work combines face and finger identification through multimodal biometrics to enhance the security and accuracy of biometric-based authentication [8]. The system utilizes a mathematical model to identify specific facial features, such as the distance between the eyes, nose, and mouth, and unique patterns on fingertips, such as ridges and valleys. By combining these biometric characteristics, the system provides a highly secure and accurate verification process [9, 10]. Multimodal biometrics is a practical approach to address the limitations of unimodal biometric systems, such as limited accuracy and susceptibility to spoofing attacks. By using multiple biometric characteristics, multimodal biometric systems provide higher security and accuracy, making them more reliable for various applications, including automated certificate creation.

## 13.1.1    Background

Haar features selection and Haar features are employed as a features detector and calculate the integral picture, which is rectangular, for face recognition. Every person has distinctive features like eyes, a nose, and a mouth, but because the area around the eyes is darker and the nose and mouth will have a different shape, these features are compared. The process of creating an integrated picture comes next [11, 12]. The rectangular rectangles are calculated at (x, y) to create a picture. After building the image, we offer AdaBoost instructions to identify visual elements from big to small sets. Cascading classifiers aggregate all the information mentioned above and eliminates the background.

A method known as PCA can be used to do feature extraction. An analysis is a practical statistical method with applications in areas like face recognition and picture reduction and is a typical method for identifying patterns in high-dimensional data [13]. It is the process of reducing the dimensionality of a data collection by specifying a new set of variables less numerous than the initial set of variables that mainly retains the information from the supplied data. PCA introduces mathematical terms like standard deviation, covariance, eigenvectors, and Eigen values [14]. It is a method for seeing patterns in data and presenting the data to bring out its similarities and contrasts. PCA is an effective method for data analysis since patterns in data might be challenging to identify in high-dimension data when the luxury of graphical representation is not accessible. One of the most used techniques for classification is K-Means clustering [15]. The primary objective of this unsupervised learning approach, which has various data analysis applications, is to categorize data into information groups. This approach entails multiple rounds of a specific process to acquire an ideal minimal answer for all data points. Let us examine this procedure in more detail: In our situation, the distance between each data point and its corresponding centroid is the function of what we aim to reduce.

$$ J = \sum_{i=1}^{k} \sum_{j=1}^{n} \left\| X_j - C_i \right\|^2 \tag{13.1} $$

Clearly defining this function may divide the procedure into numerous phases and reach the desired outcome. Our starting point is a K identifying the number of centers and a vast collection of data items. The first step is to select K random points from our points to serve as partition centers [16]. Then, after computing the distances between each data point in the collection and these centers, we record the results. We associate each location with the closest cluster centre using the computations from the previous step as support. We do this to determine the minimal distance for each point and then include that point in the designated partition set. The mathematical methodology should be used to update the cluster centre locations:

$$C_i = \frac{1}{|K_i|} \sum_{x_{j=k}} X_j \qquad (13.2)$$

Restart from the beginning of the cluster centers change. Otherwise, the K means clustering method was successfully calculated, yielding the members and centroid of the division.

We employed the fuzzy vault, based on the impossibility of the polynomial reconstruction issue, to recognize fingers. Furthermore, the fuzzy vault can handle intra-class differences in biometric data and work with unordered collections [17–19]. The fuzzy vault allows for minor differences between the encryption and the decryption sets, where the groups are unordered and are used to lock and unlock the vault. In contrast, a single-bit difference in the key of a classical cryptosystem completely prevents decryption. This fuzziness is required for usage with biometrics since successive measurements of the same biometric might frequently provide somewhat different signals due to measurement noise or non-linear distortions [20, 21]. For instance, there may be significant distortion between two impressions of the same fingerprint, and the number of features may differ. The three main parameters in the fuzzy vault scheme are:

- The number of points on a polynomial can be retrieved from the number of minute points in a user's fingerprint.
- The vault
- 's security depends on this parameter and how many chaff points are added. The security improves when more chaff points are added.

The degree of the encoding polynomial regulates the system's tolerance to biometric data inaccuracy [22, 23]. The polynomial degree is usually lower than the minimum quantity of minutia points collected from biometric data. The fuzzy vault's encoding step employs the chaff generation approach to produce random facts. These chaff points conceal the minutiae points, often called noise a point, which also secures the secret crypto-key. A few requirements must be met for any chaff points to be created. First, they should refrain from lying on the polynomial where fundamental issues are located, and second, there should be no pattern in allocating the chaff points. Finally, each chaff point must be far from every fuzzy vault member.

## 13.2   Literature Work

Several initiatives have been made to raise security to prevent unwanted access to personal information. Several face and finger recognition articles have been published to offer security levels. A Deep Neural Network Approach for Face Detection was suggested by Ye, Xueyi et al. [1]. In the proposed technique, a Deep Learning or artificial neural network classifier with four hidden layers was implemented. For trials, the LFW data set (7000) and CAS-PEAL data set (4000) were used in the suggested approach. Test findings show system performance is enhanced by correction rate (CR), missing detection rate (MDR), and false detection rate (FDR).

Ghimire et al. [2] established a reliable face detection approach using skin tone and edges. During the pre-processing stage, Skin Segmentation using the YCbCr and RGB spaces was followed by Picture Enhancement. Skin segmentation and the input pictures' edges (Canny Edge) are used to identify faces. The FRGC data set (302 Frontal Image Sample), XXXuthoriz, was used for studies in this suggested technique. According to experimental findings, the system has improved in terms of Correct Detection Rate (CDR), False Positive Rate (FPR), Missing Rate (MR), and Correct Detection Rate (CDR) of 80.1%, 3.31%, and 19.8%, respectively.

A model for face detection was suggested by Abdul Rahman et al. [3]. In the recommended technique, the segmentation of human face detection is done using the RGB-H-CbCr Skin Color Model. Experimentally, near-frontal faces could be detected successfully with reasonable rates, improving system performance. Results show a 28.29% false detection rate (FDR) and a 90.83% detection success rate (DSR).

An Edge-Based Efficient Approach to Face Detection and Feature Extraction was put out by Seyyed et al. [4]. Multi-Layer Feed- Forward NN is employed in the suggested approach to distinguish between faces and non-faces. The Viola-Jones face identification technique uses the output of this classifier as an input. Via Canny Edge detection, features are extracted. According to experimental findings, the detection rate of a neural network using AdaBoost is 94.1%, while the false positive rate is 6.5%. The limitation of this suggested methodology was that only five photographs of samples were used in the procedures.

The fuzzy vault was initially proposed by Juels & Sudan [5]. They used the Alice and Bob scenario, in which Alice seals a secret S in a fuzzy vault and locks it with an unordered set A. Only if set B considerably overlaps with set A will Bob, who also has an unordered set B, be able to open the safe. A polynomial P is created using Alice's secret key. Set A consists of polynomial points; some chaff points that don't fall on the selected polynomial are added afterwards.

Based on the fuzzy vault of Juels and Sudan, Clancy *et al.* [6] proposed a fingerprint vault. The locking set in this work is composed of many minutiae locations. In this study, the idea of employing random points, or "chaff points," that do not lie on the polynomial was put forth. Together, these fake and actual polynomial points that are on the trash comprise the fuzzy vault. The chaff points are intended to hide the minutiae points and stop the improper usage of the fuzzy vault, which is made available to the general public. With more chaff points, the vault's security is increased. This approach presupposed that the fingerprints needed to create the vault and answer the query are already aligned.

A method for template security XXXuthorize a fuzzy vault approach is proposed by Seira Hidano *et al.* [7]. Following encryption, this system saves the user template, and a fuzzy vault scheme is used to create the personal data from the user template and the requested biometric information. It includes a measure only to divulge just enough information to make it impossible to retrieve the personal data or the user template used to get it, as well as to make it possible to produce the personal data from the user's biometric information. A fingerprint authentication system is simulated in this research to assess the suggested technique's template security. This approach is also used in a fingerprint matching system by setting the number of elements "k" and the number of parity code components "g" to acceptable values. It is found that personal data may be recovered with a high probability if it is an XXXuthorized individual. This approach produces personal data from provided biometric data and a registered template, which offers extreme secrecy for both the template and the secret data.

According to Kikuchi *et al.* [8], the minutiae, a common characteristic retrieved from a fingerprint, tolerates rearranging. The problem is addressed by a novel fuzzy vault fingerprint system that assigns identifying numbers to all minutiae and chaff (false minutia) and establishes the proper order using a greedy short-distance algorithm. The basic concept is to give identity to factual and chaff minutiae to enable reordering, making it feasible to employ an effective error-collecting algorithm to address the uncertainty of biometric data. Also, the accuracy and performance of the proposed system are compared to various already-in-use techniques.

## 13.3   Proposed Work

A multimodal biometric system functions primarily as a pattern recognition system, gathering biometric information from a person, extracting a feature set from the data, and comparing the quality set to the template set in the database, as illustrated in Figure 13.2.

- **Biometric Sensor Module:** The biometric sensor gathers personally identifiable information from users. A quality-checking module evaluates the quality of the collected data to ensure the reliability of the extracted biometric data. If the collected data fails to meet the quality criteria, the module prompts the user to provide another sample.
- **Feature extractor module:** The module extracts critical characteristics from the collected biometric data, which will be used to identify the individual as their authentic self. This feature set will be saved as a biometric template for future verification. The template is designed to withstand variations within the user's biometric data and distinguish them from other users who may have similar features as shown in Figure 13.3.
- **Template database:** The template database stores the biometric templates collected during enrollment. The application determines the size of the database.

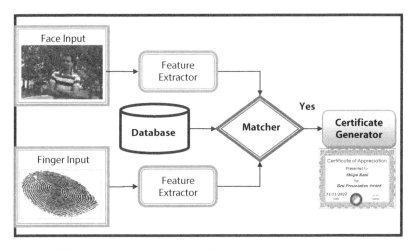

**Figure 13.2** Flowchart of proposed methodology.

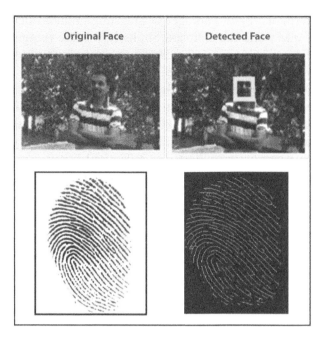

**Figure 13.3** (a) An input image of face. (b) Face detector through V-J method. (c) Input image for finger. (d) Feature extractor for finger.

- **Matching Module:** The module compares biometric query data against a saved template and generates a matching score that reflects the level of similarity between them. In fingerprint verification, for example, the matching score is

**Figure 13.4** (a) Sample certificate. (b) After verification winner certificate.

determined by the number of matching minutiae between the query and the template. Similarly, for face recognition, the score is based on the degree of similarity between the query and the template face.

- **The decision-making module**: The decision-making module uses the matching result to determine the user's identity. If both matches are successful and the result indicates that the individual is authentic, the system will immediately generate a certificate, as illustrated in Figure 13.4.

## 13.4    Experiment Result

MATLAB is an interactive system employing matrices as its primary data element, enabling quick resolution of various technical computer problems, especially matrix representations. It includes modern numerical computation software optimized for today's processor and memory architectures. MATLAB can process any image, whether stored, real-time, or otherwise. The language provides tools for noise reduction, geometric and visual data modification, texture feature extraction, visual data compression, and visual data segmentation to select a region of interest.

Our proposed approach utilizes MATLAB's image processing and captures tools. Figure 13.5 demonstrates the evaluation of the proposed module

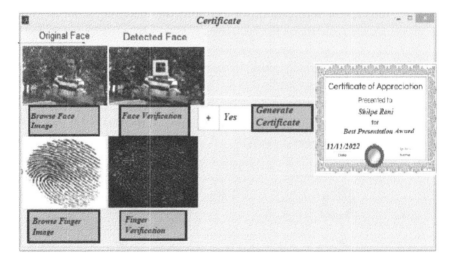

**Figure 13.5**  GUI overall module for proposed methodology.

using our own database. We captured the facial input image for authentication using the suggested methodology, followed by finger authentication after another round of facial verification. Only MATLAB can read the Excel sheet after both verification rounds are complete, and the sheet provides a list of contestants and winners to whom we must present certificates. The suggested module's last step generates an Excel file containing the certificate for the mentioned individuals. This module significantly reduces the time and effort required compared to manual processing.

## 13.5 Conclusion and Future Scope

The proposed process presents an effective solution for automatically generating certificates for significant events such as conferences and tech fests. It employs Haar, and PCA features extraction techniques for facial recognition and generates random chaff spots for finger recognition. The system automatically creates certificates for the winners once their identities have been verified. Both approaches provide high accuracy and require minimal processing time. The suggested process outperforms other methods for producing certificates at significant events, considering precision, efficiency, effort, and power consumption factors. Moreover, the system can be scaled up to handle large data sets for analysis in businesses and organizations. In conclusion, the proposed process offers a reliable and efficient way to generate certificates for significant events. Its use of advanced feature extraction techniques and image processing tools in MATLAB enables accurate and fast authentication of individuals. The proposed process has promising future scope for further development and improvement. One potential avenue for future research is to investigate the use of blockchain technology for secure and tamper-proof certificate generation. Blockchain can ensure the authenticity and immutability of certificates by storing them in a decentralized and distributed ledger. This approach can prevent the manipulation or falsification of certificates and enhance the trustworthiness of the certificate generation process. Furthermore, the proposed methodology can be extended to other applications beyond certificate generation, such as identity verification for online transactions or access control systems. The system can provide a reliable and secure solution for various identity-related applications by leveraging the same image processing and feature extraction techniques. In summary, the proposed process has promising future scope for further research and development. The system can improve its accuracy, security, and efficiency by incorporating advanced technologies such as deep learning and blockchain, making it an ideal solution for various identity-related applications.

# References

1. Ye, X., Chen, X., Chen, H., Gu, Y., Lv, Q., Deep learning network for face detection, in: *2015 IEEE 16th International Conference on Communication Technology (ICCT)*, pp. 504– 509, IEEE, 2015.
2. Ghimire, D. and Lee, J., A robust face detection method based on skin colour and edges. *J. Inf. Process. Syst.*, 9, 1, 141–156, 2013.
3. Haghighat, M., Abdel-Mottaleb, M., Alhalabi, W., Fully automatic face normalization and single sample face recognition in unconstrained environments. *Expert Syst. Appl.*, 47, 23–34, 2016.
4. Valiollahzadeh, S.M., Sayadiyan, A., Nazari, M., Face detection using adaboosted SVM-based component classifier. 76, 1–6, *arXiv*, 2008, preprint arXiv:0812.2575.
5. Ari, J. and Sudan, M., A fuzzy vault scheme‖, in: *IEEE International Symposium Information Theory*, p. 408, Lausanne, Switzerland, 2002.
6. Clancy, T., Lin, D., Kiyavash, N., Secure smartcard-based fingerprint authentication‖, in: *Proceedings of ACM SIGMM Workshop on Biometric Methods and Applications*, pp. 45–52, Berkley, CA, 2003.
7. Seira, H., Ohki, T., Komatsu, N., Kasahara, M., On biometric encryption using fingerprint and its security evaluation‖, in: *10th International Conference on Control, Automation and Robotics and Vision*, pp. 950–956, 2008.
8. Hiroaki, K., Onuki, Y., Nagai, K., Evaluation and implementation of fuzzy vault scheme using indexed minutiae‖. *Proc. IEEE*, 4413865, 3709–3712, 2007.
9. Ross, A. and Jain, A.K., Multimodal biometrics: An overview, in: *2004 12th European Signal Processing Conference*, pp. 1221–1224, IEEE, 2004.
10. Ali, Z., Hossain, M.S., Muhammad, G., Ullah, I., Abachi, H., Alamri, A., Edge-centric multimodal authentication system using encrypted biometric templates. *Future Gener. Comput. Syst.*, 85, 76– 87, 2018.
11. Malcangi, M., Developing a multimodal biometric authentication system using soft computing methods, in: *Artificial Neural Networks*, pp. 205–225, Springer, New York, NY, 2015.
12. Kumar, S., Jain, A., Agarwal, A.K., Rani, S., Ghimire, A., Object-based image retrieval using the u-net-based neural network. *Comput. Intell. Neurosci.*, 21, 14, 2021.
13. Sandeep, K., Rani, S., Jain, A., Verma, C., Raboaca, M.S., Illés, Z., Neagu, B.C., Face spoofing, age, gender and facial expression recognition using advance neural network architecture-based biometric system. *Sens. J.*, 22, 14, 5160–5184, 2022.

14. Rani, S., Swathi, G., Kumar, S., IRIS based recognition and spoofing attacks: A review, in: *2021 10th International Conference on System Modeling & Advancement in Research Trends (SMART)*, pp. 2–6, IEEE, 2021.

15. Kumar, S., Singh, S., Kumar, J., Prasad, K.M.V.V., Age and gender classification using Seg-net based architecture and machine learning. *Multimed. Tools Appl.*, 22, 3, 1–18, 2022.

16. Kumar S., Singh, S., Kumar, J., Face spoofing detection using improved SegNet architecture with blur estimation technique. *Int. J. Biom. Indersci. Publ.*, 13, 2–3, 131–149, 2021.

17. Rani, S., Kumar, S., Ghai, D., Prasad, K.M.V.V., Automatic detection of brain tumor from CT and MRI images using wireframe model and 3D Alex-Net, in: *2022 International Conference on Decision Aid Sciences and Applications (DASA)*, pp. 1132–1138, 2022.

18. Rani, S., Lakhwani, K., Kumar, S., Three-dimensional wireframe model of medical and complex images using cellular logic array processing techniques, in: *International Conference on Soft Computing and Pattern Recognition*, pp. 196–207, Springer, Cham, 2020.

19. Rani, S., Ghai, D., Kumar, S., *Reconstruction of a wireframe model of complex images using syntactic pattern recognition*, pp. 8–13, IET, Bahrain, 2021.

20. Rani, S., Ghai, D., Kumar, S., Kantipudi, M.V.V., Alharbi, A.H., Ullah, M.A., Efficient 3D AlexNet architecture for object recognition using syntactic patterns from medical images. *Comput. Intell. Neurosci.*, 21, 1–19, 2022.

21. Kumar, S., Singh, S., Kumar, J., Face spoofing detection using improved SegNet architecture with blur estimation technique. *Int. J. Biom. Indersci. Publ.*, 13, 2-3, 131–149, 2021.

22. Kumar, S., Mathew, S., Anumula, N., Chandra, K.S., Portable camera-based assistive device for real-time text recognition on various products and speech using android for blind people, in: *Innovations in Electronics and Communication Engineering*, Lecture Notes in Networks and Systems, pp. 437–448, 2020.

23. Gowroju, S. and Kumar, S., Robust pupil segmentation using UNET and morphological image processing, in: *2021 International Mobile, Intelligent, and Ubiquitous Computing Conference (MIUCC)*, pp. 105–109, IEEE, 2021.

# 14

# Face and Iris-Based Secured Authorization Model Using CNN

**Munish Kumar[1]\*, Abhishek Bhola[2], Ankita Tiwari[3] and Monali Gulhane[4]**

*[1]Department of Computer Science and Engineering, Koneru Lakshmaiah
Educational Foundation, Vijayawada, India
[2]Chaudhary Charan Singh Haryana Agricultural University,
College of Agriculture, Bawal, Rewari, Haryana, India
[3]Department of Mathematics, Koneru Lakshmaiah Educational Foundation,
Vijayawada, India
[4]Department of Computer Science and Engineering, Symbiosis Institute of
Technology (SIT) Nagpur, Symbiosis International (Deemed University) (SIU),
Pune, Maharashtra, India*

## Abstract

Biometric security is emerging as a prominent issue worldwide in data security. In the cyber world, multimodal biometric solutions for human identity detection in uncontrolled environments are gaining significant attention. This work's primary purpose is to provide multimodal biometric authentication. When compared to unimodal biometrics, which employs a single biometric indicator such as a fingerprint, face, palm print, or iris, multimodal authentication provides more effective authentication. The multimodal biometric approach with improved identification rate for smart cities remains a complex problem. This chapter offers improved multimodal biometric recognition for smart cities by combining iris and facial biometrics. In this suggested work, the face and iris of an individual are connected at the matching level, and the score level for the automatic identification of a person will calculate. By utilizing neural network-based architecture, this is accomplished. With the suggested method, accuracy rates are higher at 99.03%, and equal-mistake rates are lower at 0.15%. Multimodal biometrics is the best answer for all industries that require more precision and security.

*\*Corresponding author*: engg.munishkumar@gmail.com

Sandeep Kumar, Deepika Ghai, Arpit Jain, Suman Lata Tripathi and Shilpa Rani (eds.)
Multimodal Biometric and Machine Learning Technologies: Applications for Computer Vision,
(283–300) © 2023 Scrivener Publishing LLC

*Keywords*: Iris recognition, face recognition, image edge detection, authentication, databases

## 14.1   Introduction

A biometric system is a computerized system that recognizes a person based on behavioral or physiological attributes. It has advanced significantly in several applications, such as safety, identification, password protection, and monitoring [1]. All known biometric systems are unimodal, relying on a single source of information for identification, and have the benefit of employing biometric IDs that cannot be lost, forgotten, guessed, or easily falsified compared to possession-based identities [2, 3]. Fingerprints are the biometric trait used the most frequently out of all the others. The iris is also the most trustworthy biometric since it is distinct and consistent throughout time [4, 5].

Unimodal biometric systems have problems with noisy data, interclass similarities, nonuniversality, spoofing, etc. These problems increase accuracy, leading to subpar system performance [6–8]. Using various sources of information for authorization can circumvent some of the restrictions of unimodal biometrics. For enhanced security, the future of individual permission will rely heavily on multimodal biometrics. In the case of multimodal biometric systems, information from two or more biometric inputs is accepted [9]. Although unimodal authentication systems are more precise, they only address a few issues, such as privacy and spoofing resistance [10–12]. An approach for improving precision that is gaining popularity is combining many biometric modalities focused on rank matching. This project has already used several score-level convergence techniques [13, 14]. Fuzzy methods and optimization techniques increase the security and precision of authentication systems. Since several of their features guarantee enough population coverage, they resolve the nonuniversality issue [15, 16]. Due to the many characteristics or modalities involved in multimodal biometrics, the spoofing issue is also resolved [17]. It would be very challenging for an impostor to spoof or attack many attributes of a genuine person simultaneously.

The suggested multibiometric authentication method uses face and iris biometric characteristics for identification utilizing a convolution neural network (CNN) [18]. CNN is used in this work because its design is optimum for discovering and learning essential pictures and time-series properties. CNN has relevance in other critical disciplines, such as Medical

Imaging, Signal Processing, Item Detection, and Synthetic Data Creation [19].

In Section 14.2, the literature work is briefly discussed with past critical research studies in the domain of multimodal authentications and its other applications. Section 14.3 describes the proposed model with associated procedures such as preprocessing steps, CNN, and image fusion. In Section 14.4, the results of the proposed model are discussed in detail. Finally, Section 14.5 contains the conclusion and future scope of the presented study, followed by a reference section.

## 14.2   Related Work

The fusion methodology, feature extraction method, and classification method are only a few variables that determine the accuracy with which multimodal systems perceive things [1, 2]. Recently, several scholars have emphasized the development of dependable, multimodal biometric systems [3, 4]. The basis of the proposed models consists of at least two properties. A few examples include face and voice research [5, 6], face and fingerprint research [7, 8], face and palm print research [9, 10], face and iris research [11–13], and fingerprint and hand geometry research [12, 13]. This study suggests a biometric system based on the iris and facial features. We chose this choice because facial recognition is the most widely used technique for intuitively recognizing people, while the iris is now acknowledged as one of the most accurate biometric systems [14, 15].

J. Kulandai *et al.*, the HOG descriptor produces a feature vector for training the SVM, and the resulting results are validated against the specified test input. The experimental outcome of the method demonstrates better identification accuracy with fewer false positives, and it also verifies that the test and training image face database match appropriately under different postures and lighting situations [20].

Face characteristics were retrieved using PCA, while Gabor filters extracted iris features. The authors [18] created a face and iris-based multimodal recognition system using genetic algorithm-based selecting elements and scores level fusion.

In the suggested work [2], hybrid-level fusion for various applications has been established using the Gabor filter for feature extraction and Euclidean distance for matching.

Ashwini L. *et al.* [21] suggested an age estimate method that uses the Viola-Jones Algorithm and Euclidean distance in conjunction with SVM for feature extraction and classification. Several age categories are utilized for this database, and the recommended age estimation accuracy is 98.89%.

The author suggested [15] a unique method for multimodal biometrically protected systems based on feature-level fusion approaches. Several orientations and sizes of Gabor filters have been employed to extract facial and iris information. Ultimately, PCA will extract the essential feature from the selected characteristics for classification, which the SVM classifier will perform.

Gong [22] suggested a novel paradigm for hidden factor analysis. The person-specific features are separated from the ageing fluctuations to evaluate this model's robust age-invariant facial characteristics.

D. Gong [23] suggested a unique approach for age-insensitive face recognition, the face recognition performance of this system may be enhanced. In addition, a novel framework for matching features called identity factor analysis was developed to increase recognition performance. Experiments on the new method demonstrate its efficacy on publically available standard data sets.

Thakshila *et al.* [24] suggested classifying face photos according to gender and age. The suggested parameters are derived from the geometric facial feature differences impacted by the two sexes and the change in facial skin texture over the ageing process. The gender and age classifier has an accuracy rate of 70.5%, significantly more significant than the classification accuracy of the human brain, which is 75%.

The authors [16] proposed a multimodal face-iris biometric system that incorporates the advantages of score-level, feature-level, and decision-level fusion for optimum face and iris information. The extracted and fused optimal features are utilized to compute the optimized scores, and the ROC curves that result from score-level fusion are used to generate the optimized judgements. The authors retrieved face and iris characteristics using the Log-Gabor transform and then selected the essential features using the BSA feature selection approach.

Zhang *et al.* [25] suggested a unique approach to recognizing facial expressions by identifying the specifics of each face. Replace the whole collection of feature expressions with a single facial feature to save time and increase accuracy. Experiments demonstrate that the suggested strategy is successful on Cohn-Kanade (CK+) databases.

The study's authors [17] suggested fusing the face and iris using a weighted score-level fusion method. They used the Daugman technique for iris identification, which automatically divides the iris and pupil regions using a circular Hough transform and then encoded the iris' distinctive characteristics using 1D Log-Gabor filters and a binary template.

A technology based on PCA was used for facial recognition. The matching score for iris and face recognition was normalized using the min-max normalization method. The weighted sum approach adds the normalized scores together into one score.

A multimodal biometric identification system, fuzzy K-Nearest Neighbour, was utilized (FK-NN) for matching. Many studies have demonstrated that the system's accuracy can be increased by fusing biometric templates at various levels and using different feature extraction techniques. The cited publications use the Face94 face data set, ORL face data set, FERET faces data set, IIT Delhi iris data set, and CASIA iris data set to assess their methods. In these attempts, utilizing two distinct algorithms to extract information from the face and iris is expected, which complicates the technique. This study provides a single approach for extracting facial and iris characteristics.

## 14.3   Proposed Methodology

Using a neural network-based architecture, the proposed methodology for enhanced multimodal biometric recognition for smart cities combines iris and facial biometrics at matching and score levels. The proposed technique consists of capturing an individual's iris and facial images and extracting relevant features from these images. The extracted features are then fused using a score-level fusion approach to obtain a final score for identification.

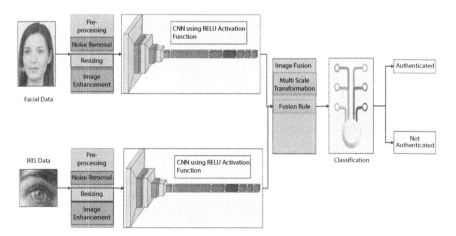

**Figure 14.1** Proposed methodology.

A detailed description is given below, and Figure 14.1 represents the architectural diagram of the proposed work.

### 14.3.1   Pre-Processing

The purpose of pre-processing is to increase the image's quality so that we may more effectively eliminate undesired distortions and improve key attributes for our application. To obtain image data prepared for model input, preprocessing is necessary. For instance, a convolutional neural network with completely connected layers required that all the images be in arrays of the same size. Preprocessing may also shorten the time needed for model training and speed up inference. If the input images are relatively large, the model can be trained substantially shorter by scaling them down without significantly affecting model performance. Preprocessing methods used in this work include, for instance, scaling, noise removal, and image enhancement.

- **Noise Removal:** Preprocessing aims to raise the image's quality for faster analysis. Image data must undergo preprocessing to be ready for model input. For instance, all photos must be in arrays of the same size for the fully linked layers of convolutional neural networks. Preprocessing a model can shorten the training process and speed up inference. Reducing the size of large input photos will drastically reduce the time needed to train the model without significantly affecting model performance. Here are several preprocessing processes from this study that are discussed: noise reduction, picture improvement, and scaling.
- **Resizing:** Resize alters the size of your photographs and, optionally, scales them to the appropriate dimensions. Moreover, additional annotations are proportionally adjusted. Stretch, fill in, fit inside, fit in, and more procedures are included in resizing.
- **Image Enhancement:** Image enhancement aims to increase a picture's utility for a specific job. During image enhancement, digital images are changed to provide better results for presentation or extra image analysis. For instance, sharpening or brightening an image might simplify spotting essential details.

## 14.3.2    Convolutional Neural Network (CNN)

Convolutional neural networks (CNNs) are a subset of deep learning architecture. It has several layers, including fully connected, convolutional, and pooling layers. After applying filters to the input picture by the convolutional layer to extract features, the pooling layer downsamples the image to save computation. The fully connected layer then makes the final prediction. The network uses gradient descent and backpropagation to learn the best filters. Each Layer takes a three-dimensional volume as input and, using a differentiable function, turns it into a three-dimensional book utilizing extra hyperparameters and other parameters. Convolutional layers, Activation Function Layers, Pooling Layers, and Fully Connected Layers are some of the several layers used in CNN.:

- Convolutional layers
  The convolutional layer combines input data, a filter, and a features map and is responsible for most processing. This layer calculates the output of neurons associated with local locations in the input by computing the dot product between the weight of each neuron and a small input volume region attached to the layer.
- Activation Function Layer
  The output of the convolution layer will be subjected to an element-wise activation function in this layer. The activation functions RELU, Sigmoid, Tanh, Leaky RELU, etc., are frequently employed. The ReLU activation function is used in this study because it accelerates and enhances the negative values to zero. This is commonly known as activation since only the active properties are transferred to the following layer. The mathematical equation for the ReLU activation function is shown in equation (14.1), and its graph is presented in Figure 14.2.

$$RELU: \max(0, x) \qquad (14.1)$$

- Pooling Layer
  This layer expedites the CNN process because the pooling process simplifies the output by lowering the number of parameters while doing nonlinear downsampling. Various pooling layers have been used, i.e. max, average, min and sum pool. The max-pooling layer produces a feature map

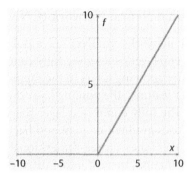

**Figure 14.2** ReLU activation function.

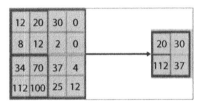

**Figure 14.3** Max pooling process.

with the standout elements from the previous feature map. An illustration of the maximum pooling is presented in Figure 14.3.

- Fully-connected layer
  As in typical neural networks, neurons in a connected layer have complete connections to all activations in the layer below. This layer performs the classification procedure using the attributes gathered via the various filters and previous layers. The activations could be calculated using a matrix multiplication and bias offset. To reliably classify inputs, fully linked layers usually use a SoftMax activation function, which yields a probability between 0 and 1. ReLU functions are commonly used in convolutional and pooling layers.

### 14.3.3  Image Fusion

The technique of fusing two or more photos to create a composite image that incorporates the data included in each image is known as image fusion. The final image has a greater information level than any of the input photos. The fusion process aims to assess the information at each pixel position in the input pictures and keep the data from that image that most accurately depicts the genuine scene content or improves the usefulness of the fused image for a given application. Image fusion involves several processes, including multiscale Transformation and Fusion Rule, which are briefly detailed below.

- Multiscale Transformation (MST)
  It decomposes the source pictures into a multiscale transform domain and reconstructs the fused images by inverting the appropriate transform after merging the transformed coefficients according to a predetermined fusion rule. These MST algorithms assume that extracting the potentially important information from the original images is possible from the decomposed coefficients.
- Fusion Rule
  Fusion rules precisely decompose the torus product of two group representations into the direct sum of irreducible representations. Instead of mixing pixels, the fusion rules do it using areas. As a result, more effective tests for selecting appropriate measurements from the source pictures may be applied before fusion, depending on a region's varied characteristics. While fusing critical information during picture fusion, the algorithms are called rules since they highlight the relevant qualities and downplay the irrelevant ones. These guidelines are essential to the fusion process since choosing sound guidelines improves the procedure's outcomes. One fusion rule cannot be created to address all application scenarios. An image fusion rule typically has four elements: Activity-level measurement is first, followed by coefficient grouping, combining, and combination of coefficients and consistency is then confirmed.

## 14.4  Results and Discussion

The IIT Delhi Iris & CASIA data set offers iris scans [29], and Faces94 & FG-NET, which contains facial images, are two publicly accessible data sets frequently used in the state-of-the-art. The two data sets were joined to create a single data set that included pictures of each person's face and iris. We used this Methodology to evaluate several multimodal classification algorithms even if the irises on the looks don't truly belong to the person (face and iris). One hundred fifty folders representing persons are present in the final data set used. Pictures of faces and irises may be found in each folder's "Face" and "Iris" subfolders. A significant issue in pattern recognition is constructing a picture from its component elements. The facial and iris images are combined in this proposed approach. The Faces94 data set, FG-NET (Face and Gesture Recognition Network), CASIA, and IITD are used to implement the results. The corrected linear activation function is then calculated using CNN (ReLU). The most current face and iris recognition detection rate is 99.65%. When compared to SVM and other methods, the proposed Methodology outperforms prior algorithms and provides more accurate estimations of accuracy. The following techniques are employed for calculations. A confusion matrix determines the accuracy, precision, recall, and F1 score of the four parameters in question. Precision and recall are crucial for knowledge retrieval, and positive class mattered more than negative class. As the model doesn't worry about anything irrelevant or not obtained when running a search, Precision and Recall merely require TP, FP, and FN (this is the actual negative situation).

- Use this equation to determine the framework's accuracy:

$$ACC = \frac{100 \times (TP + TN)}{N} \qquad (14.2)$$

- Use the following formula to determine the system's Precision and Recall:
  **Precision:** How many of the good things that were forecasted are positive?

$$Precision = \frac{TP}{TP + FP} \qquad (14.3)$$

The precision value lies between 0 and 1.
**Recall:** What proportion of the total positives are anticipated to be positive? It is equivalent to TPR (actual positive rate).

$$Recall = \frac{TP}{TP + FN} \qquad (14.3)$$

**ACTUAL**

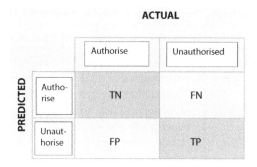

Figure 14.4 Confusion matrix for recognition.

In this case, TP stood for True Positive, TN for True Negative, FP for False Positive, FN for False Negative, and N for data set spam. Figure 14.4 depicts a confusion matrix that is used to calculate all values. False positives and negatives are okay when patterns are detected (Face & Iris), but what if we miss a significant allowed design because it is classified as an unauthorized pattern? False Positives should be as low as possible in this situation. The recall is, therefore, less effective than accuracy. While weighing many models, choosing the best one will be difficult (high precision and low recall or vice-versa). Thus, there should be a statistic that considers both of them. One such metric is the F1 score.

**F1 Score**
It is the precision and recalls harmonic mean. It accounts for both false positives and false negatives. As a result, it works well with an unbalanced data set.

$$F1\ score = \frac{2}{\dfrac{1}{Precision} + \dfrac{1}{Recall}} = \frac{2*(Precision*Recall)}{(Precision+Recall)} \quad (14.4)$$

Recall and precision are given the same weight in the F1 score.

With a weighted F1 score, we can provide recall and accuracy of various weights. Different tasks place different weights on recall and accuracy. Performance metrics for accuracy offer fewer insights into the prediction than precision, recall, and F1. Table 14.1 compares the suggested strategy to several previous approaches. With a recognition rate of 99.65%, the recommended method performs better than earlier approaches and produces superior outcomes.

**Table 14.1** The accuracy comparison between the proposed and other methods.

| S. no. | Author | Feature extraction | Matching | Accuracy |
|---|---|---|---|---|
| 1 | G. Huo et al. [15] (2015) | Several scales and orientations of a 2D Gabor filter are then transformed into an energy orientation using histogram statistics. | Support Vector Machine (SVM) | 97.81 |
| 2 | Y. Bouzouina et al. [18] (2017) | PCA and discrete coefficient transform (DCT) are used for facial features. For iris characteristics, use the 1D Log-Gabor filter technique with Zernike moment. | Support Vector Machine (SVM) | 96.72 |
| 3 | B. Ammour et al. [2] (2018) | The Gabor filter and a regression kernel discriminate analysis were combined. | Euclidean Distance | 97.45 |
| 4 | B. Ammour et al. [11] (2020) | 2D Log-Gabor filters and spectral regression kernel discriminate analysis used | Fuzzy K-NN (FK-NN) | 98.18 |
| 5 | S. Alshebli et al. [12] (2021) | Features are extracted from the data set using DWT and SVD with a 128 by 128 matrix after the data set has previously undergone pre-processing using the contrast method. | Euclidean Distance | 98.90 |
| 6 | Proposed Method | Confusion Matrix | CNN using RELU | 99.65 |

Table 14.2 displays additional comparative metrics on various data sets, such as accuracy, recall, and F1 score. Values are derived according to the confusion matrix and the algorithm mentioned above. All four data sets are subjected to the suggested technique, and a new data set is created by combining the face and iris data sets into a single data set. And with all data sets, the proposed approach blatantly exhibits a higher identification rate. An accuracy comparison graph using several techniques is shown in Figure 14.5. Figure 14.6 illustrates the results of applying the suggested strategy to all data sets and indicates that it performs better than all prior methods in accuracy.

**Table 14.2** Results calculated on different data sets by using the proposed method.

| S. no. | Data sets | Precision | Recall | F-1 score | Accuracy |
|--------|-----------|-----------|--------|-----------|----------|
| 1 | Faces94 | 0.9699 | 0.9786 | 2.936 | 98.99 |
| 2 | FG-NET | 0.9977 | 0.9913 | 2.974 | 99.30 |
| 3 | CASIA | 0.9783 | 0.9538 | 2.861 | 99.10 |
| 4 | IITD | 0.9939 | 0.9795 | 2.939 | 99.00 |
| 5 | Mixed | 0.9977 | 0.9960 | 2.988 | 99.65 |

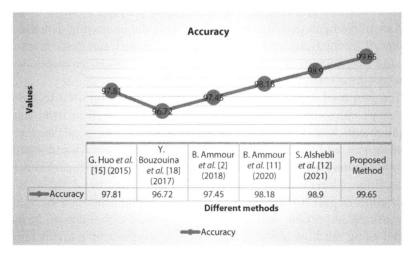

**Figure 14.5** Accuracy comparison between the proposed and other methods.

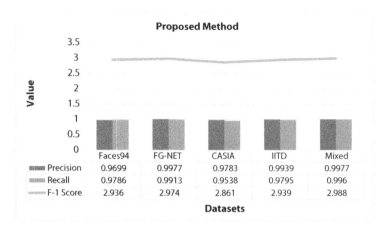

**Figure 14.6** Shows the result of the proposed method on different data sets.

## 14.5   Conclusion and Future Scope

The emerging issue of biometric security in the cyber world has led to the development of multimodal biometric solutions for human identity detection in uncontrolled environments. The proposed enhanced multimodal biometric recognition for smart cities, which combines iris and facial biometrics, offers a more accurate and secure authentication approach. Using neural network-based architecture further improves the identification rate, with a greater accuracy rate of 99.03% and a reduced rate of equal mistakes of 0.15%. Multimodal biometrics is a crucial technology for industries that require precision and security, and this chapter provides valuable insights into its implementation for smart cities. With the increasing demand for biometric authentication in various sectors, this work can guide researchers and practitioners in developing effective multimodal biometric solutions for different applications.

The proposed enhanced multimodal biometric recognition technique for smart cities can be further expanded and improved to meet future requirements. One future scope is integrating biometric modalities, such as voice, gait, and signature, to enhance the system's accuracy and security. Another future scope is to develop a real-time system to perform biometric recognition. Moreover, this work can be extended to other domains, such as healthcare and finance, where biometric authentication is becoming increasingly important. Additionally, the proposed technique can be optimized using machine learning algorithms or deep learning architectures, which can learn and improve over time, leading to even more accurate and reliable biometric recognition systems. With the increasing demand for biometric authentication in various sectors, this work can guide researchers and practitioners in developing effective multimodal biometric solutions.

# References

1. Kumar, S., Jain, A., Agarwal, A.K., Rani, S., Ghimire, A., Object-based image retrieval using the u-net-based neural network. *Comput. Intell. Neurosci.*, 22, 1, 1–17, 2021.

2. Ammour, B., Bowden, T., Boubchir, L., Face-Iris multimodal biometric system based on hybrid level fusion, in: *2018 41st International Conference on Telecommunications and Signal Processing (TSP)*, pp. 1–5, 2018.

3. Rani, S., Gowroju, S., Kumar, S., IRIS based recognition and spoofing attacks: A review, in: *2021 10th International Conference on System Modeling & Advancement in Research Trends (SMART)*, pp. 2–6, IEEE, 2021.

4. Kumar, S., Singh, S., Kumar, J., Prasad, K.M.V.V., Age and gender classification using Seg-Net based architecture and machine learning. *Multimed. Tools Appl.*, 22, 3, 1–18, 2022.

5. Kumar, S., Singh, S., Kumar, J., Face spoofing detection using improved seg-net architecture with blur estimation technique. *Int. J. Biom. Indersci. Publ.*, 13, 2–3, 131–149, 2021.

6. Rani, S., Kumar, S., Ghai, D., Prasad, K.M.V.V., Automatic detection of brain tumor from CT and MRI images using wireframe model and 3D Alex-Net, in: *2022 International Conference on Decision Aid Sciences and Applications (DASA)*, pp. 1132–1138, 2022.

7. Rani, S., Lakhwani, K., Kumar, S., Three-dimensional wireframe model of medical and complex images using cellular logic array processing techniques, in: *International Conference on Soft Computing and Pattern Recognition*, pp. 196–207, Springer, Cham, 2020.

8. Rani, S., Ghai, D., Kumar, S., Reconstruction of a wireframe model of complex images using syntactic pattern recognition, in: *4th Smart Cities Symposium (SCS 2021)*, pp. 8–13, Online Conference, Bahrain, 21-23 November 2021.

9. Rani, S., Ghai, D., Kumar, S., Kantipudi, M.V.V., Alharbi, A.H., Ullah, M.A., Efficient 3D AlexNet architecture for object recognition using syntactic patterns from medical images. *Comput. Intell. Neurosci.*, 2022, 1–19, 2022.

10. Kumar, S., Singh, S., Kumar, J., Face spoofing detection using improved SegNet architecture with blur estimation technique. *Int. J. Biom. Indersci. Publ.*, 13, 2–3, 131–149, 2021.

11. Ammour, B., Boubchir, L., Bouden, T., Ramdani, M., Face–Iris multimodal biometric identification system. *Electronics*, 9, 1, 85, 2020 Jan, Available from: http://dx.doi.org/10.3390/electronics9010085.

12. Alshebli, S., Kurugollu, F., Shafik, M., Multimodal biometric recognition using iris and face features, in: *Advances in Transdisciplinary Engineering, E-book*, vol. 15, Advances in Manufacturing Technology XXXIV.

13. Kumar, S., Rani, S., Jain, A., Verma, C., Raboaca, M.S., Illés, Z., Neagu, B.C., Face spoofing, age, gender and facial expression recognition using advance neural network architecture-based biometric system. *Sens. J.*, 22, 14, 5160–5184, 2022.

14. Gowroju, S. and Kumar, S., Robust pupil segmentation using UNET and morphological image processing, in: *2021 International Mobile, Intelligent, and Ubiquitous Computing Conference (MIUCC)*, pp. 105–109, IEEE, 2021.

15. Huo, G., Liu, Y., Zhu, X., Dong, H., He, F., Face–Iris multimodal biometric scheme based on feature level fusion. *J. Electron. Imaging*, 24, 6, 1–10, 2015, Available from: https://doi.org/10. 1117/1.JEI.24.6.063020.

16. Kumar, S., Mathew, S., Anumula, N., Chandra, K.S., Portable camera-based assistive device for real-time text recognition on various products and speech using android for blind people, in: *Innovations in Electronics and Communication Engineering*, Lecture Notes in Networks and Systems, pp. 437–448, 2020.

17. Bhola, A. and Singh, S., Visualization and modeling of high dimensional cancerous gene expression dataset. *J. Inf. Knowl. Manag.*, 18, 01, 1950001–22, 2019.

18. Bouzouina, Y. and Hamami, L., Multimodal biometric: Iris and face recognition based on feature selection of iris with GA and scores level fusion with SVM. *2017 2nd International Conference on Bioengineering for Smart Technologies (BioSMART)*, pp. 1–7, 2017.

19. Bhola, A. and Singh, S., Gene selection using high dimensional gene expression data: An appraisal. *Curr. Bioinform.*, 13, 3, 225–233, 2018.

20. Julina, J.K.J. and Sree Sharmila, T., Facial recognition using histogram of gradients and support vector machines, in: *IEEE International Conference on Computer, Communication and Signal Processing (ICCCSP)*, pp. 1–5, 2017.

21. Ingole, A.L. and Karande, K.J., Automatic age estimation from face images using facial features, in: *IEEE Global Conference on Wireless Computing and Networking (GCWCN)*, pp. 104–108, 2018.

22. Gong, D., Li, Z., Lin, D., Liu, J., Tang, X., Hidden factor analysis for age invariant face recognition, in: *Proceedings of the IEEE International Conference on Computer Vision.* pp. 2872–2879, 2013.

23. Gong, D., Li, Z., Tao, D., Liu, J., Li, X., A maximum entropy feature descriptor for age invariant face recognition, in: *Proceedings of the IEEE Conference on Computer Vision and Pattern Recognition*, pp. 5289–5297, 2015.

24. Kalansuriya, T.R. and Dharmaratne, A.T., Facial image classification based on age and gender, in: *IEEE International Conference on Advances in ICT for Emerging Regions (ICTer)*, pp. 44–50, 2013.
25. Zhang, R., Li, J., Xiang, Z.-Z., Su, J.-B., Facial expression recognition based on salient patch selection, in: *IEEE International Conference on Machine Learning and Cybernetics (ICMLC)*, pp. 502–507, 2016.

# Index

Accuracy, 283–287, 292–296
Active learning, 205–206
Adversarial learning, 205, 208
Agricultural land, 80
Analytical learning, 205, 209
Anxiety and the motivation, 148, 152
API, 39
Applications of multimodal biometric
systems,
    MBS in commercial applications,
    93–96
    MBS in government applications,
    90–92
    MBS in enterprise solutions and
    network infrastructure, 92–93
    MBS in forensic science, 90
Artificial environment, 130
Artificial intelligence, 173, 174
Artificial neural network, 1–4, 165,
    176, 195
Authentication, 1–2, 14–16, 116,
    283–285, 296–297
Autoencoder, 210
Automatically generate an exercise
    drill, 135

Bayesian learning, 205, 209
Bayesian networks,
    Bayes rule, 193
    chain rule, 193–194
    converging, 193
    diverging, 193
    d-seperated path, 194
    serial, 193

Behavioral biometrics, 119
Benchmark for effective multimodal
    biometric system, 86–87
Biometric, 251, 252, 254, 256, 261, 264,
    265
Biometric systems, 1–3, 9–11, 14–17
Biometrics, 283–287
Biometrics authentication system,
    113–115
Biometrics modalities, 89

Carbon emissions, 72
Carbon sequestration, 72–73, 77–78,
    80
CASIA, 291–292, 295–296
Certificate, 269, 270, 277, 278, 279
Classification algorithm performs
    effectively, 134
Client reviews, 54
Clustering, 195, 201–204, 206
CNN, 258
CNN architecture, 210
COMBET technique, 147, 150,
    155–156
Components of MBS, 87–88
    data store(s), 88
    input interface, 88
    output interface, 89
    processing unit, 88
Computer vision, 1, 2, 20
Concept learning, 205, 209
Confusion Matrix, 292–295
Continous authentication, 119
Control in complicated scenarios, 132

Convolutional, 288–290
Convolutional neural network, 8, 26–28
  activation function, 216
  applications, 214
  benefits, 214
  CNN flowchart, 214
  convolutional layer, 215
  fully connected layer, 217
  loss functions, 217
  pooling layer, 215
CoviShield, 34
CoWIN, 34, 35, 36, 37, 41
Criteria analysis technique, 150, 154
Curriculum learning, 210, 215–216
Curvilinear Regression,
  nonpolynomial regression, 187–190
  polynomial regression, 184–187
Customer reviews, 53–54, 63

Data mining techniques, 158–159
Decision trees, 195
Deep learning, 2, 4, 7, 9, 107–108, 167–169, 173–174
Digital image, 76
DL applications,
  automated vehicle, 218
  communications, 218
  electronics, 218
  industrial automation, 218
  medical research, 218
  satellite communication, 218

Early fusion, 116
EEG-based machine learning, 166
Enhance athletes' performances, 131
Enrolment, 116
Ensemble, 260, 264
Ensemble learning, 205, 207
Equal error rate, 115
Euclidean loss function, 218
Excel, 269, 270, 279

Face recognition, 252, 254, 260, 261
False acceptance rate, 115
False rejection rate, 115
Features 270, 271, 273
Federated learning, 205, 207
Financial evaluation, 150
Fingerprint recognition, 251, 252
Finger recognition, 270, 279
FIS, 42, 45, 46
Fitness and sports services, 148
Fusion, 251, 255, 256, 283, 285–287, 290–295
Fusion levels, 116–119
Fuzzy classification, 190
Fuzzy clustering analysis, 158–159
Fuzzy comprehensive evaluation, 147, 158
Fuzzy expert system, 165
Fuzzy integrals, 151, 156
Fuzzy logic, 31, 42, 44
Fuzzy logic and the DEA technique, 150
Fuzzy logic-based evaluation in sports, 148, 159
Fuzzy logic technique, 146, 149–150, 158
Fuzzy logic theory, 149
Fuzzy membership function,
  impulsive, 191
  left sided trapezoidal, 192
  right sided trapezoidal, 191
  triangular, 191
Fuzzy neural logic and regression analysis, 151, 157
Fuzzy rule based system, 148
Fuzzy rules,
  certainity factor, 192
  degree of importance, 192
  generalized fuzzy production rules, 192
  noise tolerance, 192
  sensitivity factors, 192
  simple fuzzy rules, 192
  weighted fuzzy production rules, 192

Gated recurrent units, 211, 213
Gaussian mixture model, 165
Gene regulatory network, 194
Google review analyzer, 54
GRU cell, 213

Haar features, 271
Healthcare,
    catastrophe, 32
    quality, 32
    workers, 34
Hierarchical clustering, 201–203
Hinge loss function, 217–218
HMD improved performance, 133
HMDs', 133, 138
Human behavior, 130
Hybrid model, 165

Identification, 17
Image processing, 76
Immersion, 130–131, 134, 139
Immersive VR, 130–131
In situ biomass, 72
Inductive learning, 205, 209
Information retrieval, 54, 56–57, 60
Intelligent model for volleyball player
    talent, 150, 154
Inter criteria analysis technique, 150
Intermediate fusion, 117
iOS, 33, 36

K-mean clustering, 201

Late fusion, 116
Leaky ReLU, 217
Linear regression,
    error, 183
    intercept, 176–177, 180–182
    slope, 176–177, 180–182
Lockdown, 35, 41
Logistics regression, 197
LSTM, 210–213

Machine learning, 1–23, 54–55, 174
Macro, meso, and micro models, 151,
    158
Meta-learning, 205
    metric learning, 208
More engaging and active, 131
More learning benefits through VR,
    132
MST, 291
Mulitmodal emotion recognition, 113
Multibiometric, 284
Multimodal, 251, 253. 254, 256, 260
Multimodal biometric system,
    106–107
Multimodal biometrics, 1–2, 9–15, 17,
    24
Multimodal colearning, 104–106
Multimodal deep learning, 107–110
Multimodal event detection, 112–113
Multimodal learning, 205, 210
Multimodality, 104–105
Multiple linear regression, 183
Multitask learning, 206
Multomodal, 269, 270, 276, 280

Natural language processing, 3, 20–23,
    55–56, 62, 258
Neural network, 255, 274
Neuropsychological evaluation using
    VR, 133
Noisy ReLU, 217
Normalized difference vegetation
    index (NDVI), 75–77

Object-oriented, 31, 44
OTP, 39, 40, 41, 44
Outline learning, 205
    incremental learning algorithm, 206
    sequential learning, 207

Pandemic, 31, 32, 35
Parametric linear units, 217

PCA, 272, 279
Performance motivation, 134
Photosynthetically active radiation, 75, 76
Physical and mental performance, 131
Physical therapy and exercise, 132, 137
Pooling, 258
Probabilistic reasoning, 146
Proposed method, 231–237
    CNN-based method, 236
    data exploitation, 237–238
    datasets used, 238–239
    DTW-based implementation, 235–236
    measures of accuracy, 245–248
    proposed model implementation, 236–237
    results of deep learning-based method, 241–244
    results of proposed method, 244–245
    results on CNN-based methods, 239–241
    SVM-based implementation, 235
    validation and training, 239

Random forest, 175, 197–199
Recognition, 283–287, 292–293, 296–297
Recurrent neural network, 173, 210–211
Regression, 175–176
Reinforcement learning, 173, 175, 203, 206
ReLU activation function, 216
Remote sensing, 72
Resolution of image, 75, 76
Restricted Boltzmann machine, 210
Risk assessment framework, 146, 149, 153
Risk assessment system based on fuzzy logic, 149, 154
Rule base, 45

Satellite data, 72, 73, 76
Self-supervised learning, 204–205
Self-taught learning, 204–205
Semantic search, 194, 195
Semisupervised learning, 204, 205
Semisupervised learning method, 166
Sensor (MODIS terra), 75, 76
Sentence segmentation, 56
Sentiment analysis, 54–56, 59–62
Sigmoid function, 197, 216
SMS, 41
Softmax loss function, 217
Spam filter, 194, 195
Spoofing, 284
Sporting rehabilitation training, 151
Sports culture industry's level of competition, 151
Sports facility, 146
Sports training, 131, 133–136, 138–140
Strength training, 146
Support vector machine, 199, 200
    hyperplane, 200
    margin, 201
Support vector machine, 165

Tanh activation function, 216
Targeted learning, 175, 205, 208
TENDIAG1 test battery, 149, 153
Text, 54
    text analysis, 64
    text-based, 54
    text categorization, 55
    text collection, 60
    text documents, 55
    text information, 55
    text information extraction, 56
    text mining, 53–58, 63–67
    text preprocessing, 55, 63
    text sample, 60
    text summarization, 61
    textual data, 54, 55, 62

Text-to-speech, 112
Transfer learning, 175, 205, 207
Tweets, 53, 62

Unimodal, 259, 260, 264
Unstructured text, 54–56, 62,
Unsupervised learning, 175, 201, 206, 209–210

Vaccination, 31–47
    vaccine slot tracker, 31, 40, 42, 46, 50
Vegetation index, 75, 76
Video description, 110
Virtual competitors, 132, 137

Virtual environment, 130–131, 132, 136
Virus, 32–34
Visual question answering, 111
VR CAVE-based training environment for athletes, 134, 139
VR environments to benefit society, 134
VR in the training process, 130
VR sports application, 134, 139
VR technology, 132, 134–136, 141
VR-based imaging (VRBI), 135, 141
VRT with sports practice to enhance the skill, 141

Wavelength reflection, 73

.

Printed and bound by CPI Group (UK) Ltd, Croydon, CR0 4YY

27/10/2024

14580129-0003